1982

the
witchcraft
papers

CONTEMPORARY RECORDS

OF THE WITCHCRAFT

HYSTERIA IN ESSEX

1560–1700

Collected and Edited by

Peter Haining

UNIVERSITY BOOKS, INC. SECAUCUS, NEW JERSEY

contents

This book is dedicated to
the memory of all those who
died because of ignorance
and bigotry in the county of
Essex 1560–1700.

acknowledgments

I should like to acknowledge my debt to numerous people for their assistance in compiling this work. Some wish to remain anonymous; those I can mention by name include the Keeper and staff of the British Museum; the Chief Archivist and staff of the Essex Records Office, Chelmsford; the Librarian and staff of the London Library; Mr. A. H. Wesencraft, Curator of the Harry Price Library at London University. I am indebted to the public libraries of Manningtree, Colchester, Safron Walden, Braintree, Chelmsford, Maldon, Epping, Brentwood, Romford, and Barking.

I must also thank Eric Maple, Professor Keith Thomas, Dr. Alan Macfarlane, and Professor R. H. Robbins, whose respective books on witchcraft, which have proved of enormous help, are specified in the main text. I have also referred to the works of Professor Wallace Notestein, C. L'Estrange Ewen, and Montague Summers, which are similarly recommended to students of this subject and this period.

Among individuals who gave generously of their time and advice I must cite Christopher Scott, who drew the map illustrating the spread of witchcraft in Essex and supervised the pictures in general, Ken Chapman, Ronald Seth, and, of course, my wife, Philippa, who assisted me in the research and so efficiently typed the manuscript.

Peter Haining
November 1973

OUTBURST OF SCANDAL IN ESSEX BACKWATER

When it comes to scandal there is always a guaranteed keen audience.

And even in a quiet Essex backwater such as Manningtree the interest in a certain scandal is taking a long time to die. At least the local Rector, Reverend Tony Smith, thinks so.

Mr. Smith is often beseiged by visitors inquiring not about the church or one of its past vicars—but the scandal of the notorious Matthew Hopkins, self-styled Witchfinder General.

Hopkins lived in Manningtree, from where he carried out a witch-finding campaign which swept fear throughout Essex during the 17th Century.

Where is he buried? Where did he live? Can I see his death entry in the registers? These are the questions constantly put to Mr. Smith.

"The interest in scandal during the past few years, from Matthew Hopkins here to the Watergate Affair in America, has been so great the present era could become known as the Scandalous Seventies," said Mr. Smith.

But he is far from annoyed by the outburst of 'Hopkinsmania'.

He has taken a great deal of interest in the life of Hopkins and says he enjoys telling people about the whole era of Witchcraft terror in Essex.

East Anglian *Daily Times*
August 6, 1973.

introduction

The county of Essex, a flat, low-lying area on the eastern coast of England, has retained a timeless and rural charm despite the encroachment of nearby London and the determined efforts of those arms of the commuter, roads and railways, to penetrate to its farthest corners. Still it is a county, of small, quaint villages, of towns dominated by the agricultural pursuits of the region, and of city centers so full of historical buildings and monuments as to have resisted the tide of shopping complexes and multistory car parks. It is a county of history and tradition, an area of stability where families can be found who have lived in the same districts—even in the same houses—for generations. It is a place rich in history, a county that has played host to royalty, sent men to the far corners of the earth, and nursed writers and artists of the highest quality.

Essex County also became the center of, and the most bloody contributor to, the terrible witchcraft hysteria that blighted the English countryside from the mid-1560s to the close of the seventeenth century. This earned the county, for all time, the epithet of "The Witch County."

As anyone with even the most perfunctory knowledge of the subject will know, witchcraft has a long and complex history—stretching back into the mists of antiquity if you accept its origins as being in the ancient fertility cult Wicca or, alternatively, as a somewhat later invention of the Church and its bloody tribunal the Inquisition, which was established in the Middle Ages to expose and punish religious unorthodoxy. Whichever the case, the hysteria which erupted in the sixteenth and seventeenth centuries was almost entirely due to the prevailing climate, which, politically, was fraught with tension and unease and, socially, revealed people to be intensely superstitious and convinced that any activity that could not be rationally explained—in other words, anything *super*natural—was the work of the devil. Two quotations by eminent men of the period will perhaps better define the situation.

Sir Matthew Hale, the chief justice of the king's bench and widely held to be one of the brightest luminaries of the law, put the common viewpoint into these succinct words in 1604: "That there are such creatures as witches be in no doubt at all; for, first, the scriptures have affirmed so much. Secondly, the wisdom of all nations has provided laws against such persons, which is an argument of their confidence of such a crime. And such has been the judgement of this kingdom, as appears by that Act of Parliament which has provided punishments proportionable to the quality of the offence."

Likewise, James Howell, the historiographer royal to Charles II, expressed what must have been the opinion of high and low when he wrote to a friend in Paris in 1646: "We have multitudes of Witches among us, for in Essex and Suffolk alone there were above two hundred indicted within these two years, and above the one half of them executed: More, I may well say, than ever this Island bred since the Creation. I speak it with horror. God guard us from the Devil, for I think he was never so busy upon any part of the Earth that was enlightened with the beams of Christianity; nor do I wonder at it, for there's never a Cross left to frighten him away."

At this time, then, the devil was seen by virtually everyone to be a literal being, and his servants—and even those suspected of being in league with him—were to be feared and, wherever possible, rooted out and put to death.

It has been much debated why Essex should have played a larger part in this history of persecution than any other county. Certainly, other counties were as rural, as full of superstitious backwaters, and as strongly ruled by church and state; yet here, in the period in question, the belief in witchcraft was more pronounced than anywhere else. "The indictments for witchcraft in Essex," C. L'Estrange Ewen has reported in his study *Witch Hunting and Witch Trials* (1929), "actually outnumber those of the four counties of Hertfordshire, Kent, Surrey and Sussex combined." (The total for Essex was 473, with the next-largest 132 in Kent.) Wherever one turned, men, women, and children were being put to death or imprisoned for the slightest hint of witchcraft. A person merely had to accuse a neighbor of the practice, presenting the most absurdly circumstantial evidence, and what passed for justice fell on the accused with barbaric savagery.

The history of witchcraft throughout England at this time has been fully and carefully documented in numerous studies,[1] and Essex has naturally received extensive consideration in them all. Its major trials have been discussed and analyzed, the most famous witches and those who hunted them carefully studied, and the effects on society as a whole carefully plotted. However, all this material has been produced in hindsight, with the light of subsequent discoveries and evaluations at hand. Certainly, it was founded on original records, but with few exceptions it was weighted to the particular writers' purposes.

But just how did those who were present *at the time* view the events? What did they see, hear, and feel? How were their views shaped amid the hysteria? Did common sense and rationality prevail at all? Did anyone give a damn for justice and the basic human rights of man?

These are the questions *The Witchcraft Papers* sets out to answer. Herein are assembled some of the most important documents, trial reports, essays, and studies relative to the witchcraft outbreak in Essex. This study benefits from several important facts: First, the opening witchcraft trial in England (1565) took place in Essex County, at Chelmsford; second, the county saw the worst of all witch prosecu-

1. The best of these are undoubtedly Professor Wallace Nottestein, *A History of Witchcraft in England 1558–1718*, published in 1911 and reprinted in 1968 by Thomas Y. Crowell, New York; Professor G. L. Kittredge, *Witchcraft in Old and New England*, Oxford University Press, 1929; and Keith Thomas, *Religion and the Decline of Magic*, London: Weiedenfeld and Nicholson, 1971. All these are recommended to the reader seeking a fuller background to the witchcraft hysteria.

tions, directed against a group of women from the small village of St. Osyth's; third, Matthew Hopkins, the most infamous name in the annals of witch persecution, conducted the worst of his horrendous forays in the county; and, fourth, the last recorded witch hunt that ended in the death of the suspect also took place in the county (1699).

With these four cornerstones we have not only a framework on which to build a comprehensive picture of witchcraft in Essex, but also a means of indicating what was happening elsewhere throughout the nation. This structure allows the editor to fill in the intervening gaps with all manner of other material to show the ebb and flow of the persecution. The "Papers" have, naturally, differing values. Some are of the utmost importance and of extreme rarity, having been taken from manuscript originals; others are of a less weighty nature—ballads and poetry, for instance—but all show, I think, the many and varied aspects of witchcraft in Essex from 1560 to 1700.

Before proceeding to the "Papers," the reader would probably benefit from learning a little of Essex itself, to enable him or her to appreciate the documents more fully against their background.

In the middle of the sixteenth century the county of Essex consisted of approximately 420 villages and 7 boroughs; the largest town was Colchester (also, incidentally the oldest recorded town in Britain), followed by Chelmsford and the fishing and trading port of Maldon. Population figures at this period are extremely difficult to obtain and are usually unreliable, but it seems reasonable to estimate that the population of the county was slightly more than 100,000. The area was predominantly agricultural, and most villages contained only a few hundred people, living in about thirty to fifty households. Many such communities consisted of only three or four different families, who alternately feuded or intermarried with each other. Because of the isolation of most of the villages, the lack of education, and the primitive conditions in which they lived, the people were intensely superstitious and paid great regard to "magic spells" used for either good or evil.

Traditionally, old people were believed to be the repository of cures for illness, and as long as they lived within the community with relatives, little harm came to them. But if they were widowed or forced to live alone for any reason, they almost invariably became ostracized; and if, in time, old age brought with it senility, the accusation of "witch" was not long in following. The records of the period, including some in this book, clearly show that many of these accusations arose from quarrels between families or neighbors. It was very convenient to say that someone who fell ill after a row had been bewitched by the other party—just as it was easy to blame crop failure, animal diseases, or food spoilage on the muttered remarks of an old village dotard.

Documents also clearly illustrate how, once the accusation of witchcraft had been uttered against someone, however ill judged it might be, it was virtually impossible to stop the story from circulating. When the witchcraft persecution began in earnest, of course, the rumors flew thick and fast, and at its worst a person needed only to be old, ugly, and poor to be labeled a witch. (Some authorities, including Richard Bernard and John Gaule, have also said that a similar charge was frequently leveled against those leading a "lewd and naughty kind of life"!)

As we shall see, the law took all such charges seriously during much of the period we are considering, but on the rare occasions when the evidence was too ridiculous for even the magistrates, the villagers of Essex were not above handing out their own kind of rough justice. These mobs, as has always been the case, were most active when the suspect was a widow or an unmarried woman, so that repercussions were unlikely.

For all this superstition, Essex was a profoundly religious county and displayed its inherent Puritanism perhaps most vividly when Cromwell began his opposition to King Charles I, the county proving one of the first strongholds of Cromwell's campaign. This climate also undoubtedly contributed to the fervor with which people joined in the hysteria of persecution and the way they accepted the most literal definition of the devil. (It is interesting to note in this context, however, that there are few actual descriptions in contemporary documents of the devil's appearing; he usually appears disguised as a small cat or a ferret.)

Against these general statements of the conditions of the time, it is possible to weigh the actual statistics garnered from the Essex court rolls and indictments of the period. (The reader should bear in mind that the law concerning witchcraft changed twice during the time covered by this study. The first English witchcraft statute was introduced in 1542 by Henry VIII and then repealed in 1547. In 1563 it was reintroduced by Queen Elizabeth I, only to be repealed and replaced with a still more severe charter by James I in 1604. This subsequent law remained untouched on the statute books until 1736. Fuller details of the laws and their punishments will follow in the appropriate sections.)

Between 1560 and 1680, about 2,300 people were involved in witchcraft cases in Essex, as either suspects or victims, and of these more than 500 were prosecuted at the assizes, quarter sessions, or ecclesiastical courts. This total, however, probably represents less than two thirds of all those believed to have actually been accused during the period. About 70 percent of the accusations related to the death or illness of human beings by witchcraft, and most of the remainder related to injuries to animals. The witches were almost invariably women—fewer than 5 percent were men—and the vast majority were between fifty and seventy years old. (A proportion are also shown to have still been married, "though they quarreled much and were commonly known as scolds," to quote one case.) It appears, too, that it was women more than men who suffered the attentions of the witches.

If we turn now to the actual yearly assize-court figures assembled by Professor Ewen, the rise and fall in the number of people brought before the magistrates illustrates far more graphically than words the pattern of the hysteria.

Period	Accused	Indicted
1560–1579	52	82
1580–1599	111	195
1600–1619	44	78
1620–1639	25	35
1640–1659	63	83*
1660–1679	12	14

* Of this total, 50 people were indicted in 1645 alone—the first year of Matthew Hopkins' reign of terror.

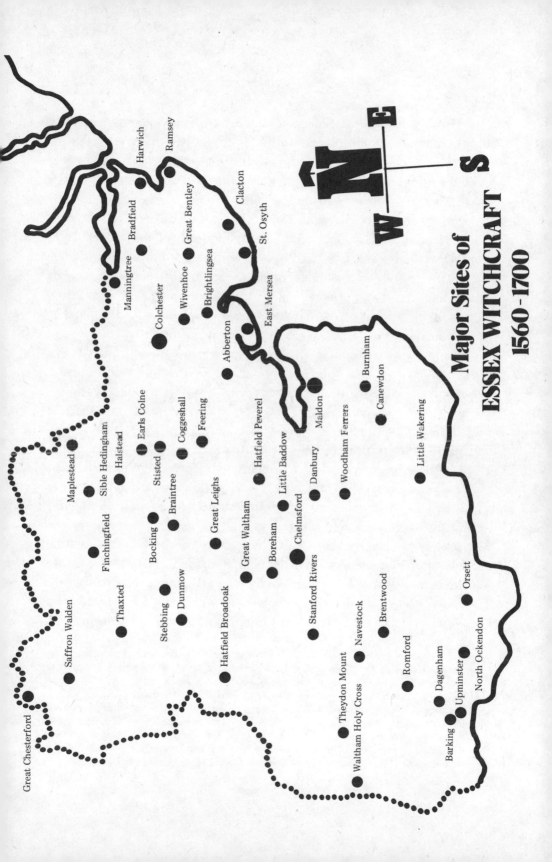

Major Sites of
ESSEX WITCHCRAFT
1560 - 1700

Great Chesterford

Saffron Walden

Maplestead

Thaxted

Finchingfield

Sible Hedingham

Halstead

Earls Colne

Stebbing

Dunmow

Bocking

Braintree

Stisted

Coggeshall

Feering

Great Leighs

Hatfield Broadoak

Great Waltham

Boreham

Hatfield Peverel

Little Baddow

Chelmsford

Stanford Rivers

Danbury

Woodham Ferrers

Maldon

Burnham

Canewdon

Little Wakering

Manningtree

Bradfield

Harwich

Ramsey

Colchester

Wivenhoe

Great Bentley

Brightlingsea

Clacton

St. Osyth

Abberton

East Mersea

Theydon Mount

Waltham Holy Cross

Navestock

Brentwood

Romford

Dagenham

Upminster

Barking

North Ockendon

Orsett

From still closer examination of the rolls, it appears that the most intensive area of prosecution was the northern part of the county, with one particularly virulent outbreak in the northeast at Manningtree. Chelmsford, Braintree, and Halstead, in the center, also have high percentages. However, even the most cursory glance at the accompanying map shows how, in reality, the prosecutions stretched across the length and breadth of the county. Indeed, of the county's 420 villages, more than half were involved with at least one witchcraft case.

Hanging was the punishment prescribed by law for conviction of causing death by witchcraft under the statute of Queen Elizabeth— merely practicing witchcraft was enough under James I's law—and as a consequence, eighty-two Essex people ended their days on the rope during our period. Imprisonment was also widely used in Elizabeth's time, but whether this was preferable is doubtful, since prison conditions were so appalling that at least fifty Essex men and women are known to have died of "jail fever" while under sentence or awaiting trial.

The form of the trial for witchcraft varied little during the period. Anyone suspecting another of witchcraft would lay information against that person with the constable or local justice. It was then up to the official to decide whether to seize the suspect or to begin an inquiry, taking statements from others who might have information. In the latter case, once the statements were complete, the suspect would be taken into custody by warrant, examined, and indicted to appear before the next assizes at Colchester, Chelmsford, Braintree, or Brentwood.[2] Bail was available but rarely allowed in witchcraft cases. In court, a presentation of the facts was made by the prosecutor; then came the

2. The assize-court records for Essex contain a variety of indictments, the majority being traditional accusations for bewitching people, animals, or goods; but among them are some that are more unusual. One such, from the Chelmsford summer sessions of 1616, shows the traditional form of the indictment but contains details of a charge not often encountered at this time: "The jurors for the Lord the King [James I] do present that Susan Barker, of Upminster in the county of Essex, wife of the late Henry Barker, being a common witch and enchantress, not having God before her eyes, but seduced by the instigation of the Devil, on 28 September at Upminster aforesaid in the county aforesaid, feloniously did take up a skull out of a certain grave in the burying ground of the parish church of Upminster,

appearance of witnesses; and finally an offer was made to the suspect to confess before sentence was passed. (Matthew Hopkins, it will be seen, circumvented much of this procedure by finding the suspects himself and then having them confess even before they went in front of the examining magistrate, let alone the assize court!)[3]

A horrifyingly large number of cases, in Essex particularly, were based on the statements of young children. Not a few of these infants actually accused their relatives, and two of the worst cases held in the county, in 1579 and 1589, featured youngsters giving evidence against their own mothers. "Many go so farre," George Gifford commented in his *Dialogue* (1594), "that if they can intice children to accuse their parents they thinke it a good worke." Since it was widely believed that witchcraft was hereditary, it has been argued that the children blamed others to save their own necks. Nevertheless, we shall see several instances of this side of witchcraft in the "Papers."

Another facet of the witchcraft story deals with the alleged white, or good, witches—the "cunning men" who were said to be the opponents of the witches and able to counter their power. These men—they were almost without exception males—were much sought after by the people of Essex to cure illness and remove spells. They, too, generally lived in isolation from the community, but they were held in high

being part of the body of a certain deceased man lately buried there, with intent to use the said skull in certain evil and devilish arts, namely witchcraft, charms and sorceries with intent to bewitch and enchant a certain Mary Stevens against the form of the statute in this case lately made and provided, and against the peace of the said lord the now King, his crown and dignity."

3. Perhaps the most extraordinary "confession" Hopkins extracted was that of a Dorothy Ellis of Brentwood in 1646. It reads, "She saith that about thirtie yeares since she being much troubled in her minde, there appeared unto her the Devell in the likeness of a great catt and spoke and demanded of hir hir blood which she gave hime, after which the spirit in the likness of a catt sucked upon hir body. And the first thing that she commanded her spirit to doe was to goe and bewitch 4 of the cattell of Thomas Hitchal which cattell presently died. Further she confesseth that she sent hir catt spirit to bewitch and take away the life of Marie the daughter of Thomas Salter which spirit forthwith kild the child of the said Marie. Also she confesseth she commanded her spirit to lame the mother of the said child old Marie Salter which was done accordingly; and she commanded hir spirit to goe and bewitch and lame John Gotobed because he cald her an old witch and flung stones at her, which command was performed by her spirit and the said Gotobed lamed. X (Dorothy Ellis, hir mark.)"

regard and it was more likely for a villager who consulted a "cunning man" to be prosecuted if he was found out then for the man himself to be brought before the magistrate.

These men were said to provide small items to wear around the neck or carry in the pocket to ward off the influence of witches, and they supposedly sacrificed small animals to make their spells more powerful. There was much debate about their alleged powers and they carefully avoided controversy by refusing payment until success was achieved. The most famous of these men, Miles Blomfield, was said to be an alchemist as well as a "cunning man." He was so revered that in 1582 he was made a churchwarden at Chelmsford. "Cunning men" enjoyed continuing support in Essex until quite recently.

As a matter of record the last case of witchcraft to appear before the Essex quarter sessions was in 1664, and the last before the assizes was in 1675. The county's final witchcraft execution was in 1646, and the last in England at Exeter in 1684. There were informal accusations in the county after 1675, of course, but none ever reached the courts.

That, then, is the background to *The Witchcraft Papers*. They represent a sad and terrible era in English history that must in part be to blame for the subsequent bloody drama at Salem in 1692. For many of the settlers there were of English—not to mention Essex—origin and had carried with them to the new world most of the old fears and prejudices relating to witchcraft. As for Essex itself, the stain remains.

As a resident of Essex and a visitor to many of the places featured in this study, I know how by night a special kind of eeriness creeps across the county, an atmosphere that can give rise to all sorts of fantasies in even the most sophisticated mind. On the marshes near St. Osyth strange shapes rear up on winter nights, and even in the countryside around the busy town of Colchester, there is a haunting and remote beauty that cannot have changed in hundreds of years. There can be no excuses for the terrible things that happened here in the name of God and Christianity—but for those who search in the records, in the pages of this book, and in the district itself, there are explanations to be found. . . .

Peter Haining, Birch Green, Essex

deposition against a witch

Anonymous

Although the trial at Chelmsford in July 1565 is widely accepted to herald the opening of witchcraft persecution in Essex—and indeed in England—there was in fact an earlier and completely overlooked instance in the county that arose almost immediately after the introduction of Queen Elizabeth's new witchcraft statute in 1563. This decree had been produced mainly on the instigation of the Protestant clergy, who were worried that the sudden outbreak of witchcraft in Europe—which was being put down with great determination—might spread to England. (At this time there were no laws against Witchcraft, the last statute of Henry VIII having been repealed in 1547 by Edward VI.) There was also much talk of sorcery in the air, and a deeply rooted concern was growing among the English noblemen that supporters of the Roman Catholic ruler of Scotland, Mary, Queen of Scots, were resorting to magic in their plots against Elizabeth. (In fact, at this same time Mary was herself passing an antiwitchcraft bill!)

Against this background, and the predictable hostility among the population whenever the word "witchcraft" was mentioned, it is not difficult to understand how readily legislation was put forward and accepted. The chief provisions of the new act called for the death penalty for murder by sorcery and a year's imprisonment for witchcraft "not deadly." As more than one commentator has subsequently remarked, despite its comparative rationality, this act quite literally began the century of witch mania in England.

Essex, as indicated, was the first area to see the new law put into effect, and this was particularly approved by the bishop of the diocese, Edmund Grindal, a rigid Calvinist and avowed witch hunter who had already complained that "our ecclesiastical punishment is too slender for sorcery." His influence was no doubt another of the reasons why the vast majority of indictments for witchcraft during Elizabeth's reign were to be handed down in Essex.

This first instance concerned Elizabeth Lewys, of Waltham, who was accused before the 1563 summer assizes at Chelmsford of "exercysinge her wytcherie" and causing animals to die and people to fall ill. Her case is particularly interesting, not only because it is the first recorded prosecution of an alleged witch, but also because the statements of her accusers paint a revealing picture of life in rural Essex at the opening of the "Witchcraft Era." The record of the trial is to be found in the *Archdeaconry Act Book of Essex*, which is of considerable antiquity and now housed in the Essex Records Office. The pages are so faded as to make it impossible to include more than three of the half dozen testimonies made against Elizabeth Lewys and only a section of her defense. In the light of the astonishing evidence, it was perhaps only just that the poor woman was in a position to be able to fall back on one of the oldest English judicial provisions to avoid imprisonment or execution—she pleaded pregnancy and was allowed to go free!

The Deposition of Henry Geale, aged 80, a resident of Waltham for six or seven years.

Said that John Lewys and his wife Elizabeth, about this time two years ago had stolen a capon [a rooster fattened for cooking] from this deponent, and when he came to demand it they denied it utterly, till at last when they saw this deponent would go further the said John Lewys confessed and offered him money, but no certain sum. And he said he had sold it to one Mary Barnard, Lewys' wife's sister, which capon the said Lewys then fetched. He would have delivered it, but this deponent refused so to do, and told him to come into this deponent's house. For this deponent had been to see Thomas Gryges, the Constable, who told him to send for some other man at the receipt of the capon. And the delivery of the capon was made in the presence of Thomas Wignall. . . .

The said capon delivered they fell into talk. The said Wignall said to John Lewys in this wise. "For shame Lewys, being an old man wilt not thou leave thy pilfering?" Then said Lewys, "I pray you end this matter and I will never do so more." To whom again Wignall said, "Thou has been a pretty man in thy days has thou not?" "Yes" said Lewys, "I may thank my wife for my lameness for she has bewitched me lame, and when I sent for the Cunning Man of Witham he told me it was my wife's doing." . . .

And then and there Lewys' wife and her mother who lived with them fell to vexations, and she, the said Elizabeth Lewys, said that being weary of exercising her witcherie because her mother was stronger in bewitching than she was, she would devour herself. And upon that her husband, being in fear of her, went into the street. And when coming home he found her hanging in the house. She had hanged herself until she was dead [*sic*]. And her husband cut the rope. And being relieved, Thomas Wignall and others demanded of her why she did so and she said that she did it to the end that her mother should be hanged because she was the stronger witch.

The Deposition of Agnes Devenyshe, aged 47, a resident of Waltham for eight years.

She said that she had heard a common rumour that Lewys' wife was a witch. About March last, she went to the said Lewys' wife's house, and they talked about a sore arm of hers. And she, Lewys, counselled her to go to a woman under Munckewood, and going there, the folks told her that she was a witch. . . .

That this deponent going to Lewys' wife for money which she had lent, could not be repaid, and after that she had two pigs and one of them suddenly died, and the other pined until she was forced to sell it. And she judged that it was the doing of the said Lewys' wife. And then this deponent fell sick with her husband and child with all in pain and grief. . . .

That one May evening, being at John Canell's house, his child being sick, it lay with the neck twisted, the face under the left shoulder and the right arm clasped with the hand backward, and the body lying not right but writhing, and the right leg turned backwards behind the body—contrary to all nature; and they suppose the very doing of the said Lewys' wife.

The Deposition of Philippa Geale, aged 32 of Great Waltham.

That Elizabeth Lewys, wife of John Lewys, and this deponent fell to arguing about the taking in of work, and that the said Lewys' wife went to John Barnard's wife and said that this deponent would spin no more of her work. Thereupon at the next meeting they fell out. And this deponent told her [Lewys] that she lied and had told a wrong talk. And, among other talk, this deponent said that she said, "If it be as folk say, thou art a witch?" To which the said Lewys' wife answered, "If I be a witch, the devil thee touch." And immediately upon that this deponent fell into a great quivering and quaking. And soon after that she went home, continuing to suffer from that day [Saturday] to Wednesday, at which day she fell down dead [*sic*] and was so sick for fourteen days that nobody thought she would have lived. And then her neighbours sent for the priest, to whom she told it all. And then he sent for the said Lewys' wife, threatening her if this deponent died she should be hung for a witch, and after her coming this deponent mended.

The Examination of Elizabeth Lewys.

Whether she in her yard or house, kneeling, standing or lying flat, spoke these words, "Christ, my Christ, if thou be a saviour come down and avenge me of my enemies, or else thou shall not be a saviour." This she denies. . . .

Whether she confessed that she killed a lamb by witcherie, and cried "Why not feed dogs with the meat of children?" when it was being fed with milk and white-bread. She admitted that she came into a house where a woman was feeding a lamb with milk and white-bread and said, "What, must it be fed with white-bread and milk?" and then the woman put down the lamb, and the next day it died by eating too much white-bread and milk. . . .

Whether she counseled Agnes Devenyshe to go to the Woman of Munckewood for witchcraft to aid her recovery from illness. She replied that she had not willed the woman to go there for witchcraft. . . .

Whether she played a part in the hurting of John Canell's child for he affirms that his child sickened and was so deformed as never was seen, *viz.* the right arm turning completely contrary, and the leg contrary to that, and both rising to the head of the child. She denied this and said she was not the doer of it, nor of any of the other acts of witcherie alleged against her.

the first witch trial in england

by John Philip

The first major Essex witchcraft trial took place in 1565 at Chelmsford and was carefully recorded in several legal and ecclesiastical documents that have survived to the present day. Perhaps more detailed, and certainly more colorful, than these was a vivid pamphlet, the first of its kind, published a few days after the event. It captured much of the drama of the proceedings, which took up two hot summer days in July 1565. The judges were Sir John Fortescue, who later became the chancellor of the exchequer, and Mr. Justice Southcote of the queen's bench. The prosecutors were a fervent and silver-tongued local minister, the Reverend Thomas Cole, and the attorney general, Sir Gilbert Gerard. (That he should have attended the trial shows the importance the authorities placed on it.)

What these four men deliberated and decided was to serve as a precedent for many later witchcraft trials. During the evidence—recorded in the pamphlet "verbatim as neere as could be gathered" by the scribe, a London hack named John Philip—not only was the testimony of a twelve-year-old child, Agnes Brown, admitted, but the cat made its first appearance as a "familiar" in the history of witchcraft. The pamphlet, "Imprynted at London by Willyam Powell for

Wyllyam Pickeringe dwelling at Sainte Magnus Corner. Anno 1566, the 13 August," falls into two sections, the first covering the trial and the second the "confession" of one of the accused, Mother Waterhouse.

The three accused witches, Elizabeth Francis, Agnes Waterhouse, and her daughter Joan, all came from the tiny village of Hatfield Peverel, near Chelmsford, but the only real connection between them was that Elizabeth Francis had allegedly passed on her familiar, the cat named Sathan, to Mother Waterhouse. At the end of the trial, Mother Waterhouse was found guilty of "bewitching to death" and sentenced to be executed. (She was hanged two days later, the first woman to be put to death in England for witchcraft.) Her daughter Joan—having given evidence against her for the crown—was found not guilty and released.

Elizabeth Francis was found guilty of bewitching and sentenced to the statutory one year's imprisonment, but her story does not end there. Shortly after her release, she was again accused of bewitching and once more committed to prison for a year. Still, she appeared not to have learned the value of keeping out of trouble, for less than a decade later she was back in court yet again, accused with three other women of practicing witchcraft. This time, however, there was to be no mercy—she was found guilty and hanged.

But to return to the original case and the pamphlet describing it—a single copy of which still exists, in the British Museum:

The examination and confession of certain wytches at Chelmsford in the Countie of Essex, before the Quenes Majesties Judges, the xxvi days of July, Anno 1565 at the Assize holden there as then, and one of them put to death for the same offence, as their examination declareth more at large.

The second examination and Confession of Mother Agnes Waterhouse and Joan her daughter, upon her arainement, with the questions and answeres of Agnes Browne the Childe on whom the spirite haunteth at this present, deliberately declared before Justice Southcote and Master Gerard the Quenes atturney, the xxvii day of July Anno 1566, no less wonderfull than most true.

The Ende and laste Confession of Mother Waterhouse at her death which was the xxix day of July 1566.

The examination of them with their confession before Doctor Cole and master Foscue at the same Sise verbatum, as nere as coulde be gathered, and firste of Elizabeth Frauncis who saide as here foloweth.

Fyrst she learned this arte of witchcraft at the age of xii yeres of hyr grandmother whose nam mother Eue of Hatfyelde Peurell, disseased. Item when shee taughte it her, she counseiled her to renounce GOD and his worde, and to geue of her blodde to Sathan (as she termed it) whyche she delyuered her in the lykenesse of a whyte spotted Catte, and taughte her to feede the sayde Catte with breade and mylke, and she dyd so, also she taughte her to cal it by the name of Sathan and to kepe it in a basket.

When this mother Eue had geuen her the Cat Sathan, then this Elizabeth desired firste of the sayde Car (callinge it Sathan) that she might be ryche and to haue goodes, and he promised her she shoulde—askinge her what she would haue, and she sayde shepe (for this Cat spake to her as she confessed in a straunge holowe voice, but such as she vnderstode by vse) and this Cat forthwith brought shepe into her pasture to the number of xvii, blacke and whyte, whych continued with her for a tyme, but in the ende dyd all weare awaye she knewe not howe.

Item, when she had gotten these shepe, she desired to haue one Andrew Byles to her husband, which was a man of some welth, and the cat dyd promyse she shold, but that he sayde she must fyrste consent that this Andrew shuld abuse her, and she so did.

And after when this Andrew had thus abused her he would not mary her, wherefore she willed Sathan to waste his goodes, which he forthwith did, and yet not beyng contentid with this, she wild him to touch his body whych he forthewith dyd whereof he died.

Item, that euery time that he did any thynge for her, she sayde that he required a drop of bloude, which she gaue him by prycking herselfe, sometime in one place and then in an other, and where she pricked her selfe there remayned a red spot which was styl to be sene.

Item, when this Andrew was dead, she douting her selfe with childe, willed Sathan to destroye it, and he bad her take a certayne herbe and drinke it, whych she did, and destroyed the childe forthwyth.

Item, when she desyred an other husbande he promysed her an other, naminge this Frauncis whom shee nowe hath, but said he is not so rich as the other, willynge her to consent vnto that Frauncis in fornycation which she did, and therof conceaued a daughter that was borne within a quarter of a yere after they were maried.

After they were maryed they liued not so quietly as she desyred, beinge stirred (as she said) to much vnquietnes and moued to swearing and cursinge, wherfore she willed Sathan her Cat to kyll the childe, beinge aboute the age of half a yere olde, and he did so, and when she yet founde not the quietnes that she desyred, she wylled it to lay a lamenes in the leg of thys Frauncis her husbande, and it did in this maner. It came in a morninge to this Frauncis shoe, lying in it lyke a tode, and when he perceived it puttinge on his shoe, and had touched it with his fote, he being sodenly amased asked of her what it was, and she bad him kil it and he was forthwith taken with a lamenes which will not heal.

After all this when shee had kept this Cat by the space of xv or xvi yeare, and as some saye (though vntruly) beinge wery of it, she came to one mother Waterhouse her neyghbour (a pore woman) when she was going to the oven and desired her to geue her a cake, and she wold geue her a thing that she should be the better for so long as she liued, and this mother Waterhouse gaue her a cake, where vpon she brought her this cat in her apron and taught her as she was instructed before by her grandmother Eue, telling her that she must cal him Sathan and geue him of her bloude and bread and milke as before, and at this examination woulde confesse no more.

Mother Waterhouse of Hatfylde peuerell of the age of lxiiii yeares being examined the same day confessed as followeth, and the xxix daye suffered.

Fyrst she receyued this cat of this Frances wife in the order as is before sayde, who wild her to cal him Sathan, and told her that yf she made muche of him he would do for her what she wolde haue him to do.

Then when she had receyued him she (to trye him what he coulde do) wyld him to kyll a hog of her owne, which he dyd, and she gaue him for his labour a chicken, which he fyrste required of her and a drop of her blod. And thys she gaue him at all times when he dyd anythynge for her, by pricking her hand or face and puttinge the bloud to hys mouth whyche he sucked, and forthwith wold lye downe in hys pot againe, wherin she kepte him, the spots of all the which priks are yet to be sene in her skin.

Also she saythe that another tyme being offended with one Father Kersye she toke her catte Sathan in her lap and put hym in the wood before her dore, and willed him to kyll three of this father Kersyes hogges, whiche he dyd, and retourning agayne told her so, and she rewarded hym as before, wyth a chicken and a droppe of her bloud, which chicken he eate vp cleane as he didde al the rest, and she cold fynde remaining neyther bones nor fethers.

Also she confessed that falling out with one widdow Gooday she wylled Sathan to drowne her cow and he dyd so, and she rewardid hym as before.

Also she falling out wyth another of her neyboures, she killed her three geese in the same maner.

Item, shee confessed that because she could haue no rest (which she required) she caused Sathan to destroye the brewing at that tyme.

Also beying denyed butter of an other, she caused her to lose the curdes ii or iii dayes after.

Item fallinge out with an other of her neybours and his wife, shee wylled Sathan to kyll him with a bludye flixe, whereof he dyed, and she rewarded him as before.

Likewyse shee confessed, that because she lyued somwhat vnquietly with her husbande, she caused Sathan to kyll him, and he doid so about ix yeres past, syth which tyme she hath lyued a widdow.

Also she said that when she wolde wyl him to do any thinge for her, she wolde say her Pater noster in laten.

Item, this mother Waterhouse confessed that shee fyrst turned this Cat into a tode by this meanes, she kept the cat a great while in woll in a pot, and at length being moued by pouertie to occupie the woll, she praied in the name of the father and of the sonne, and of the holy ghost that it wold turne into a tode, and forthwith it was turned into a tode, and so kept it in the pot without woll.

Also she said, that going to Brackstede a lyttle before her apprehentyon, this Sathan wylled her to hye her home, for she shulde haue great trouble and that shee shoulde be eyther hanged or burned shortly, more at this tyme she woulde not confesse.

Jone Waterhouse daughter to this mother Waterhouse, beinge of the age of xviii *yeres, and examined confesseth as foloweth.*

Fyrst that her mother this laste wynter woulde haue learned her this arte, but she lerned it not, nether yet the name of the thinge. She saith she neuer saw it but once in her mother's hand, and that was in the likenes of a tode, and at that time comming in at a sodeyn when her mother called it oute to worke some thynge withall, she herde her to call it Sathan, for shee was not at any time truely taught it, nor did neuer exercise it before this tyme as foloweth:

Item she confessed that when her mother was gone to Breackstede, in her absence lacking breade, she went to a gyrle a neybours chylde, and desired her to geue her a pece of brede and cheese, whiche when denied and gaue her not, or at the least not so muche as wolde satisfye her, shee goinge home dydde as she had seene her mother doe, callynge Sathan, whiche came to her (as she sayd) she thoughte out of her mothers shewe from vnder the bedde, in the lykenes of a great dogge, demaundynge what she wolde haue wherewithal she beyng a fearde, sayd she wold have him to make such a gyrle a ferd naminge this gyrle, then asked hee her what she wolde geue hym, and she saide a red kocke, then sayde hee no, but thou shalt geue me thy body and sowle, whereby she beinge soore feared, and desyrous to be rydde of hym, sayd she wold: And herewith he went to this gyrle in the lykenes of an euyll fauoured dogge with hornes on his head, and made her very muche afearde, and dothe yet haunt her, nowe can not these witches (as they saye) cal hym in agayn, because they dyd not let hym out. And more (sayth shee) she never dydde, but this her doinge was the reuealyng of all the rest.

The Confession of Agnes Waterhowse the xxvii *daye of July in Anno* 1566 *at Chelmsforde before Justice Southcote and M. Gerard the quenes atturney.*

Fyrst being demaunded whether that shee were gyltye or not gilty vpon her araynement of the murtheringe of a man, she confessed that she was gilty, and then vppon the euidence geuen agaynst her daughter Jone Waterhouse, she sayde that she hadde a white Cat, and wylled her cat that he shuld destroy many of his neyghbours cattell, and also that he shoulde kyll a man, and so he dyd, and then after she must go ii or iii mile from her house, and then she toke thoughte howe to kepe her catte, then she and her catte concluded that he the sayde Catte wolde become a tode, and then she shuld kepe him in a close house and geue hym mylke, and so he wolde continue tyll she came home againe, and then being gone forth, her daughter hauing ben at a neyghbour's house there by, required of one Agnes Browne, of the age of xii yeres or more, a peece of breade and cheese, and the sayde Agnes saide that shee had none, and that she had not the key of the milkhouse dore, and then the sayde Jone went home and was angry with the said Agnes Broun and she saide that she remembred that her mother was wonte to go vp and downe in her house and to call Sathan Sathan she sayde she wolde proue the like, and then she went vp an downe the house and called Sathan, and then there came a black dogge to her and asked her what she woulde haue, and then she saide she was aferd and sayd, I wold haue thee to make one Agnes Browne afrayde, and then he asked her what she wold giue him and she saide she wold geue hym a red kock, and he said he wolde haue none of that, and shee asked him what he wolde haue then, and he sayde he wold haue her body and soule, and so upon requeste and feare together she gaue him her body and soule, and then sayde the quenes atturneye *Howe vvylt thou do before God.* O my Lord, I trust God wyll haue mercy vpon mee, and then he saide *thou saiste vvell,* and then he departed from her, and then she saide that she herde that he made the sayde Agnes Browne a fearde.

The said Agnes Brown, was then demaunded and called for, and then she came in, and beinge asked what age she was of she sayde she thoughte she was xii yeres old, and then the quenes atturney asked her what shee could say, and then shee saide that at suche a day, naming the daye certayne that shee was chirning of butter and there came to her a thynge lyke a black dogge with a face like an ape, a short taile, a cheine and a syluer whystle (to her thinking) about his neck, and a peyre of hornes on his heade, and brought in his mouth the keye of the milkehouse doore, and then my lorde she saide, I was afearde, for he skypped and leaped to and fro, and satte on the toppe of a nettle, and then I asked hym what he wolde haue, and he saide he woulde haue butter, and I saide I had none for him and then he saide he wolde haue some or he went, and then he dyd run to put the keye into the locke of the mylkehouse dore, and I sayde he sholde haue none, and he sayde he wolde haue some, and then he opened the dore and went vppon the shelfe, and there vpon a new chese laid downe the key, and being a whyle within he came out againe, and locked the dore and said that he had made flap butter for mee, and so departed, and then she saide shee tolde her aunte of it, and then she sent for the priest, and when he came he bad her to praye to God, and cal on the name of Jesus, and soo the nexte day my lord he came again to me with the keye of our milkehouse dore in his mouthe, and then I saide in the name of Jesus what haste thou there, and then he layed downe the key and sayde that I spake cuyll woordes in speakyng of that name, and then hee departed, and so my aunte toke up the key, for he had kept it from vs ii dayes and a nyghte, and then we went into the milkhouse and there we dyd se the print of butter vpon the chese, and then within a few daies after hee came againe with a beane pod in his mouth, and then the queenes atturney asked what that was, and so the other Justices declared, and then shee sayde my lorde I saide in the name of Jesus what hast thou there, and so then he laid it downe and saide I spake cuil wordes and departed and came agayne by and by with a pece of breade in his mouth, and I asked hym what he wold haue, and he sayde butter it was that he wold haue, and so he departed, and my lord I dyd not see hym noo more tyll wenseday laste, whiche was the xxiiii day of July, why said the quenes atturneye was he with the on Wenseday last, ye she said, what did he then to thee sayde he, my lorde saide shee he came with a knyfe in his mouthe and asked me if I were not dead, and I saide No I thanked God, and then hee sayde if I wolde not dye that hee wold thrust his knife to my harte but he wold make me to dye, and then I sayde in the name of Jesus lay down thy knyfe, and he sayde he wolde not departe from his sweete dames knyfe as yet, and then I asked of hym who was his dame, and then he nodded and wagged his head to your house mother Waterhouse, then the queenes attourneye asked if she sayde Agnes Waterhouse what she saide to it, then she demanded what maner knife that it was, and Agnes Browne said it was a daggar knife, there thou liest saide Agnes Waterhouse, why, quod the quenes atturney, mary my lord (quod she) she saith it is a daggar knife and I haue none such in my house, but a greate knyfe, and therein she lieth, yea yea, my lord quoth Jone Waterhouse she lieth in that she saith it hadde a face like an ape, for this that came to mee was like a dogge, well sayde the quenes attourney, well, can you make it come before us nowe, if ye can we will dyspatche you out of prison by and by, no saith saide Agnes Waterhouse I can not, for in faith if I had let hym go as my daughter did I could make hym come by and by, but now I have no more power ouer him, then said the queenes atturneye, Agnes Waterhouse when dyd thye Cat suck of thy bloud neuer saide she, no saide hee, let me se, and then the jayler lifted up her kercher on her heade, and there was diuerse spottes in her face and one on her nose, then sayde the quenes atturney, in good faith Agnes when dydde he sucke of thy bloud laste, by my fayth my lord sayde she, not this fortnyght, and so the jurye went together for that matter.

The ende and last confession of mother Waterhouse at her death, whiche was the xxix *daye of July. Anno* 1566.

Fyrste (beinge redi prepared to receiue her death) she confessed earnestly that shee had bene a wytche and vsed suche execrable sorserye the space of xv yeres, and had don many abhominable dede, the which she repented earnestly and unfaynedly, and desyred almighty Gods forqeueness in that she had abused hys most holy name by her deuyllishe practyses, and trusted to be saued by his most vnspekeable mercy. And being demaunded of the by standers, shee confessed that shee sent her Sathan to one Wardol, a neibour of hers, beinge a tayler (with whom she was offended) to hurte and destroye him and his goodes. And this her Sathan went therabout for to haue done her wyll, but in the ende he returned to her agayne, and was not able to do this myschiefe, she asked the cause, and he aunswered because the said Wardol was so strong in fayth that he hadde no power to hurte hym, yet she sent hym dyuerse and sundry time (but all in vayne) to haue mischeuid hym. And being demaunded whether she was accustomed to go to church to the common prayer or deuine seruice, she saide yea, and being required what she dyd there she saide she did as other women do, and prayed right hartely there, and when she was demanded what praier she saide, she aunswered the Lordes prayer, the Aue Maria, and the belefe, and then they demaunded whether in laten or in englyshe, and shee sayde in laten, and they demaunded why she saide it not in englyshe but in laten, seing that it was set out by publike aucthoritie and according to Goddes word that all men shoulde pray in the englyshe and mother toung that they best vnderstande, and shee sayde that Sathan wolde at no tyme suffer her to say it in englyshe, but at all tymes in laten: for these and many other offences whiche shee hathe commytted, done and confessed, shee bewayled, repented, and asked mercy of God, and all the worlde forgyuenes and thus she yelded vp her sowle, trusting to be in joye with Christe her Sauiour, which dearely had bought her with his most precious bloudde. Amen.

the memoirs of a
witchcraft judge

by Sir Thomas Smith

During the era of the English witchcraft trials a number of judges rose to prominence, but perhaps because of the bias of their judgment and the severity of their punishments, most have subsequently been consigned to oblivion. Certainly they were all subject to considerable social and official pressures, but it is sad to find so few who displayed anything approaching rationality in an age when prejudice and bigotry rode roughshod over the lives of men and women in all but the wealthiest and most noble classes. In the light of this, it is perhaps all the more remarkable to find that one of the few judges still recalled in history came from Essex, the very hotbed of witchcraft. He was Sir Thomas Smith, a nobleman and one of the country's senior justices.

Although not far removed from many of his colleagues in his unbending attitude toward witchcraft, Sir Thomas does at least seem to have been receptive to common sense, and he was a patient listener, not given to cajoling or threats. Where he does surpass his contemporaries is in the records he has left of his life and work, and his court proceedings in particular.

Born in Saffron Walden in 1512, Thomas Smith was the son of the high sheriff of Essex and proved himself an exemplary scholar at

Cambridge. After leaving the university, he was for a brief spell a lecturer before being recruited into the diplomatic service, serving thereafter as an ambassador to several European courts. In 1567 he decided to retire from public life for a few years and settled on his estate near Epping. However, he did agree to serve as a local justice of the peace, and in this capacity he came into contact with witchcraft at first hand and played a significant role in several cases.

In the closing years of his life, Sir Thomas became principal secretary of state to Queen Elizabeth and was much sought after for his wide knowledge of medicine, chemistry, mathematics, astronomy, and history. He died in 1577.

The following report of his examination of two women accused of witchcraft, recorded by John Strype and last reprinted in 1820, is another fascinating picture of rural Essex—Sir Thomas's own area—and typical in its way of many of the cases that passed before the benches of Essex justices in the second half of the sixteenth century.

Among other cases that came before Sir Thomas, there happened certain matters of supposed witchcraft, which occasioned much disturbance among his neighbours; arising especially from two women, viz. one, Malter's wife of Theydon Mount, the parish where Sir Thomas himself dwelt; and the other, Anne Vicars of Navestock, not far off.

The examination of the former he took in April 1570: against whom one evidence deposed, that about two years past she bore her husband in hand that he was bewitched: and as a remedy thereof, she caused a trivet to be set, and certain pieces of elder and white hazel wood to be laid upon the trivet across, with a fire under it; and then him, who was at that time not well in his wits, to kneel down and say certain prayers, as she taught him: and thereby, she said, he should be delivered of his bewitching, or his witch should consume as the fire did; which, when this evidence rebuked her for doing, as using witchcraft, she conceived an ill-will towards him. And as he having a sheep-shearing about that time, and not inviting her thereto, being his neighbour, she, as he supposed, bewitched two of his sheep; for immediately after they were taken with sickness, their hinder legs so indisposed that they only could crawl, and died. The same man had a sow, being well when the sun went down, which the next morning was found dead, with her nose lying upon the groundsel of this woman's house, where she never was fed, nor wont to come before.

Another witness deposed, that she being servant to a farmer's wife in the said parish of Theydon Mount, this goodwife Malter came to her mistress, who was going to London market, and desired her to bring her home some sprats; but she saying she came always loaden from London, denied her. Upon this, the deponent, then her hired maid, came from milking; and as she set her milk in the pan upon a loft, there was a speckled bird, as she thought, which fluttered among the milkpans, and with her feet and wings slubbered therein: her mistress in the meantime called her away; but she endeavoured by a broom to sweep or drive away this bird; but it would not away, but went fluttering from pan to pan, and could not fly but skip and hop. At the last, it went from the loft where the milk and wheat was, into the cheese loft; and then, being often called by her mistress, she came down, and being blamed for her long tarrying, she related how she was troubled with such a bird; and then her mistress came herself into the milk loft, and found it come down stairs a very toad; which after it was once come into the buttery, she could never see it more. And for the space of six weeks after, by no means nor diligence, nor change of churn or cloths, could they have any butter; until that her mistress did bid her carry her milk, and churn at a neighbour's house; and there the milk made butter as it was wont to do before, and in the same milk-pans. Other evidences there were against this woman.

In May, Sir Thomas took the depositions of several against Anne Vicars. A woman deposed, that about three years past, she was taken with a strange sickness; her body disfigured, her lips great and black, and she almost out of her wits. She suspecting that she was bewitched by the said Anne, went to one Cobham of Romford, who was thought to be cunning in such matters; and he declared to her that she was bewitched by the same woman, telling her the words which passed twixt Anne Vicars and her, whereby she conceived displeasure against her, and wrought her that mischief: and Cobham promised her, that as long as he lived she should have no power over her. And so it happened: for during his life she was recovered and continued well; but shortly after his death she fell again into her disease.

Another woman of Stapleford Abbots said, that about three years past she was coming from Romford market with this Anne Vicars, and suddenly the said Anne cast up her nose into the air and smelt; which the other marvelled at, and asked her if she saw anything, or if there were any carrion there? And she said, she smelt either a whore or a thief. At last she espied the wife of one Ingarsole, going a great way before them: whereat the said Vicars cried out with an oath, "I told you, I smelt either a whore or a thief"; and making great haste to overtake her, when she came at her, she cast her apron upon the side of her face next unto her; and then went backwards a great way, with her face towards the said Ingarsole's wife, casting her apron over it, and making many crosses, saying, as it were, certain prayers; but what, this examinant could not tell; but marvelled much at her behaviour, and said she was to blame to slander her that was an honest woman, and so known among her neighbours for twenty years. But upon this, Ingarsole's wife fell extremely sick, and lost one of her eyes with a stroke, as she thought, that came unto her she could not tell how, in the plain field, where neither was bush nor tree, or other creature.

And the said Maud, Ingarsole's wife, examined, said that the said Anne Vicars' daughter, about the time that this calamity befell her, did fell wood that was assigned in the common to her the said Maud; whereupon she forbade her to do so any more, or else she would take away her bill. The next day the said wench came again; but she would not suffer her to carry away the wood: whereupon the said Anne Vicars fell out with her, and wished she might not be delivered of that she went with, being then great with child. This falling out was on the Monday, and on the Thursday she lost one of her eyes with a sudden stroke, as she thought, where no creature nor thing was by to hurt her; besides that she was extreme sick, and in great danger of her life.

Also one Agnes, wife of Thomas Combres, being examined, said that since Michaelmas last, the said supposed witch fell out with her, and upon that she fell a cursing and banning at her, and wished her eyes out: whereupon within two days she fell down as dead, extremely sick, and hardly recovered it: and since that time she had marvellous pain in her eyes. These and divers more depositions Sir Thomas now took against this woman, of her supposed witchcraft, exercised upon her neighbours.

Thereafter at the end of May, Sir Thomas did commit both the said Malter's wife and Anne Vicars to the Assizes the next month, with a note that he did consider there was much idle gossip in the stories; whereafter at the Assizes the said Malter's wife and Anne Vicars were separately committed to prison for one year each on the good office of Sir Thomas Smith's judgement.

the witchcraft apprentice

by Raphael Holinshed

As Queen Elizabeth's reign continued, the witchcraft hysteria increased. In 1579 the second major Essex trial took place, at Chelmsford. In many respects it was a replica of the first, and indeed, one of the defendants was Elizabeth Francis, who had been among the accused in 1565. The judges were Sir Thomas Gawdy and Mr. Justice Southcote (the same man who had been a judge at the first trial), and before them were four women, all accused of bewitching. Three of the women, Elizabeth Francis, Ellen Smythe (allegedly the daughter of a witch), and Alice Noakes, were said to have bewitched people to death and were committed to the gallows. The fourth, Margery Stanton, was accused only of bewitching cattle and, because of a lack of evidence, was set free.

Unremarkable though the trial was in comparison to some others, it did excite interest on a national scale. And with this trial one can find the first reports of such occurrences written by writers of distinction, rather than just the poor hacks penning sensation for the pamphlet-buying public. The most famous of these writers was certainly Raphael Holinshed (c. 1530–1580), the translator and author of *The Chronicles of England, Scotland and Ireland,* which not only are regarded as classic works, but provided much of the material from which Shakespeare created his plays. Holinshed, who was born in Cheshire, settled in

London as a young man and worked almost exclusively producing material for the legendary printing house of Reginald Wolfe. His major work was the *Chronicle,* published in two volumes in 1577, and the massive wordage and scholarship of the work certainly bear evidence that he must have been assisted by two or three other contributors.

Holinshed dealt primarily with national and international politics, particularly emphasizing the wars going on between several of the European nations, but he also included some delightful anecdotes about "monstrous births," earthquakes, and strange crimes. Witchcraft, then so much a topic of public attention, could also hardly have failed to capture his interest, and the *Chronicles* include two important references. The first deals with the case of a Kent woman, Joan Cason, who was tried for invoking spirits, found guilty, and executed. The other concerns a much more unusual occurrence involving a teenage Essex boy who was said to be the assistant of a notorious Suffolk conjuror, or wizard. Holinshed was obviously intrigued by the allegation of a boy participating in witchcraft (although the tone of his report seems to indicate some skepticism) and wrote the case up from contemporary reports. It appears here, from an edition of the work published in 1684, containing numerous additions from the original manuscript that had been deleted by the first publisher, Reginald Wolfe.

The eighth and twentieth day of November [1579] were arraigned in the King's Bench, William Randall of Ipswich for conjuring in Essex to know where treasure was hid in the earth and goods feloniously taken were become. Also Thomas Elks, Thomas Lupton, Rafe Spacie and Christopher Waddington, for being present, aiding and procuring the said Randall to the conjuration aforesaid.

With Randall was a child of 13 years called Thomas Lever who was said to be his assistant and helper in all matters of conjuration. That one of such tender years should be in this association aroused much discussion and I think it fit to insert his story herewith.

The child was seized with his master Randall in the last year and committed to the county gaol in Essex on matters touching conjuration. It was said the conjurer could bewitch and summon spirits and call the Devil to his tune; and that the boy Thomas Lever, mixed his potions and was familiar with all his workings.

In his practise of witchcraft, Randall was said to invoke wicked spirits, and four men and one woman gave evidence against him. Although they were all very poor people, yet would they rather accuse him, for his offence was very odious to them.

The deposition against Randall said that he did make secret workings at a place near Halsted in company with Thomas Elks, Thomas Lupton, Rafe Spacie and Christopher Waddington, and did call upon the Devil to reveal to the company assembled where the lost goods were.

In time the matter came to nought and when the men found none of the items which were lost, they began to counsel among themselves that Randall was a cheat. Their quarreling, so it appears, soon brought them to justice.

In the last year, Randall, the child and the others, Elks, Lupton Spacie and Waddington, were all arraigned and committed to the county gaol of Essex in Colchester to await their trial. Between times the mother of the said child Lever did humbly petition the Privy Council in London that he was imprisoned, had done no witchery himself, and should be set free.

Their Lordships did consider the matter on January 16 of this year, directing a letter to Lord Brian Darcye and Sir Thomas Lucas in Essex, wherein they stated that they could not see any particular cause why the child should remain so long as he had done in gaol without committal. They did therefore require them, in case they knew no sufficient cause why he should be any further detained, to give order for his setting at liberty; but if they found good cause why he should be detained, then to advise their Lordships thereof, to the end that his mother may be satisfied with a reasonable answer.

Still receiving no reply to their request in July, their Lordships enquired again concerning Thomas Lever and this time were informed that Randall and the others were for trial this November. At their trial, Randall, Elks, Spacie and Waddington were found guilty, and had judgements to be hanged. Randall was executed, the others were reprieved.

Of the child, he still languishes in the Colchester gaol, but on what charges, if there be any, none can say.

That her Majesty is sore oppressed by these witches and devil-mongers is now common knowledge, but that a child should be in such company is a singular and amazing thing.

an alleged witchcraft plot against queen elizabeth

Privy Council Report

The English politicians, as we have seen, were much preoccupied with witchcraft, and indeed their concern had had a very early stimulus when, barely a month after Elizabeth had been crowned, a lord, Sir Anthony Fortescue, was arrested for alleged sorcery. Sir Anthony was said to have cast a horoscope of the Queen's life and therein found that she "should not live passing the next spring." He and his accomplices were indicted for committing treason, although they pleaded they had "meant to attempt nothing in the Queen's lifetime." Such was the feeling that even the most unlikely incident might lead to insurrection, that the privy council (mentioned in the previous report by Holinshed), whose function was to protect the sovereign and ensure that justice was properly and effectively carried out, devoted much time to investigating alleged cases of witchcraft and sorcery.

Essex was to feature in their deliberations again, in 1580, when they inquired into another incident not unlike that concerning Sir Anthony Fortescue but far more sinister in its implications. This was no mere horoscope casting but, if we accept any of the evidence, a plot to destroy the Queen, body and soul, by the use of witchcraft. The case was based on an overheard conversation about a plan to make a waxen image of the Queen that would then be destroyed with pins and fire. This was an old witchcraft practice, frequently recorded, intended to cause the person in whose likeness the image was made to fall ill and die slowly in the most excruciating pain.

As one can see from this report, taken from the actual contemporary records of the privy council, it is impossible to tell exactly what had happened and whether there was any truth in the allegations. To the council members' credit, they seemed far from convinced that there was enough in the charges to warrant more than routine inquiry. Nonetheless, the document is another vivid example of the development of the witchcraft hysteria both in Essex and in England as a whole. (The author's further inquiries revealed that the main suspect in the plot, Nicolas Johnson, was apparently committed to prison for "safekeepinge" and languished there for some years before finally being set free for lack of evidence to convict him.)

A Meeting of the Privy Council
in London to Discuss Reports
of a Plot against the Sovereign.
Held on the 1 day of November Anno 1580

Those present:

Lord Chancellor	Lord Hunsdon
Lord Treasurer	Mr. Treasurer
Lord Admiral	Mr. Comptroller
Lord Chamberlaine	Mr. Vice-Chamberlaine
Earl of Warwick	Mr. Secretary Walsingham
Earl of Leicester	Mr. Secretary Wilson

It was decreed that a letter should be sent to Lord Robert Rich, Earl of Warwick, now on the Queen's business in Essex, signifying receipt of his letter of the 28th of October with certain examinations of John a Lee, Thomas Glascocke and others concerning a matter of sorcery said to have been practised by Nicholas Johnson of Woodham Ferrers in the county of Essex.

Their Lordships do yield to him their right and hearty thanks for the pains he has taken in this matter. And forasmuch as their Lordships find not that the words alleged by one Potter to have been uttered by the said John a Lee to

Glascocke accusing Johnson for making of her Majesty's picture in wax, etc., confirmed by Glascocke and one Crowe, witnesses produced to certify the same to have been spoken by Lee, and Johnson doth likewise deny the speaking and practising of any such thing.

If, therefore, upon further examination of the matter, there should appear no better proof to charge the one or the other, his Lordship is required, taking bonds of the said Lee and Johnson and of the others for their appearance at the next Assizes, to set them at liberty.

In the meantime, his Lordship is desired to examine the conversation of the said Johnson, and whether he hath heretofor been a dealer in sorcery and such like lewd practises, to the end he may then answer as well for any further matter to be proved against him, as for that he resteth now charged with all, returning unto him the examinations sent hither by his Lordship for his better direction in that behalf, wherewith he may acquaint the Justices at the time of the next Assizes.

Their Lordships do wish earnestly to state that they are much concerned over the reports of witchcraft and do wish to do all in their power to put it down in her Majesty's name. And that they will exercise the utmost punishment on those who by any such ways of the Devil should attempt to attack or harm the person of Her Majesty, the State or the peoples of this realm.

the saint osyth witch trial

by "W. W."

Just as Essex had been the site of the first witch trial in England, so in 1582 it was the place where the most infamous of all English trials was held. The proceedings took place again at Chelmsford, but concerned thirteen women from the small fishing village of Saint Osyth. Although then considered remote and backward, Saint Osyth had an illustrious history and had actually been part of King Canute's royal demense in the eleventh century. It was also the place where one of the most famous of Essex legends had occurred in 1171, when a "huge dragon" had swept across the village at such a speed that a fire had been kindled, burning down many of the houses and outbuildings.

The trial of the Saint Osyth witches is now one of the blackest spots in the black history of persecution. The amazing way in which hearsay evidence, the tales of small children, and the most vicious prejudices were accepted without question seems incredible in even such an incredible age as the sixteenth century. The preliminary hearings were conducted by the local lord of the manor and county-sessions judge, Lord Brian Darcy (whose name we encountered in the sad story of the thirteen-year-old boy, Thomas Lever, accused of being apprenticed to a conjuror), and the evidence he accepted and the manner in which he attempted to obtain admissions from defendants with cajolery and promises earn him a special place of infamy in the annals of English witchcraft. (Some authorities have noted that his evident maliciousness may be explained in part by the fact that his father was believed to have been bewitched to death.)

The trial took several weeks, and after the various indictments and testimonies had been taken in Saint Osyth, the proceedings moved to Chelmsford and trial before a jury. In all, Lord Darcy presented thirty-eight testimonies, which gave details of the twenty-three people allegedly bewitched to death and the numerous other villagers and their livestock who had supposedly fallen ill under the spell of the thirteen accused. In hindsight, it appears that the only saving grace of the trial was that the jurymen, mostly simple people like the accused, saw through much of the evidence and found in it only vindictive accusations and village feuds of the kind they themselves had probably suffered. They had the courage to condemn only six of the women.

The pamphlet that records this infamous event is interesting in that although the author is stated to be one "W. W.," it is now widely believed that he was in fact Lord Brian Darcy himself. Certainly the preface represents precisely his own merciless viewpoint and the phraseology of many of the testimonies is in exactly the same style as other essays that he did admit to writing. The only surviving copy of the pamphlet, which was printed in London by Thomas Dawson in 1582, is now in the British Museum, and it is from this that the following text was taken. This version has been slightly modernized and edited to eliminate the undue repetition of the original and to make for easier reading. The flavor of the original, however, has been retained.

A true and just Recorde of the Information, Examination, and Confession of all the Witches, taken at St. Osyth in the County of Essex; whereof some were executed, and some others entreated according to the determination of law. Wherein all men may see what a pestilent people Witches are, and, how unworthy to lyve in a Christian Commonwealth. Written orderly, as the cases were tryed by evidence, by W.W.

PREFACE.

If there hath been at any time, any means used to appease the wrath of God, to obtain his blessing, to terrifie secret offenders by open transgressors' punishments, to witdraw honest natures from the corruption of evill company, to diminish the great multitude of wicked people, to increase the small number of virtuous persons, and to reform all the detestable abuses which the perverse wit and will of man doth daily devise, this doubtless is no less necessary than the best, that Sorcerers, Wizzardes, or rather Dizzardes, Witches, Wise women (for so they will be named), are rigorously punished. Rigorously, said I?—why it is too mild and gentle a tearm for such a merciless generation; I should rather have said most cruelly executed; for that no punishment can be thought upon, be it in never so high a degree of torment, which may be deemed sufficient for such a devilish and damnable practice.

The first complaint of this trial was laid against *Ursula Kemp,* alias Gray, of St. Osyth, by her neighbour, Grace Thurlowe who spoke thus to the magistrate, the right honourable and good lord, Lord Brian Darcy.

About twelve months since, said Grace, her son Davy was strangely taken and greatly tormented. Ursula came, like the rest of the neighbours, to see him; but, unlike the rest, she thrice took the child by the hand, saying each time, "A good childe, how are thou loden", going out of the house and returning between each phrase, which was evidently a charm, and no holy way of pitying a sick child. After this she said to Grace, "I warrant thee, I, thy childe shall do well enough," and sure it was so, for that night the child slept well, and after another such cantrip visit from Ursula, mended completely.

Then a bit after, she, Thurlowe, was delivered of a woman child, and asked not Ursula to be her nurse; whereat sprung up a quarrel, and the child in consequence fell out of the cradle and brake its neck; not because it was clumsily laid, or carelessly rocked, but because Ursula was a witch and had a grievance against Grace. And to this mischance, when she heard of it, all that the old dame said, was, "It maketh no matter; for she might have suffered me to have the keeping and nursing of it." Then a trouble and a "fratch" ensued, and Ursula threatened Grace with lameness, whereat Grace answered, "Take heed, Ursula, thou hast a naughtie name;" but in spite of her warning the old witch did her work, so that Grace was taken with such lameness that she had to go upon her hands and knees. And thus it continued; whenever she began to mend her child fell ill, and when her child was well she was cast down lame and helpless.

The next complainant was Annis Letherdall of St. Osyth who deposed as after. She and Ursula had a little matter of commerce between them, but Annis failed the suspected woman, "knowing her to be a naughtie beast." So

Ursula in revenge bewitched Annis's child, and that so severely that Mother Ratcliffe, a skilful woman, doubted if she could do it any good; yet for all that she ministered unto it kindly. And, as a proof that it was Ursula and only Ursula, who had so harmed the babe, and that its sad state came in no wise from bad food, bad nursing, and filthy habits, the little creature of only one year old, when it was carried past her house, cried "wo, wo," and pointed with its finger windowwards.

So then, to clinch the matter and strike fairly home, the magistrate examined Thomas Rabbet, Ursula's "base son" a child of barely eight years of age, and got his version of the mother's life. His mother had four imps at home, he said—Tyffyn, like a white lamb; Tettey, a little grey cat; Pygin, a black toad; and Jack, a black cat; and she fed them, at times with wholesome milk and bread, and at times they sucked blood from her body. He further said that his mother had bewitched Johnson and his wife to death, and that she had given her imps to Godmother Newman who put them into an earthen pot which she hid under her apron and so carried them away.

One Lawrence Kemp then said that she had bewitched his wife who lay a drawing at home, and continued so a day and a night, all the parts of her body were cold like a dead creature's, and yet at her mouth did appear her breath to come and go. Thus she lingered, said her husband, until Ursula came in unbidden, turned down the bedclothes, and took her by the arm, when immediately she gasped and died.

Confession of the said Ursula Kemp. At first she would confess nothing save being troubled about ten or eleven years ago with a lameness in her bones, for the cure of which she went to see one Cook's wife of Weeley, who said she was bewitched. This woman taught her a charm by which she might unwitch herself, and it instructed her to take hog's dung and charnell, and put them together and hold them in her left hand, and to take in the other hand a knife, and to prick the medicine three times, and then to cast the same into the fire, and to take the said knife and to make three pricks under a table, and to let the knife stick there: and after that to take three leaves of sage, and as much of herb John (alias herb grace) and put them into ale, and drink it last at night and first in the morning, and that she taking the same, had ease of her lameness. This charm had also never failed with her neighbours. All other of the charges she denied.

But upon the good lord, Lord Darcy, promising the said Ursula that if she would deal plainely and confess the truth that she should have favour, so by giving her fair speech she confessed as followeth. Bursting out with weeping and falling on her knees, she said, yes, she had the four imps her son had told of, and that two of them, Tettey and Jack, were hes whose office was to punish and kill unto death; and two, Tiffin and Pygin, were shes, who punished with lameness and bodily harm only, and destroyed goods and cattle. And she confessed that she had killed all the folk charged against her; her brother-in-law's wife, and Grace Thurlowe's cradled child, making it to fall out of its cradle and break its neck solely by her enchantments; and that she had bewitched a little babe of Annis Letherdall's and in fact, that she had done all the mischief with which she was charged. Then, not liking to be alone, she said that Mother Bennet had two imps; the one a black dog, called Suckin, the other red like a lion, Lyerd; and that Hunt's wife had a spirit, too, for one evening she peeped in at her window when she was from home, and saw it look out from a potcharde from under a bundle of cloth, and that it had a brown nose like a ferret. And she said that her spirit Tiffin informed her of all these things.

Putting herself upon the country, she was nonetheless found guilty to be a witch and executed when her turn came.

Joan Pechey, widow, of St. Osyth, was then brought forward; and Alice Hunt, herself an accused witch, deposed against her that she was angry because at a distribution of bread made by the said Brian Darcy, she had gotten a loaf which was too hard baked for her; whereat in a fit she said it might have been given to some one younger, and not to her, with no teeth to eat through the crust. And then Alice watched her home, and saw her go in alone to her own house where no human soul was; but there she heard her say, as to someone, "Yea, are you so sawsie; are ye so bold; you were not best to be so bold with me. For if you will not be ruled, you shall have Symonds sawse; yea," said the said Joan, "I perceive if I do give you an inch you will take an ell." All of which talk Alice Hunt found was to no Christian creature, but to her foul and wicked imps.

The which testimony her sister, Margerie Sammon, confirmed, saying that old Joan was as clever as their own mother (a noted witch, one Mother Barnes), or any one else in St. Osyth skilled in sorcery and magic.

And then the accuser, *Alice Hunt,* wife of William Hunt of St. Osyth, mason, was made to take the place of the accused, and listen to the catalogue of her own sins. The chief witness against her was her little daughter-in-law, Phoebe, of the age of eight or thereabouts, who deposed to her having two little things like horses, the one black the other white, which she kept by her bedside in a little low earthen pot with wool, colour white and black, and which she fed with milk out of a black trening dish.

When the Commissioners went to search the place they found indeed the board which Phoebe said was used to cover them, and she pointed out the trening dish whence they were fed; but the little things like horses were gone; when Phoebe said they had been sent to Hayward of Frowicke.

After a time Alice Hunt was brought to confess not only to two, but four imps; two like colts, black and white, called Jack and Robbin; and two like toads, Tom and Robyn. Mother Barnes, her mother, gave them to her, she said, when she died; and she gave her sister, Margerie Sammon, two also.

When Margerie was confronted with Alice and heard what she had deposed she got very angry and denied the whole tale, saying "I defie thee, though thou art my sister," saying that she had never any imps given to her on her mother's death-bed, or at any other time. But Alice took aside and whispered something in her ear; after which Margerie, with great submission and many tears, confessed that she had in truth these two imps given to her by her mother as her sister had said, and that she had carried them away that same evening in a wicker basket filled with black and white wool. Her mother had said that if she did not like to keep them old Joan Pechey would be glad of them; but she did not part with them just then; and that she was to feed them on bread and milk, otherwise they would suck her blood. Their names were Tom and Robyn, and last evening she took them away and went into Read's ground, where she bade them go. Immediately they skipped out of the wicker basket toward a barred gate going into Howe Lane, to Mother Pechey's house, whereat she, Margerie, said "All evil go with you, and the Lord in heaven bless me from ye."

Examined by the Lord Darcy, the said Mother Pechey denied having any spirits and all the charges. She was threescore year and onwards, she said, and had lived forty years in St. Osyth's in honour and good repute. She knew Mother Barnes, yet knew her for no witch, nor ever heard her to be so accompted, or to have skill in any witchery; nor was she at her death-bed; nor knew she of her imps. For her own part she denied that she had any puppets, spirits, or mammettes, nor had had any spirits conveyed to her by Margerie Sammon, or since Mother Barnes' death. She denied all that Alice Hunt had said and that she had had any hand in Johnson's death, as she had been accused of, but when he died said only he was a very honest man: she also denied some very shocking passages with her son, which he, however, had been brought to confess; and when questioned more closely concerning her imps, said that she had had only a kitten and a dog at home. When asked of what colour were they? she answered "Ye may go and see." She was thereafter committed to prison.

Alice Newman of St. Osyth was also condemned and executed; being obstinate to the last: denying the four counts with which she was charged, viz. her imps, the slaughter of her own husband, of John Johnson, and of his wife. But William Hooke deposed that on his death-bed her husband had been perpetually crying out against her, saing, "Dost thou not see—dost thou not see?" meaning the imp with which she tormented him, and which he strove vainly to beat away. Seeing her obstinacy, the Lord Brian Darcy told her that he would sever her and her spirits asunder; to which she answered quickly, "Nay", sayth she, "that shall ye not, for I will carry them with me if I have any."

Elizabeth Bennet, wife of John Bennet of St. Osyth, denied that she had had any hand in the bewitching to death of Johnson, or his wife, saying that the aforesaid Alice had done it all. But one William Byett of St. Osyth accused her of bewitching his wife, for she, being sickly and sore troubled, the said Elizabeth used speeches unto her, saying "A good woman, how art thou loden?" and then clasped her in her arms and kissed her. Whereupon presently after her upper lip swelled and was very big, and her eyes much sunked into her head, and she hath lain since in a very strange case.

The said Bennet was at first silent and would confess to nothing beyond that she had certainly a pot, but no wool therein, and no imps to lay on it.

Then did the Lord Darcy speak directly to her: "For so it is, there is a man of great cunning and knowledge, come over lately unto our Queen's Majesty, which hath advertised her what a company and number of witches be within England: whereupon I and other of her Justices have received commission for the apprehending of as many as are within these limits, and they which do confess the truth of their doings, they shall have much favour; but the other they shall be burnt and hanged."

And hearing these words she fell upon her knees, distilling tears, and spoke openly to confess. William Byett and she dwelt as neighbours together, she said, living as neighbours should, well and easily; but latterly they had fallen out, because he called her "old Trot" and "old witch", and did ban and curse her and her cattle. So she replied with calling him "knave", saying, "Wind it up, Byett, for it will light upon yourself." And Byett's beast died forthwith. Then Byett's wife beat her swine with great gybels, and made them sick; and once she ran a pitchfork through the side of one so that it was dead, and when the butcher who bought it came to dress and cut it up, it proved a messel, so she had no money for it, for the butcher would not keep it and she was forced to take it back again.

The Examinate then said that two years past there came to her two spirits one called Suckin, being black like a dog, the other called Lyerd, being red like a lion and as she was coming from the mill Suckin came unto her and took her by the coat, and held her so that she could not go forward nor remove by the space of two hours asking her if she would go with it. Enquiring in the name of God what art thou? Thou will not hurt me? it said "No," and she then praying to Almighty God to deliver her from it, the spirit departed from her. The next day Suckin brought Lyerd, but upon her mentioning the name of God, both disappeared. Afterwards Suckin endeavoured to push her into the oven, whereby she burned her arm. On another occasion Suckin in the likeness of a black dog, and Lyerd as a hare, sat beside her when milking, whereupon the cow snorted and ran away, spilling the milk. Upon praying to the father, the son, and the holy ghost, they departed. Afterwards she sent Lyerd to kill William Byett's beasts, but the spirit instead plagued Byett's wife to death. She was thereafter condemned and sent to the gallows with the aforementioned Ursula Kemp.

The next before Lord Darcy was *Alice Manfield,* widow of Thorpe, aged 63 years, who after the evidence did confess that she received from *Margaret Grevell* of Thorpe some twelve years since, four imps called Robin, Jack, William and Puppet alias Mamet, two hes and two shes, all like unto black cats, kept in wool in a box. Mother Grevell sent Robin to torment a bullock of Joan Cheston, and Jack to plague Robert Cheston upon the great toe unto death. The latter imp, after its labour, sucked blood of Margaret, and received beer and bread. Robin told her that he had been sent by Margaret to vex her husband who accordingly suffered from strange sores until he died. Examinate sent her imp Puppet alias Mamet to plague Joan Cheston's beasts with lameness and rewarded it with blood from her body; on another occasion it stayed John Sayer's cart because he would not let his thatcher cover in an oven for her, and received beer for its labour. The four imps being granted leave to go into Clacton, they burnt a barn stored with corn belonging to Ross, on which occasion being away from home a seven night, they were fed by one Celles. Puppet, on its return sucked the left shoulder of the Examinate, but the others were rewarded with beer. Mother Grevell caused the imps to destroy several brewings of beer, batches of bread, etc. But Margaret Grevell denied it all, even when Alice was confronted with her; denied also that she had bewitched John Carter's two brewings, so that half a seam had to go to the swill tub, all because he would not give her Godesgood. The brewing was only unbewitched when John's son managed to stick his arrow in the brewing vat. He had shot twice before, but missed, though he was a good shot and stood close to the vat—which was evident sorcery. Margaret denied also that she had bewitched Nicholas Strickland's wife so that she could make no butter, because Nicholas, who was a butcher, refused her a neck of mutton. She was committed to prison.

Elizabeth Eustace of St. Osyth, aged 53 years, was accused that she had bewitched Robert Sanneuet, drawing his mouth all awry so that it could not be got into its place again only with a sharp blow; and that she had killed his brother Crosse, three years ago, and bewitched his wife when with child and quite lusty and well, so that she had a most strange sickness and the child died soon after its birth; that she made his cows give blood instead of milk; and caused his hogs to skip and leap about the yard in a strange sort. And she hurt all Felice Okey's geese, and in particular her favourite goose, because she, Felice, had turned hers out of her yard; all of which Elizabeth Eustace denied to the face of Alice Manfield and her other Accusers. And as, on being searched, she was found to have no "bigges" or witch marks, she was sent to prison instead of the gallows.

Agnes Glascocke, wife of John Glascocke, sawyer, was charged by Mychel, the shoemaker, of being a naughtie woman and accused of bewitching to death Martha, daughter of Michael Stevens, Abraham Hedge and Charity, daughter of William Page, all of St. Osyth. She was thereupon searched and a few marks like well-sucked spots were found upon her body. And she did abuse Ursula Kemp who had accused her of sundry things, and said she had bewitched her and made her like to herself, she Agnes Glascocke, all the time ignorant and innocent of her devilish arts. She was nonetheless condemned and taken to prison.

Next was heard *Cicely Celles,* wife of Henry Celles of Little Clapton who was accused of bewitching Richard Rosse's horses, because he had refused Cicely a bushel of malt which she had come for, bringing a poke to put it in. Testimony was given by Henry Celles, son of accused, aged nine years, who affirmed that at Candlemas last past about midnight there came to his brother John a spirit, which took him by the left leg and also by the little toe, and which was like his little sister, only that it was black. At which his brother cried out, "Father, father come help me; there is a black thing that hath me by the leg as big as my sister." Whereat his father said to his mother, "Why thou whore, cannot you keep your imps from my children?" Whereat she presently called it away from her son, saying "Come away, come away." At which speech it did depart. He further said that his mother fed her imps daily with milk out of a black dish; that there names were Hercules, Sotheons, or Jack, which was black and a he, and Mercury, white and a she; that their eyes were like goose eyes; and that they lay on some wool under a stack of broom at the old crab-tree root. And also that his mother had sent Hercules to Ross for revenge; at which his father when he heard of it, said, "She was a trim fool."

Another Joan Smith of the same place, deposed that one day, as she was making ready to go to church, holding her babe in her arms, her mother, one Redworth's wife, and Cicely were all at her door, ready to draw the latch as she came out, whereat the grandmother to the child, took it by the hand, and shook it, saying "A mother's pug, art thou coming to church?" and Redworth's wife, looking on it, said, "Here is a jolly and likely child—God bless it." After which speeches Celles his wife said, "She hath never the more children for that, but a little babe to play withall for a time." And she saith within a short time after her said child sickened and died. But, she saith, that her conscience will not serve her to charge the said Cicely or her husband to be the causers of any such matter, but prayeth God to forgive if they have dealt in any such sorte.

Then Thomas Death accused Cicely Celles and one Barker's wife of bewitching George Battell's wife and his own daughter Mary, who got such good of the witches by a wise man's ministering that she saw her tormentor standing in bodily shape before her; and Alice Baxter was pricked to the heart by a white imp like a cat which then vanished into the bushes close by, and so badly holden that she could neither go nor stand nor speak and did not know her own master when he came by, but was forced to be taken home in a chair by two men. All of which Cicely Celles denied; especially the story of the imp and the children, but denial did her no good, for Cicely had witch marks, so was condemned.

A very crowd of witnesses came to testify against the accused *Agnes Heard* of Little Oakley. Of some she had bewitched the cream, of others the milk; of some the cows, the pigs or the wives.

Thomas Cartwright testified that after words with Agnes Heard he had trouble with his cattle, caused, he thought, by the witchery of the said Agnes Heard.

Bennet, wife of William Lane, said that after obtaining two pence from Agnes Heard, and giving her milk, the next day she would have fleet her milk bowl, but it would not abide the fleeting, but would rop and roll as it were the white of an egg, also the milk being on the fire it did not so soon seath but it would quail, burn by and stink, which she said she thought might be long of the feeding of her beasts, or else that her vessels were not sweet, whereupon she scalded her vessels, and scoured them with salt, but it was never the better. Finally she put a red-hot horseshoe into the milk, and could then seath her milk, fleet her cream, and make her butter in good sort as she had before.

Then spoke Agnes Dowsing, base daughter of Agnes Heard, aged seven years, who, asked if her mother had imps, said yes. In one box she had six "avices" or blackbirds, and in another box six like cows as big as rats, with short horns lying in the boxes on white or black wool. And she said that her mother gave her one of the cow imps, a black and white one, called Crowe; and to her little brother one, red and white, called Donne; and that she fed the avices or blackbirds with wheat and barley and oats and bread and cheese; giving to the cows wheat straw, bean straw, oat straw, or hay, with water or beer to drink. When her brother saw these blackbird imps come a tuitting and tetling about him, she said, he put them in the boxes. Some of them sucked on her mother's hands, and some on her brother's legs, and when they showed her the marks she pointed them out one by one, saying "Here sucked aves and here blackbird."

Thereafter followed the testimony of the minister of Beaumont, which did cause much excitement among those who were present and is given in full hereunder.

Richard Harrison, cleric, parson of Beaumont, said that he and his late wife did dwell in little Oakley in a house of his wife, and that he, Richard Harrison, had also the parsonage of Oakley in farm. And about summer twelve-month, he being at London, his wife had a duck sitting on certain eggs under a cherry tree in a hedge. And when the duck had hatched, his wife did suspect one Agnes Heard a light woman and a common harlot, to have stolen her ducklings; and that his wife went unto Agnes Heard and rated her an all-to chid her. But she could get no knowledge of her ducklings, and so came home and was very angry against Agnes.

And within a short time after, Richard Harrison went into a chamber and there did read on his books for the space of two or three hours, bidding his wife to go to bed with the children, and that he would come to her. And she so did. And being awhile laid down in her bed, his wife did cry out, "Oh Lord, Lord, help me and keep me!" And he running to her asked her what she ailed. And she said, "Oh Lord! I am sore afraid, and have been divers times, but that I would not tell you." And said, "I am in doubt, husband, that yonder wicked harlot Agnes Heard, doth bewitch me." And Harrison said to his wife, "I pray you be content and think not so, but trust in God, and put your trust in him only, and he will defend you from her, and from the Devil himself also." And he said moreover, "What will the people say, that I being a preacher, should have my wife so weak in faith?"

This examinate saith that within two months after, his wife said unto him, "I pray you, as ever there was love between us (as I hope there hath been, for

I have five pretty children by you, I thank God), seek some remedy for me against yonder wicked beast [meaning the said Agnes Heard]. And if you will not, I will complain to my father, and I think he will see some remedy for me. For," said she, "if I have no remedy, she will utterly consume me." Whereupon this examinate did exhort his wife as he had before, and desired her to pray to God, and that he would hang her, Agnes Heard, if he could prove any such matter.

And after, he went to the parsonage, and there he saith he gathered plums. And the said Agnes Heard came to the hedge side, and Anwick's wife with her, and said unto him, "I pray you give me some plums, sir." And this examinate saith unto her, "I am glad you are here, you vile strumpet!" Saying, "I do think you have bewitched my wife, and, as truly as God doth live, if I can perceive that she be troubled any more as she hath been, I will not leave a whole bone about thee. And besides, I will seek to have thee hanged!" And saith he said unto her that his wife would make her father privy unto it, and that "Then I warrant thee, he will have you hanged, for he will make good friends, and is a stout man of himself." And saith that then he did release divers things to her that were thought she had bewitched, as geese and hogs. And as he was coming down of the tree, she, the said Agnes, did depart suddenly from him without having any plums.

This examinate saith (after which speeches so by him used unto her, and before Christmas) his wife was taken sore sick and was at many times afraid both sleeping and waking. And did call this examinate, her husband, unto her not above two days before her death and said unto him: "Husband, God bless you and your children, for I am now utterly consumed with yonder wicked creature." And within two days after his wife departed out of this world in a perfect faith, repeating these words, "Oh Agnes Heard, Agnes Heard! She hath consumed me!"

Before the Lord Darcy, Agnes Heard confessed that she was certainly angry with the churl Cartwright for taking a bough away which she had laid over a flow in the highway, but she had not bewitched him or his; and that she had, truly, kept Lane's wife's dish fourteen days or more, as Lane's wife had said, and that Lane's wife had sent for the twopence which she, Agnes, owed her, and that she had grumbled with her—also with this neighbour and that neighbour, according to the habits of St. Osyth's—but that she had bewitched none of them. And she denied the avices and the blackbirds and all and sundry of the stories of Crowe or Donne; likewise of the bewitching to death of the minister's wife. She was acquitted.

Lastly came another witch, *Joan Robinson*, who was accused by various people of Walton. It was testified that a cat did eat blood from the accused's nose, and that following rebuffs to her on different occasions, a great wind nearly blew down a house, a cow could not calve, a goose deserted its nest, beasts broke their necks, a mare died, and a dog which fed of it died, a beast was drowned in a ditch where there was but a little water, a sow behaved as if mad, a farrow of pigs died, and horses strayed in a pond. She was found guilty and executed.

So ended the trial and it was thankfully seen how the good Lord Darcy had brought to a termination the devilish acts of 13 witches in the county of Essex.

ADDENDUM

The names of 13 witches and those that have been bewitched by them.

The names of those persons that have been bewitched and thereof have died, and by whom, and of them that have received bodily harm, &c. As appeareth upon sundry enformations, examinations, and confessions taken by the worshipfull Brian Darcy, Esquire; and by him certified at large unto the Queen's Maiestie's Justices of Assise of the Countie of Essex, the 29 of Marche, 1582.

St. Osyth's.	The witches 1. Ursula Kemp, alias Gray	bewitched to death	Kemp's wife, Thurlow's childe, and Stretton's wife.
	2. Alice Newman and Ursula Kemp	bewitched to death	Letherdall's childe, and Stretton's wife.
Confessed by Ursula and Elizabeth.	The said Alice and Ursula Kemp	bewitched	Stratton's childe, whereof they Grace Thurlow, did languish.
	3. Elizabeth Bennet	bewitched to death	William Byet, and Joan his wife, and 3 of his beasts. The wife of William Willes, and William Wittingalle.
	Elizabeth Bennet	bewitched	William Bonner's wife, John Butler, Fortune's childe; whereof they did languish.
	Alice Newman	bewitched to death	John Johnson and his wife, and her own husband, as it is thought.

Confessed the cattell.	4. Alice Hunt	bewitched to death	Rebecca Durrant and 6 beasts of one Hayward's.
	5. Cicely Celles	bewitched to death	Thomas Death's childe.
Little Clapton.	Cicely Celles	bewitched	Ross's Maide, Mary Death, whereof they did languish.
Thorpe.	Cicely Celles and 6. Alice Manfield		bewitched Richard Ross's horse and beasts and caused their Impes to burne a barne with much corne.
Confessed by Alice Manfield.	7. Alice Manfield and Margaret Grevell	bewitched to death	Robert Chesson, and Grevell husband to Margaret.
	Alice Manfield and Margaret Grevell		bewitched the widow Cheston, and her husband, 5 beasts and one bullocke, and severall brewings of beere, and batches of bread.
Thorpe.	8. Elizabeth Eustace	bewitched to death	Robert Stanneuet's childe, and Thomas Crosse.
	Elizabeth Eustace		bewitched Robert Stanneuet, 7 milk beasts, who gave blood in steede of milke, and severall of his swine dyed.
Little Okley.	9. Annis Heard	bewitched to death	Richard Harrison's wife, and two wives of William Dowsing, as it is supposed.
	Annis Heard		bewitched Cartwright two beasts, made, sheepe, and lambes 20; West swine, and pigs; Diborne, a brewing of beere, and severall other losses of milke and creame.
Walton.	10. Joan Robinson		bewitched beasts, horses, swine, and pigs, of severall men.
	Annis Glascocke 12. Joan Pechey 13. Joan Robinson		These have not confessed any thing touching the having of spirits.
	Annis Glascocke	bewitched to death	Michael Stevens' childe. The base childe at Pages'. William Page's childe.

The said Ursula Kemp had foure spyrites, viz., their names Tettey a he like a gray cat, Jack a he like a black cat, Pygin a she like a black Toad, and Tiffin a she like a white Lambe. The hes were to plague to death, and the shes to punish with bodily harme, and to destroy cattell.

Tiffin, Ursula's white spirit, did tell her alwayes (when she asked) what the other witches had done: and by her the most part were appelled, which spirit telled her alwayes true. As is well approved by the other witches' confession.

The said Alice Newman had the said Ursula Kemp's spirits to use at her pleasure. Elizabeth Bennet had two spirits, viz., their names Suckin, a he like a blacke Dog: and Lyerd, red like a lion or hare.

Alice Hunt had two spirits like colts, the one blacke, the other white.

11. Margerie Sammon had two spirits like toads, their names Tom and Robyn.

Cicely Celles had two spirits by severall names, viz., Sotheons, Hercules, Jack, or Mercury.

Alice Manfield and Margaret Grevell had in common by agreement, 4 spirits, viz., their names Robin, Jack, Will, Puppet, alias Mamet, whereof two were hes, and two were shes, like unto black Cats.

Elizabeth Eustace had 3 impes or spirits of colour white, grey, and blacke.

Annis Herd had 6 impes or spirites, like avices and black birds, and 6 other like kine, of the bygnes of kats, with short hornes; the avices she fed with wheat, barley, otes, and bread, the kine with straw and hay.

¶A true and iuſt Recorde, of
the Information, Examination
and Confeſſion of all the Witches, taken at
S. Oſes in the countie of Eſſex: whereof
ſome were executed, and other ſome entreated according to the determination of lawe.

Wherein all men may ſee what a peſtilent
people Witches are, and how vnworthy to lyue
in a Chriſtian Commons
wealth.

Written orderly, as the ca-
ſes were tryed by euidence,
By W. W.

¶*Imprinted in London at the*
three Cranesin the Vinetree by
Thomas Dawſon
1582.

The contemporary pamphlet of the infamous St. Osyth Witch Trial, in all probability
written by the Judge himself!

Essex witch and her familiars; late sixteenth century manuscript

Rural Essex today—

Elizabeth I, who introduced the new Witchcraft Statute of 1563

unchanged for hundreds of years

Witch practicing necromancy.
Seventeenth century woodcut

¶The ende and last confession of mother Waterhouse at her
death, whiche was the
xxix. daye of July.
Anno. 1566.

Mother wa-
terhouse.

IF yrste (beinge
redi prepared
to receiue her
death) She confessed
earnestly that shee
had bene a wytche
and vsed suche exe-
crable sorserye the
space of. xv. yeres,
and had don many
abhominable dede,
the which she repē-
ted earnestly & vn-
faynedly, and desy-
red almyghty God
forgeuenes in that
she had abused hys
most holy name by
A   her

Confession of Mother Waterhouse, from extremely rare pamph
describing the first Essex Witch Trial in 1566

Elizabeth Lewys of Chelmsford, first person tried in England for witchcraft, 1563

A Detection
of damnable driftes, practized by three VVitches arraigned at Chelmiffozde in Effex, at the laste Affifes there holden, whiche were eyecuted in Apzill.

1579.

Set fozthe to difcouer the Ambufhementes of Sathan, wherebp he would furpzife vs lulled in feruritie, and hardened with contempte of Gods vengeance thzeatened foz our offences.

Imprinted at London for Edward White, at the little North-dore of Paules.

tle page of tract describing the second major trial of witches,
elmsford, 1579.

The Witchcraft Judge, Sir Thomas Smith (1512–1577)

Bill of indictment against Ellen Smythe of Maldon, accused of bewitching Susan Webbe, aged four years, "who languished for a year until she died." Issued March 7, 1579

Skeleton found in St. Osyth early this century, believed to be a witch because of method of burial and rivets in the thigh bones to prevent the corpse leaving the grave as a vampire

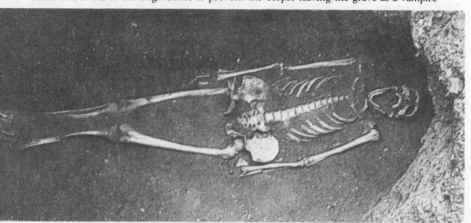

Three witches of Dagenham; Joan Cony, Joan Upney, Joan Prentice. Hanged after the trial at Chelmsford, 1589, and the subject of both pamphlet and ballad

The diſcouerie of Witchcraft.

¶ *The firſt Booke.*

An impeachment of Witches power in meteors and elementarie bodies, tending to the rebuke of ſuch as attribute too much vnto them.

The firſt Chapter.

ℌℰ ꜰables of Witchcraſt haue taken ſo faſt hold and dæpe rœt in the heart
of man, that ſewe o꜏ none can (nowadaies)
with patience indure the hand and co꜏recti-
on of God. Fo꜏ if any aduerſitie, græfe, ſick-
neſſe, loſſe of child꜏en, co꜏ne, cattell, o꜏ libertie happen vnto them; by & by they erclaime
vppon witches. As though there were no God in Iſrael that o꜏dereth all things ac- Iob.ſ.
co꜏ding to his will; punishing both iuſt and vniuſt with græfs,
plagues, and afflictions in maner and fo꜏me as he thinketh gœd:
but that certeine old women hære on earth, called witches,
muſt næds be the contriuers of all mens calamities, and as
though they themſelues were innocents, and had deſerued no
ſuch punishments. Inſomuch as they ſticke not to ride and go
to ſuch, as either are iniurioullie tearmed witches, o꜏ elſe are
willing ſo to be accounted, ſæking at their hands comfort and
remedie in time of their tribulation, contrarie to Gods will and
commandement in that behalfe, who bids vs reſo꜏t to him in all Matth.11.

C.i.   our

First page of the vastly influential book *The Discoverie of Witchcraft* (1584) written by
Reginald Scot as a direct result of the St. Osyth Trial

the fables of witchcraft

by Reginald Scot

Repercussions from a trial such as that of the Saint Osyth witches were inevitable and predictable, with much delight among the witch-hunting fraternity, who redoubled their efforts. One result, however, could hardly have been foreseen and is much to be applauded. "The affair at St. Osyth undoubtedly made a great noise," Professor G. L. Kittredge noted in his classic study *Witchcraft in Old and New England*, "and appears to have been the chief immediate impulse to Reginald Scot's famous book, 'The Discovery of Witchcraft'."

Today, Scot's book is widely held to be one of the most important works on witchcraft, and it stands like a beacon of common sense and rationality amid all the prejudice and hysteria of the age in which it was written. Although it is unlikely that he actually attended the trial, Scot certainly read "W. W.'s" pamphlet and composed his attack on the witchcraft delusion and the supposed existence of the devil "to the everlasting and inexcusable shame of the witch mongers."

In careful and reasoned prose, Scot retold the history of witchcraft, demonstrated how the confusions around it had emerged, and attempted to prove that its very existence was probably false. Since he was attacking the basis of a law, he had to publish the book himself, and not surprisingly it existed virtually in secret until most copies were seized and burned in 1603 by King James, who considered it "damnable."

Scot was born in 1538 of a Kentish country family. After having failed to obtain a degree at Oxford, he returned to Kent to lead the life of a country gentleman. He did serve briefly as a government official and member of parliament but seems to have devoted much of his time to writing and study. Among his works is *The Perfect Platform of a Hop-Garden*, which is credited with introducing hop growing into England.

His name, however, was established with *The Discovery of Witchcraft*, which was both the first book in English on witchcraft and the inspiration for those who were either to attack or to rationalize the subject for the next two hundred years until the repeal of the witchcraft act. The whole tone of the book is sarcastic, and the light style of the author's pen makes it still an eminently readable work. Because of King James's action, only a single copy is believed to exist of the first edition (in the Cornell University Library), but there was a subsequent exact reprint in 1651, of which a few more copies survive.

Of the work, several authorities have told us that Scot had "for years before he put pen to paper been investigating alleged cases of witchcraft, attending trials, closely questioning magistrates and divines." He actually wrote the book, however, "in some haste, after the S. Osees affair, to strike lustily whilst the iron was hot." In the book, apart from a passing mention of the trial, there is only one other specific reference to Essex. "There is a justice in Essex," he writes, "whome for diverse respects I have left unnamed [in all probability Lord Brian Darcy], not long since thought he was bewitched, in the verie instant while he examined the witch; so as his leg was broken thereby &c; which either was false or else this rule that such men are immune from witches is untrue, or both rather injurious unto God's providence." In selecting an extract for this collection, I have settled upon Scot's introductory notes, which not only clearly demonstrate the manner of his argument but also indicate public attitudes during the closing years of Elizabeth's reign.

The fables of Witchcraft have taken so fast hold and deepe root in the heart of man, that fewe or none can (nowadaies) with patience indure the hand and correction of God. For if any adversitie, greefe, sicknesse, losse of children, corne, cattell, or libertie happen unto them; by & by they exclaime uppon witches. As though there were no God in Israel that ordereth all things according to his will; punishing both just and unjust with greefs, plagues, and afflictions in maner and forme as he thinketh good: but that certeine old women heere on earth, called witches, must needs be the contrivers of all mens calamities, and as though they themselves were innocents, and had deserved no such punishments. Insomuch as they sticke not to ride and go to such, as either are injuriouslie tearmed witches, or else are willing so to be accounted, seeking at their hands comfort and remedie in time of their tribulation, contrarie to Gods will and commandement in that behalfe, who bids us resort to him in all our necessities. ,

Such faithlesse people (I saie) are also persuaded, that neither haile nor snowe, thunder nor lightening, raine nor tempestuous winds come from the heavens at the commandement of God: but are raised by the cunning and power of witches and conjurers; insomuch as a clap of thunder, or a gale of wind is no sooner heard, but either they run to ring bels, or crie out to burne witches; or else burne consecrated things, hoping by the smoke thereof, to drive the divell out of the aire, as though spirits could be fraied awaie with such externall toies: howbeit, these are right inchantments, as *Brentius* affirmeth.

But certeinlie, it is neither a witch, nor divell, but a glorious God that maketh the thunder. I have read in the scriptures, that God maketh the blustering tempests and whirlewinds: and I find that it is the Lord that altogither dealeth with them, and that they blowe according to his will. But let me see anie of them all rebuke and still the sea in time of tempest, as Christ did; or raise the stormie wind, as God did with his word; and I will beleeve in them. Hath anie witch or conjurer, or anie creature entred into the treasures of the snowe; or seene the secret places of the haile, which GOD hath prepared against the daie of trouble, battell, and warre? I for my part also thinke with Jesus Sirach, that at Gods onelie commandement the snowe falleth, and that the wind bloweth according to his will, who onelie maketh all stormes to cease; and who (if we keepe his ordinances) will send us raine in due season, and make the land to bring forth hir increase, and the trees of the field to give their fruit.

But little thinke our witchmongers, that the Lord commandeth the clouds above, or openeth the doores of heaven, as *David* affirmeth; or that the Lord goeth forth in the tempests and stormes, as the Prophet *Nahum* reporteth: but rather that witches and conjurers are then about their businesse. ,

The *Martionists* acknowledged one God the authour of good things, and another the ordeiner of evill: but these make the divell a whole god, to create things of nothing, to knowe mens cogitations, and to doo that which God never did; as, to transubstantiate men into beasts, &c. Which thing if divels could doo, yet followeth it not, that witches have such power. But if all the divels in hell were dead, and all the witches in *England* burnt or hanged; I warrant you we should not faile to have raine, haile and tempests, as now we have: according to the appointment and will of God, and according to the constitution of the elements, and the course of the planets, wherein God hath set a perfect and perpetuall order.

I am also well assured, that if all the old women in the world were witches; and all the priests, conjurers: we should not have a drop of raine, nor a blast of wind the more or the lesse for them. For the Lord hath bound the waters in the clouds, and hath set bounds about the waters, untill the daie and night come to an end: yea it is God that raiseth the winds and stilleth them: and he saith to the raine and snowe; Be upon the earth, and it falleth. The wind of the Lord, and not the wind of witches, shall destroie the treasures of their plesant vessels, and drie up the fountaines; saith *Oseas*. Let us also learne and confesse with the Prophet *David,* that we our selves are the causes of our afflictions; and not exclaime upon witches, when we should call upon God for mercie.

The Imperiall lawe (saith *Brentius*) condemneth them to death that trouble and infect the aire: but I affirme (saith he) that it is neither in the power of witch no divell so to doo, but in God onelie. Though (besides *Bodin,* and all the popish writers in generall) it please *Daænus, Hyperius, Hemingius, Erastus,* &c. to conclude otherwise. The clouds are called the pillars of Gods tents, Gods chariots, and his pavillions. And if it be so, what witch or divell can make maisteries therof? S. *Augustine* saith, *Non est putandum istis transgressoribus angelis servire hanc rerum visibilium materiem, sed soli Deo:* We must not thinke that these visible things are at the commandement of the angels that fell, but are obedient to the onelie God.

If it were true that witches confesse, or that all writers write, or that witchmongers report, or that fooles beleeve, we should never have butter in the chearne, nor cow in the close, nor corne in the field, nor faire weather abroad, nor health within doores. Or if that which is conteined in *M. Mal. Bodin,* &c: or in the pamphlets late set foorth in English, of witches executions, shuld be true in those things that witches are said to confesse, what creature could live in securitie? Or what needed such preparation of warres, or such trouble, or charge in that behalfe? No prince should be able to reigne or live in the land. For (as *Danæus* saith) that one *Martine* a witch killed the emperour of *Germanie* with witchcraft: so would our witches (if they could) destroie all our magistrates. One old witch might overthrowe a royal armie: and then what needed we any guns, or wild fire, or any other instruments of warre? A witch might supplie all wants, and accomplish a princes will in this behalfe, even without charge or bloudshed of his people.

If it be objected, that witches worke by the divell, and christian princes are not to deale that way; I answer, that few princes disposed to battell would make conscience therin, speciallie such as take unjust wars in hand, using other helpes, devises, & engines as unlawfull and divelish as that; in whose campe there is neither the rule of religion or christian order observed: insomuch as ravishments, murthers, blasphemies and thefts are there most commonlie and freelie committed. So that the divell is more feared, and better served in their camps, than God almightie.

But admit that souldiers would be scrupulous herein, the pope hath authoritie to dispense therewith; as in like case he hath doone, by the testimonie of his owne authors and friends. Admit also, that throughout all christendome, warres were justly mainteined, and religion dulie observed in their camps; yet would the Turke and other infidels cut our throtes, or at least one anothers throte, with the helpe of their witches; for they would make no conscience thereof.

Alas! what creature being sound in state of mind, would (without compulsion) make such maner of confessions as they do; or would, for a trifle, or nothing, make a perfect bargaine with the divell for hir soule, to be yeelded up unto his tortures and everlasting flames, and that within a verie short time; speciallie being through age most commonlie unlike to live one whole yeare? The terror of hell fire must needs be to them diverslie manifested, and much more terrible; bicause of their weaknesse, nature, and kind, than to any other: as it would appeere, if a witch were but asked, Whether she would be contented to be hanged one yeare hence, upon condition hir displesure might be wreked upon hir enimie presentlie. As for theeves, & such other, they thinke not to go to hell fire; but are either persuaded there is no hell, or that their crime deserveth it not, or else that they have time enough to repent: so as, no doubt, if they were perfectlie resolved heereof, they would never make such adventures. Neither doo I thinke, that for any summe of monie, they would make so direct a bargaine to go to hell fire. Now then I conclude, that confession in this behalf is insufficient to take awaie the life of any body; or to atteine such credit, as to be beleeved without further proofe. For as *Augustine* and *Isidore*, with the rest of the sounder divines saie, that these prestigious things, which are wrought by witches are fantasticall: so doo the sounder decrees of councels and canons agree, that in that case, there is no place for criminall action. And the lawe saith, that The confession of such persons as are illuded, must needs be erronious, and therefore is not to be admitted: for, *Confessio debet tenere verum & possibile*. But these things are opposite both to lawe and nature, and therfore it followeth not; Bicause these witches confesse so, *Ergo* it is so. For the confession differeth from the act, or from the possibilitie of the act. And whatsoever is contrarie to nature faileth in his principles, and therefore is naturallie impossible.

The lawe also saith, *In criminalibus regulariter non statur soli confessioni rei.* In criminall cases or touching life, we must not absolutelie stand to the confession of the accused partie: but in these matters proofes must be brought more cleare than the light it selfe. And in this crime no bodie must be condemned upon presumptions. And where it is objected and urged, that since God onelie knoweth the thoughts, therefore there is none other waie of proofe but by confession: It is answered thus in the lawe, to wit: Their confession in this case conteineth an outward act, and the same impossible both in lawe and nature, and also unlikelie to be true; and therefore *Quod verisimile non est, attendi non debet.* So as, though their confessions may be worthie of punishment, as whereby they shew a will to commit such mischeefe, yet not worthie of credit, as that they have such power. For, *Si factum absit, soláque opinione laborent, é stultorum genere sunt;* If they confesse a fact performed but in opinion, they are to be reputed among the number of fooles. Neither may any man be by lawe condemned for criminall causes, upon presumptions, nor yet by single witnesses: neither at the accusation of a capitall enimie, who indeed is not to be admitted to give evidence in this case; though it please *M. Mal.* and *Bodin* to affirme the contrarie. But beyond all equitie, these inquisitors have shifts and devises enow, to plague and kill these poore soules: for (they say) their fault is greatest of all others; bicause of their carnall copulation with the divell, and therefore they are to be punished as heretikes, foure maner of waies: to wit; with excommunication, deprivation, losse of goods, and also with death.

And indeede they find lawe, and provide meanes thereby to mainteine this their bloudie humor. For it is written in their popish canons, that As for these kind of heretikes, how much soever they repent and returne to the faith, they may not be reteined alive, or kept in perpetuall prison; but be put to extreame death. Yea, *M. Mal.* writeth, that A witches sinne is the sinne against the Holie-ghost; to wit, irremissible: yea further, that it is greater than the sinne of the angels that fell. In which respect I wonder, that *Moses* delivered not three tables to the children of Israell; or at the leastwise, that he exhibited not commandements for it. It is not credible that the greatest should be included in the lesse, &c.

But when these witchmongers are convinced in the objection concerning their confessions; so as thereby their tyrannicall arguments cannot prevaile, to imbrue the magistrates hands in so much bloud as their appetite requireth: they fall to accusing them of other crimes, that the world might thinke they had some colour to mainteine their malicious furie against them.

a new ballad of the life and death of three chelmsford witches

Anonymous

Apart from the pamphlets that so graphically described the witchcraft trials—and indeed any other event or scandal of public interest—another form of quickly disseminating the news was the broadsheet. These atrociously written and abominably printed single sheets of paper were hurried to the streets of London and provincial towns hot on the heels of the events they depicted. The more sensational the details, the more bloodthirsty the happenings (murders were especially popular and were invariably illustrated with the most gruesome pictures of the actual killings), the more quickly the hacks who wrote the scripts would be urged to produce their lines for the waiting printers, often in ballad form.

The sheets were sold for a halfpenny or less, and such was the enthusiasm and delight displayed by those eager persons who purchased them that today copies of all but a few have been completely worn out or destroyed.

One of the first broadsheet ballads to depict a witchcraft trial dealt with the third major trial in Chelmsford, and although it was sold widely in London, it seems unlikely that more than a few second- or third-hand copies ever found their way to the actual locality of the trial. This third trial bore many similarities to the earlier two, again featuring a group of women (although this time there was a single man with the nine females included in the indictment) accused of bewitching several people to death. The now familiar trappings of the witch trial were present—personal animosity, witch marks, and familiars—and again the major witnesses to the prosecution were small children. Three of the witches, Joan Cony, Joan Upney and Joan Prentice, all from the Dagenham area, were condemned by their own children and, although confessing they had "sinned grievously and been deceived by the Deville," were nonetheless sentenced to be hanged. The authorities apparently wasted no time after the verdict was given—just two hours later all three were dangling from the gallows outside the court! The ballad that recorded this trial—now in the author's collection—is so faded and torn as to make its reproduction in full quite impossible; therefore, I have selected several key verses that are still virtually intact and added just a few words to complete them, retaining as best as possible the style and intention of the original.

Students of the "street" ballad have observed how outrageously the writers stole phrases from each other, to finish their work as quickly as possible, and the author has managed to trace several earlier and later ballads that contain similar lines to those below—not one of them dealing with witchcraft! Nonetheless, as representative of one of the sixteenth century's most popular forms of disseminating the latest scandal, this "Newe Ballad" is perhaps as good as any still to be found.

A NEWE BALLAD OF THE LIFE AND DEATHS OF THREE
WITCHES ARRAYNED AND EXECUTED AT CHELMSFORD.
5 JULY 1589
(To the tune of "Bragandary Down", & etc)

I

List Christians all unto my Song
'Twill move your Hearts to Grace,
That Dreadful Witchcraft hath been done,

Of late about this place;
But Three that cried the Devil's Name
With those who did them follow,
Now to Justice are brought home
To swing upon our Gallow.

II

There's scarse a Month within these Years
But Witchcraft foul is done,
And many are the weeping tears
These Satan's Fiends have rung;
Though they sought Mercy ere the rope
Soon as the Judgment's read,
Who gainsays the Devil's Hope
Is all when they are Dead?

III

A vile long life they have run on
Regarding not their End,
Their Hearts still bent to cruelty
Not minding to Amends;
Men and cattle they Bewitched
No Peace they gave to Rest,
But yet, in turn the parts were switched
By Marks upon their Breasts.

IV

As to the Story now to tell
The Truth I will Declare,
It was the Witches' Children small
That they did not Beware;
For God into these Infants' Hearts
Did pour the Light of Reason,
And all against their Mothers spoke
Of Witchcraft and of Treason.

V

Evil were the tales of their demands
Sprung from the Depths of Hell,
And terrible the work of their Commands
As did the children tell;
Now has the Judge the Sentence read
And ended in our town,
The rule of Imps and Spells and Dread
For many miles aroun'.

VI

So listen Christians to my Song
The Hangman's swung his rope,
And on these Gallows hath been done
An end to Satan's Hope;
Give the News from Chelmsford Town
To all the world be spread,
A crew of Evil Witches have gone Down
Hang'd by the neck, all three are Dead.

(Repeat)

a dialogue concerning witches and witchcraft

by George Gifford

In the closing years of Queen Elizabeth's reign, a second important witchcraft book was published. This book, like Scot's *Discovery*, drew its inspiration from the events in Essex. This work was from the pen of a Nonconformist clergyman, George Gifford, who lived in Essex at Maldon. The town of Maldon, still today one of the most attractive small harbor ports on the coast of Essex, had been a center of alleged witchcraft occurrences since long before the passing of Elizabeth's witchcraft act. Several old women were widely referred to as witches, and there were stories of a broom that swept by itself and a group of local treasure seekers who were said to have employed the aid of the notorious necromancer Dr. Dee in their quests.

George Gifford, vicar of All Saints' Church in Maldon and an Essex man born and bred, was deeply versed in local knowledge and was a spectator at witchcraft trials in the borough court in 1574, 1579, and 1592. From all this he drew the material for two books, *Discourse of the Subtle Practices of Devils by Witches and Sorcerers* (1587) and *A Dialogue Concerning Witches and Witchcrafts* (1593). The second work was by far the more important and, despite dealing only with local occurrences, subsequently established its author as the most valuable authority on Essex witchcraft. The book had a similar dramatic effect on readers to that of Scot's *Discovery*, but although Gifford was also an opponent of the "witchcraft delusion," he did not deny the existence of witches or doubt that they had dealings with the devil.

The work takes the form of a discussion among a superstitious countryman and his wife, a schoolmaster who believes in witchcraft, and a skeptic named Daniel. Through these characters—obviously modeled on local people Gifford knew—the author argues that the sickness and death ascribed to witchcraft are mostly due to natural causes, that spectral and hearsay evidence should not be taken seriously in the courts, and that no one should be convicted except on the most conclusive evidence. Because of the manner in which the book's writing is couched, Gifford did not suffer the indignities of Scot, but admittedly he did lard his text with fiction as well as fact to make it more widely acceptable. As a result of his inquiries, the author believed that Essex was a "bad county for witches, I think even one of the worst in England."

Such is the importance of Gifford to this study, that his *Dialogue* is reprinted in full. No doubt the reader will find himself agreeing with Thomas Ady, a later contributor to this collection, who said of the preacher that he "had more of the spirit of truth in him than many of his profession." Sadly, the book's message, like that of Scot's *Discovery*, was more than half a century away from earning anything like widespread acceptance.

THE SPEAKERS.

Samuel.   Daniel.   The wife of Samuel.   M. B.
schoole-maister.   The goodwife R.

Sam. You are wel met, old acquaintance, I am glad to see you looke so well, how do all our good friends in your country?

Dan. I trust they be all in good health: they were when I came from home, I am sory to se you look so pale: what have you bene sicke lately?

Sam. Truly no, I thanke God I have had my health pretily well, but yet me thinke my meate doth me no good of late.

Dan. What is the matter, man, do you take thought and care for the world? take heede of that, for the Scripture saith, worldly sorrow worketh death. (2 Cor. vii. 10.) It is a great sinne rising from unbeleefe, and distrust in Gods providence, when men be over pensive for the world.

Sam. Indeede my mind is troubled, but not for that which you say, for I hope in God I shall not want so long as I live.

Dan. Is it any trouble of conscience for sinne? if it be, that may turne to good.

Sam. O no, no, I know no cause why.

Dan. Why what is it then, if I may be so bold, I pray you tell me. I thinke you take me for your friend.

Sam. Indeede I have alwayes found you my verie good friend, and I am sure you will give me the best counsell you can: truely we dwell here in a bad country, I thinke even one of the worst in England.

Dan. Is it so! I thinke you dwell in a fine country, in a sweete wholesome aire, and fruitfull grounds.

Sam. Aire, man! I find no fault with the aire, there be naughtie people.

Dan. Naughtie people! where shall a man dwell, and not find them? swearers, liers, railers, slaunderers, drunkards, adulterers, riotous, unthrifts, dicers, and proud high minded persons, are every where to be found in great plentie.

Sam. Nay, I do not meane them, I care not for them. These witches, these evill favoured old witches do trouble me.

Dan. What, do you take your selfe to be bewitched?

Sam. No, no, I trust no evill spirit can hurt me, but I heare of much harme done by them, they lame men and kil their cattel, yea they destroy both men and children. They say there is scarse any towne or village in all this shire, but there is one or two witches at the least in it. In good sooth, I may tell it to you as to my friend, when I go but into my closes, I am afraid, for I see now and then a hare, which my conscience giveth me is a witch, or some witches spirit, she stareth so upon me. And sometime I see an ugly weasill runne through my yard, and there is a foule great cat sometimes in my barne, which I have no liking unto.

Dan. You never had no hurt done yet, had you by any witch?

Sam. Trust me I cannot tell, but I feare me I have; for there be two or three in our town which I like not, but especially an old woman. I have bene as careful to please her as ever I was to please mine own mother, and to give her ever and anon one thing or other, and yet methinkes she frownes at me now and then. And I had a hog which eate his meat with his fellows, and was very well to our thinking over night, and in the morning he was starke dead. My wife hath had five or sixe hens even of late dead. Some of my neighbours wish me to burne something alive, as a hen or a hog. Others will me in time to seeke help at the hands of some cunning man, before I have any further harme. I would be glad to do for the best.

Dan. Have you any cunning man thereabout, that doth helpe?

Sam. There is one, they say, here a twentie miles off at T. B. which hath holpe many. And thus much I know, there was one of mine acquaintance but two miles hence, which had great losses; he lost two or three kine, sixe hogs, he would not have tooke fifteene shillings a hog for them, and a mare. He went to that same man, and told him he suspected an old woman in the parish. And I thinke he told me, that he shewed him her in a glasse, and told him she had three or foure impes, some call them puckrels, one like a grey cat, another like a weasel, another like a mouse, a vengeance take them, it is a great pitie the country is not rid of them, and told him also what he should do: it is half a yeare ago, and he never had any hurt since. There is also a woman at R. H. five and twentie miles hence, that hath a great name, and great resort there is daily unto her. A neighbour of mine had his child taken lame, a girl of ten yeares old, and such a paine in her backe, that she could not sit upright. He went to that woman, she told him that he had some bad neighbour, the child was forespoken, as she suspected; marie, if he would go home, and bring her some of the clothes which the child lay in all night, she would tell him certainely. He went home, and put a table napkin about her necke all night, and in the morning tooke it with him, and she told him the girle was bewitched indeed, and so told him what he should do, and he had remedie: the girle is well at this day, and a pretie quicke girle. There was another of my neighbours had his wife much troubled, and he went to her, and she told him his wife was haunted with a fairie. I cannot tell what she bad him do, but the woman is merrie at this houre. I have heard, I dare not say it is so, that she weareth about her S. Johns Gospell, or some part of it.

Dan. If you have such cunning men and woman, what need you be so much afraid?

Sam. Alas, man, I could teeme it to go, and some counsell me to go to the man at T. B. and some to the woman at R. H. And between them both, I have lingred the time, and feare I may be spoiled before I get remedie. Some wish me to beate and claw the witch, untill I fetch bloud on her, and to threaten her that I will have her hanged. If I knew which were the best, I would do it.

Dan. I perceive your danger is betweene two stooles.

Sam. It is very true, if I had heard but of one, I should have gone ere this time, and I am glad that I met with you. I pray you let me have your best counsell; I trust you beare me good-will.

Dan. Truly, I will give you the best counsell I can, which I am sure shall do you good, if you will follow it, for indeed I pittie your case, it is most certaine you are bewitched.

Sam. Bewitched, do you thinke I am bewitched? I feele no harme in my bodie, you make me more afraid.

Dan. Nay, I do not thinke that the old woman hath bewitched you, or that your body is bewitched, but that the divell hath bewitched your mind with blindnesse and unbeleefe, to draw you from God, even to worship himselfe, by seeking help at the hands of divels. It is a lamentable case to see how the divel hath bewitched thousands at this day to runne after him, and even to offer sacrifice unto him.

Sam. I defie the divell: worship him? fie upon him, I hate him with all my heart. Do you thinke any seeke help at his hands? we seeke help against him. I thinke he never doth good, he hurteth, but he never helpeth any.

Dan. It is not in these matters to be taken as we imagine, but as the word of God teacheth. What though a man thinke he worshippeth not divels, nor seeketh not help at their hands, as he is perswaded, nor hath any such intent, is he ever the nerre, when as yet it shall be found by God's word, that he doth worship them, and seeke unto them for help?

Sam. Do you thinke, then, that there be no witches? Doth not God suffer wicked people to do harme? Or do you thinke that the cunning men do helpe by the divell? I would be glad to reason with you, but I have small knowledge in the Scriptures. We have a schoole-maister that is a good pretie scholler (they say) in the Latine tongue, one M. B., he is gone to my house even now, I pray you let me intreate you to go thither; you two may reason the matter, for you are learned.

Dan. I could be content, but it will aske some time, and I am going to such a place upon speciall businesse.

Sam. I pray you let me intreate you: foure or five houres is not so much.

Dan. Well, I will go with you.

Sam. Wife, I have brought an old friend of mine, I pray thee bid him welcome.

The Wife. He is verie welcome. But truly, man, I am angrie with you, and halfe out of patience, that you go not to seeke helpe against yonder same old beast; I have another hen dead this night. Other men can seeke remedie. Here is M. B. tels me, that the goodwife R. all the last week could not make her butter come. She never rested untill she had got her husband out to the woman at R. H.; and when he came home, they did but heate a spit red hot, and thrust into the creame, using certaine words, as she willed him, and it came as kindly as any butter that ever she made. I met the old filth this morning; Lord, how sowerly she looked upon me, and mumbled as she went, I heard part of her words. Ah, (quoth she) you have an honest man to your husband, I heare how he doth use me. In truth, husband, my stomacke did so rise against her, that I could have found in my heart to have flowne upon her, and scratched her, but that I feared she would be too strong for me. It is a lustie old queane. I wished that the goodwife R. had bene with me. I pray you, good husband, let me intreate you to go to that same good woman: you may ride thither in halfe a day.

Sam. Wife, I pray thee be content, I have intreated this mine old friend to reason with M. B., for he tels me that we be in a verie foul errour.

M. B. I suppose, so farre as my learning and capacitie do extend, that small reasoning may serve. The word of God doth shew plainely that there be witches, and commaundeth they should be put to death. Experience hath taught too too many what harmes they do. And if any have the gift to minister help against them, shall we refuse it? Shall we not drinke when we are athirst? shall we not warme us when we are a cold? It is pitie that anie man should open his mouth any way to defend them, their impietie is so great.

Dan. For my part, I go not about to defend witches. I denie not but that the divell worketh by them. And that they ought to be put to death. We ought also to seeke remedy against them, but, as I told my friend, the divel doth bewitch men by meanes of these witches, and leade them from God, even to follow himselfe, to offer sacrifice unto him, to worship him, to obey his will, to commit many grievous sinnes, and be drowned in manifold errours.

M. B. If you have this meaning, that witches and sorcerers are bewitched by the divel, that they forsake God, and folow him, that they worship and obey him, and do sacrifice unto him, and commit many hainous sins, I agree with you, for I take it, they even vow themselves to the divell, or else he would not be so redie to do them service. But if you meane that such as seeke remedy against them, and would have them rooted out, be so seduced and mis-led by the divell, as you speake, I say your speech is rash and foolish, for they that be earnest against witches, be earnest against the divell, they defie the divell, they seeke to resist him, and to roote out his instruments. Now, if you were a man that had any learning, you should see, that contraries cannot be in the same subject, at one instant, in the same part, and in the same respect: how then can a man hate the divell, defie the divell and his works, and yet follow him at one time?

Dan. I know that witches and conjurers are seduced and become the vassals of Satan, they be his servants, and not he theirs, as you speake. But I meane indeed that multitudes are seduced and led from God, to follow the divell, by meanes of witches and conjurers: yea I speake it of those, not which are caried of a godly zeale, but of a blind rage and mad furie against them. If I speake this rashly and foolishly, as you say, and your self learned as you boast, and I unlearned, I shall be the more easily overthrowne. But I speake so truly, and can so well justifie all that I have said by the word of God, that your learning and best skill shall not be able to disproove the same. Your logicke at the first doth faile you. Not that contraries can be in the same subject at the same instant, in the same part, and in the same respect. But herein you are utterly blind and deceived, that you name contraries, and take it that the first of them, as namely to hate the divell, to defie him and his workes, are in them, when as indeede they are in them but in imagination. For if men say and think they defie the divel and his workes, and through blindnes and infidelitie, are even bewitched, and seduced to follow the divell, and to do his will, doth their speech and blind imagination make the things indeede to be in them? What if a poore begger woman say and thinke that she is a queene: is she therefore no begger, begging still her bread? or is she rid of her lice?

M. B. Nay, if you judge, I have done. If men be earnest against the divell, and defie him and all his workes, are you to judge of their conscience, and to say they defie him but in imagination, and follow him, and worship him indeed? is not God alone the judge over men's hearts? Againe, do you compare those that are in their right mind, with such as be mad, or out of their wits?

Dan. I know that God alone is the searcher of the heart, touching the things which lie hid in secret: but where things are open and manifest, the tree is knowne by the fruites, so farre we may go. As if a man professe the faith of Jesus Christ soundly, in all points according to the word of God, and doth frame his life thereafter in doing good workes: it is very wicked for any man to judge of him, that he is a hypocrite, and that he doth all of vaine-glorie. And yet it may be that the Lord, who discerneth the secret intents of the heart, seeth indeed that he is but a hypocrite. On the contrarie part, where a man professeth in words that he doth defie the divell and all his workes, and yet when it cometh to the triall of Gods word, he is found to be seduced, and wrapped in blind errors of the divell, in infidelitie, and evill workes, in which he fulfilleth the will of Satan, and honoureth him in the place of God, shall we say that this is a good man because of his words and imaginations, that he defieth the divell and his works? *Woe be to them that call good evill, and evill good,* Esa. v. We may say they are in a bad case, except they repent, and turne from following Satan. But yet I say, that a faithfull man may erre in some of these things through weakenesse of faith, and through ignorance. And therefore, here men may not be too rash in judgment. And now whereas you find fault, that I make comparison between such as be mad and those that be in their right mind: it is your ignorance, which do not consider that there be two kinds of madnes, or being out of their right mind, the one for matters of this world, the other for things spirituall and heavenly. There be which are in their wits for this world, which touching spiritual things are as far awrie in their imaginations, as the poore beggar, which thinketh she is a goodly queene. Doth not the holy apostle say, that *because men receive not the love of the truth, God will send them strong delusion to beleeve lies,* 2 Thes. ii. And what is that, but that Satan shall seduce, illude, and bewitch their minds, to make them beleeve that they worship and follow God, when they worship and follow him?

M. B. Do you take that to be St. Pauls meaning? Doth Satan bewitch mens minds, and leade them into falshood and errour making them beleeve they worship God, when they worship divels?

Dan. S. Paul speaketh there indeed of the comming of the great Antichrist in the power of the divell. Now those which are seduced and worship Antichrist, thinke they worship God, but marke what S. John saith, *All the world wondred, and followed the Beast, and worshipped the Dragon which gave power to the Beast: and they worshipped the Beast.* Revelat. xiii. And looke in the twelfth chapter of the Revelation, and you shall find that the Dragon, which the Poperie doth worship in stead of God, is the divell.

M. B. Truly I like your words well, I am persuaded the divell doth seduce and bewitch mens minds: but touching those that seek help at the hands of cunning men and women against witches, I cannot thinke so hardly of them. I may be awrie, I see well: I will not be obstinate if the word of God shew me mine errour. Let us even friendly conferre of the matter. Be not offended with me, and for my part I will speake all that I know or thinke.

Dan. I must intreate you likewise to beare with my plaine speeches. And let us in the matters proceede from one point to another, standing onely upon that, wherein we shall be found to differ in judgement: and let Gods word be the judge betweene us.

Sam. I like this well: though I can say but litle, I will sit and heare you.

Dan. What is the first question that we shall handle?

M. B. I heard you say, if I did not mistake your speech, that there be witches that worke by the divell. But yet I pray you tel me, do you thinke there be such? I know some are of opinion there be none.

Dan. It is so evident by the Scriptures, and in all experience, that there be witches which worke by the divell, or rather, I may say, the divell worketh by them, that such as go about to proove the contrarie do shew themselves but cavillers.

M. B. I am glad we agree in that point, I hope we shall in the rest. What say you to this? that the witches have their spirits, some hath one, some hath more, as two, three, foure, or five, some in one likenesse, and some in another, as like cats, weasils, toades, or mise, whom they nourish with milke or with a chicken, or by letting them suck now and then a drop of bloud: whom they call when they be offended with any, and send them to hurt them in their bodies, yea to kill them, and to kill their cattell?

Dan. Here is great deceit, and great illusion; here the divell leadeth the ignorant people into foule errours, by which he draweth them headlong into many grievous sinnes.

M. B. Nay, then, I see you are awrie, if you denie these things, and say they be but illusions. They have been proved, and proved againe, even by the manifold confessions of the witches themselves. I am out of all doubt in these, and could in many particulare lay open what hath fallen out. I did dwel in a village within these five yeares, where there was a man of good wealth, and sodainly within ten dayes space, he had three kine died, his gelding worth ten pounds fel lame, he was himself taken with a great paine in his back, and a child of seven yeeres old died. He sent to the woman at R. H. and she said he was plagued by a witch, adding moreover, that there were three women witches in that town, and one man witch: willing him to look whom he most suspected: he suspected one old woman, and caused her to be caried before a Justice of Peace and examined: with much ado at the last she confessed all: which was this in effect: that she had three spirits, one like a cat, which she called Lightfoot, another like a toade, which she called Lunch, the third like a weasill, which she called Makeshift. This Lightfoote she said, one Mother Barlie, of W., sold her above sixteene yeares ago, for an oven cake, and told her the cat would do her good service, if she would, she might send her of her errand: this cat was with her but a while, but the weasil and the tode came and offred their service. The cat would kill swine, the weasil would kill horses, the toade would plague men in their bodies. She sent them all three (as she confessed) against this man. She was committed to the prison, and there she died before the assises. I could tell you of many such: I had no mind to dwell in that place any longer.

Dan. You mistake me, I do not meane that the things are not, but my meaning is, that the divell by such things doth beguile and seduce ignorant men, and lead them into errours and grievous sinnes. And let us examine every parcell of that which you set downe in your speech, and you shall see no lesse.

M. B. That is it which I would faine see. You confesse they have spirits, some one, some more, and in such likenesses: what errour be the people led into by that?

Dan. First consider this, that there be multitudes and armies of divels, as we see in the Gospel, that many divels were entered into one man, and Christ saying *What is thy name?* answer is made, *Legion, for we are many.* Marke v. Now, although the divels be many, yet they be all caried with such hatred against God, with such desire to have him dishonored and blasphemed, and burne with such bloudie malice and crueltie against men, that they bend their study al together, one helping and furthering another what they can in their worke: insomuch that the Scripture doth speake of them, as if they were but one divell: for St. Peter saith, *Your adversarie the divell goeth about like a roaring lion seeking whom he may devoure.* (1 Pet. v.) And in the Revelation, (chapter xii.) all the divels make that great red dragon, and our Saviour doth shew how close they joyne in one, when he saith, *If Satan be devided against Satan, or if Satan cast foorth Satan, how shall his kingdome endure?* (Matth. xii.) Now then, whether the witch deale, as she supposeth, with one spirit, or with many, it commeth all to one effect, thus farre, that one dealeth not alone, but with the help of others. So that he or she that hath familiaritie with one divel, it is as much as if it were with an hundred. Moreover, the divels be spirits, they have no bodily shape or likenesse, but yet can make an appearance of a shape, as appeareth by the inchaunters before Pharao, when their rods were turned into serpents in shew. (Exod. vii.) And then one divel can seeme to be foure or five, and foure or five can seeme to be one: it is therefore but the craft of Satan, to make shew of more or lesse.

M. B. Do you not thinke then, that where the more divels be, there is the greater power of Satan?

Dan. Yes, but it cannot be discerned, be his appearing to the witch in shew of more or lesse, for one can seeme ten unto her, and ten can seeme one.

M. B. Well, I do not mislike all this, I pray you proceede forward.

Dan. Then further marke well how the holy Scriptures do paint out the divels to be mightie terrible spirits, full of power, rage, and crueltie, compared to a great fierie red dragon; (Revel. xii.) to a greedie or hungrie lion, that roareth after the prey, (1 Pet. v.) and called by S. Paul principalities and powers, the rulers of the darknesse of this world: now when they take upon them the shapes of such paltrie vermin, as cats, mice, todes, and weasils, it is even of subtiltie to cover and hide his mightie tyrannie and power, which he exerciseth over the hearts of the wicked. It is most necessarie for us all to know, what strong adversaries we have to encounter withall, that we may flie unto the Lord God, and seek to be armed with his power against them.

M. B. Well, what will you inferre upon this? I can not denie but that the Scriptures do paint out the divels to be mightie terrible spirits, and so they may be, although they appeare but like cats or weasils.

Dan. I do not say that they be not mightie and terrible, because they appeare in such shapes: but I affirme, that their appearing so, is to cover and hide their mightinesse and effectual working, which they exercise in the dark hearts of men. And marke well, I pray you, the power of divels is in the hearts of men, as to harden the heart, to blind the eyes of the mind, and from the lustes and concupiscenses which are in them, to inflame them unto wrath, malice, envie, and cruell murthers: to puffe them up in pride, arrogancie, and vaine-glorie: to intice them unto wantonness and whooredomes, and all uncleannesse. And about these things they work continually, and with such efficacy, that without the power of the glorious passion and resurrection of our Lord Jesus Christ, which we have by faith, they cannot be withstood, and they will seeme to be but meane fellows, busied about making drinke that it shal not work in the fat, in keeping cheese from running, and butter from comming, in killing hens or hogs, or making men lame.

M. B. May they not do both the one and the other?

Dan. Yea, but this is my meaning, that while they be occupied about the greatest things, as in stirring up tyrants and wicked men to persecute, to reproch, and blaspheme the Gospell, which pulleth them downe, to set division and wars betweene kingdoms and kings, hatred and discord betweene man and wife, and contention betweene brethren: yea, to set all in a broile and confusion: they would seeme to be busied about trifles, and about these they busie mens minds, that they may not observe and take heed of them in those other.

M. B. I perceive your meaning, but yet I do not conceive whereunto you chiefly tend: for do not they which looke upon these harmes done by witches, confesse that the divell doth all those things which you mention?

Dan. The ignorant sort which are so terrified by witches, do in words after a sort confesse so much as you say, but when it commeth to the matter, they denie it in effect. For marke this, the divels continually compasse the soule of man about, to shoote it full of their fierie darts, (Ephes. vi.) even to wound it to death with all wicked sinnes. *The divell goeth about like a roaring lion, seeking whom he may devoure.* (1 Pet. v.) And they by this craft which they use by meanes of the witches, make the blind people imagine that they never come nigh them, but when the witches are angrie and do send them, and that they are easily driven away when they do come, as by burning some quick thing, as hen, or hog, or by beating and drawing bloud upon the witch. Such people as can thus drive him away, or by thrusting a spit red hote into their creame, are farre from knowing the spirituall battell, in which we are to warre under the banner of Christ against the divell, much lesse do they know how to put on (as S. Paul willeth), the whole armour of God, to resist and overcome him. (Ephes. vi.) He may deale with their soules even as he listeth, when they take him not present but upon such sending, and where such hurt doth follow in their bodies or goods.

M. B. I do not denie, but that the divels seeke chiefly for to destroy the soules of men: but (as I take it) you confesse, that they being sent by the witches, do also those bodily harmes: and as yet I see no reason why they may not seeke remedie against such harmes, and drive him away by any good meanes; doth the word of God forbid us to use meanes? If I be sicke, shall I not take phisicke? If I be thirstie, shall I not drinke? Indeed, I am of your mind, though I did not know so much before, that the divell dealeth subtilly in this, that by dealing in such small matters, he covereth himself in the greater, as though he came not neere, nor did not meddle but in such manner: but here standeth the case, I resist him in those greater, may I not also use those helpes which drive him away in the lesser? I will, if I can, drive him away in all things.

Dan. How the divels are sent by the witches, and how they do those bodily harmes, we are not yet come unto, and there lie two of the chiefest subtilities of the divell in them, by which he deceiveth the multitude. But by occasion we are fallen into the mention of remedy to drive them away. Because (I say), such as thus drive him away, know not the spiritual battel, much lesse how to put on the whole armour of God to overcome the divell: order doth require that we speake first of his sending, and then of those bodily harmes which he doth, afterward of these meanes which are used to repell him. Let us therefore step one step backe againe, if you agree to the rest which I have spoken.

M. B. With a good will: for so we shall omit no part. But I thought we had fully agreed in this, that the witches do send their spirits, and do many harmes both unto men and beasts: because we have it confirmed by daily experience: and unlesse you will denie that which is manifest, I doubt not but we shall accord in these.

Dan. I say the witches do send their spirits.

M. B. What shall we neede then to stand upon that point in which we are agreed?

Dan. Yes, though we agree that they send them, yet we may dissent in divers things about this sending. As first, tell me, whether do you thinke that the witch or the divell is the servant; which of them commaundeth, and which obeyeth?

M. B. How can I tell that? It is thought he becommeth her servant, and where she is displeased and would be revenged, she hireth him for to do it. The witches themselves have confessed thus much: and for my part, I thinke no man can disproove it.

Dan. They that do the will of God, are the children and servants of God. And they which fulfill the lustes of the divell, and obey him, are his children and his servants. (John viii. 44, Acts xiii. 10.) Are they not?

M. B. I grant all this.

Dan. The divels are the rulers of the darknesse of this world. (Ephes. vi. verse 12.)

M. B. The text is plaine.

Dan. The darknesse of this world, is not meant of the darkness of the night, which is but the shadow of the earth, but it is the spirituall darknesse, which consisteth in the ignorance of God, in infidelitie, and in sinne.

M. B. I am of your mind in this also.

Dan. And do you not thinke then that the divell hath his throne, his dominion, and kingdome in the hearts of ignorant blind infidels?

M. B. I must needes thinke he hath; the word of God doth force me thereunto, seeing he is the prince of darkenesse.

Dan. And is there any greater infidelitie and darknesse in any, then in witches, conjurers, and such as have familiaritie with divels?

M. B. I take it they be deepest overwhelmed in darknesse and infidelitie of all other.

Dan. Lay all these things together which you confesse, and see whether it doth not follow upon the same, that the witch is the vassall of the divell, and not be her servant; he is lord and commaundeth, and she is his drudge and obeyeth.

M. B. Yea, although he be lord, yet he is content to serve her turne, and the witches confesse, they call them forth and send them, and that they hire them to hurt such in their bodies, and in their cattell, and they be displeased withall.

Dan. I am sorie you are so farre awrie: it is pitie any man should be in such errour, especially a man that hath learning, and should teach others knowledge.

M. B. Nay, I may returne this upon you; for, if you will denie this, it is but a folly to reason any further. I will never be driven from that which I know.

There was one old mother W. of Great T. which had a spirit like a weasill: she was offended highly with one H. M.: home she went, and called forth her spirit, which lay in a pot of wooll under her bed, she willed him to go and plague the man: he required what she would give him, and he would kill H. M. She said she would give him a cocke, which she did, and he went, and the man feel sicke with a great paine in his belly, languished, and died: the witch was arraigned, condemned, and hanged, and did confesse all this.

Dan. I told you before that I do not deny these things, but you are deceived about the doing: you marke not the cunning sleights of the divell: tell me, is not this the truth which S. Peter speaketh, *that the divell goeth about like a roaring lion, seeking whom he may devoure?* (1 Pet. 5)

M. B. What then?

Dan. What then? can you be so simple as to imagine that the divell lieth in a pot of wooll, soft and warme, and stirreth not, but when he is hired and sent? The divels conspire together in their worke, they bestirre them, and never take rest night nor day: they are never wearie, they be not cold, they care not for lying soft; these be fooleries, by which he deceiveth the witches, and bewitcheth the minds of many ignorant people: and whereas you say he is hired, it is but deceit: for, let me aske you two or three questions more if neede be.

M. B. What be your questions?

Dan. You say the witch commeth home angrie, who hath kindled this wrath in heart but the divell? Who inflameth her mind with malice, to be revenged, and to do mischiefe but the divell? doth he not rule in her heart? Tell me what you thinke of this.

M. B. I must needs confesse he stirreth her up to wrath and malice.

Dan. Then he lieth not at home in his pot of wooll: nor he is not hired to this: hitherto she is his drudge, and obeyeth him, and not he her, being led by his suggestion. Then tell me, is not the divell like a red or fierie dragon (*Revelat.* xii.) burning in malice against God, and with all bloudie and cruell hatred that may be against men? And is he not farre reddier unto all mischiefe, then any man or woman?

M. B. The divell is more fierce then any man or woman; none can denie this.

Dan. If none can denie this, and he be the worker of the wrath and malice in the heart of the witch, then what needeth he to be hired? he stirreth her up, and if he would, he could turne her mind from sending him, and must he be hired? doth he care for a cocke or a chicken? is he hungrie, or needeth he somewhat to eate?

M. B. Nay, but it is thought he taketh those things to witnesse against the witch that she is his.

Dan. Let it be, there were somewhat in that which you speake, yet he hath a farre deeper reach, for the truth is, he would and doth perswade the blind people, that he medleth litle, but when he is even hired and sent, and that then his medling is but in such matters: and hereupon all is on a broyle against old women, which can any wayes be suspected to be witches, as if they were the very plagues of the world, and as if all would be well, and safe from such harmes, if they were rooted out, and thus they fall a rooting out without all care: for it is thought that the witch which hath her spirits, is even like a man which hath curst dogges, which he may set upon other mens cattell, which yet in the nature of dogs would never stirre but when they are bidden: and so the harmes do come from the man which owneth those dogs. They thinke that the country might be rid of such spirits, if there were none to hoister them, or to set them a work. They imagine that they and their cattel should then go safe. Alas, poore creatures, how they be deluded! how litel do they understand the high providence of Almighty God, which is over all!

M. B. Do you thinke then that witches ought not to be rooted out? or do you thinke it were not much safetie to the countrey from harmes, if it could be rid of them?

Dan. For the rooting out of witches, the Scripture is plaine: *Thou shalt not suffer a witch to live*: but we are not yet come to that point. But whether they be to be rooted out that men may be safe from harmes, as the people in furie and blindnesse imagine, that is next.

M. B. Men feele the smart and the harmes which they do, and it is no marvell, though they be earnest to have them rooted out, and a good riddance it were if the whole land could be set free from them.

Sam. Truly, M. B., I am of your mind, I would they were all hanged up one against another: we should not (I hope) stand in such feare of their spirits. But I interrupt you too.

The Wife. They that would not have them hanged or burnt, I would they might even witch them unto hell. If I had but one fagot in the world, I would carie it a mile upon my shoulders to burne a witch.

Dan. Well, good woman, spare your fagot awile, and ease your shoulders, and let us reason the matter a litle further. I pray you let me aske you this question, Doth the witch or the divell the harme unto men and cattell?

M. B. Why the divell doth it at their sending, though I confesse it must needes be as you said, that the divell worketh all in the mind of the witch, and mooveth her to send him.

Dan. The divell hath a kingdome, but it is in darkenesse and corruption of sinne. He hath no right nor power over Gods creatures, no not so much as to kill one flie, or to take one eare of corne out of any mans barne, unlesse power be given him. You know when Christ cast the divels out of the man possessed, they aske leave for to go into the heard of swine. Then tell me, who giveth the divell this power then, when the witch sendeth him, to kill or to lame man or beast? doth the witch give it him? Do you thinke he had power to do harme, but no mind till she moved him? Or do you take it that her sending giveth him power which he had not?

M. B. It is a question indeed worth the asking: for doubtlesse the divell hath not power until it be given him, to touch any creature, to hurt or to destroy the body, but only to tempt and to lead into sin. I am also sure that the witch cannot give him power, but only God above.

Dan. Lay these two together then, that the divell only hurteth, and that none can give him power, neither man nor woman, but only God, and tel me whether the people be not wonderfully caried awry in a rage. For, when as they should consider, that the divell is the Lords executioner: and then finding that he hath any power given him to molest, to hurt and vexe them in their bodies or goods, to know certainly it cometh from the Lord, and then gather from thence (as the truth is), that the Lord is displeased with them for their offences, and so seeke unto him, humbly craving pardon and deliverance from this enemy seeking to be armed with the mighty power of faith, to cast him foorth and resist him, as the Lord willeth, (1 Pet. v.): here is no such matter, no looking so high among the people, but running deeper into error, and into sinne, as if the witches did it, and that it commeth from their anger, and not from their own sinnes and infidelity. Here is no repentance, no humbling themselves by fasting and prayer, but running for helpe unto divels, using meanes which those divels by the cunning men and women appoint, scratching and clawing, thirsting often after guiltlesse bloud, and raging against those whom they imagine to be witches, which many times are not, because they imagin, that if there were no witches, there should be no such plagues. As if they had no foule sins nor unbeleefe, or that there remained not a just revenging God to punish, or as if he had not the divels still the executioners of his wrath.

M. B. Truly, your words do make me affraid: for I am even guiltie of those things my selfe, if they be so grievous as you set them out: and by Gods grace I wil consider better of the matter: for I have counselled many to seeke unto those cunning folks, and to use such helps as they prescribe: and you say it is to seeke helpe at divels. To see that point we shal come anone: now I would be resolved about somewhat in your last speech, as namely, do you cleare the witches, because God and not they giveth the divel power, and do you thinke that the divels should kill men and their cattell, if they were not sent by witches? Should the harmes still follow, if there were not witches?

Dan. That I say God alone, and not the witches, giveth power unto the divels to plague and torment: it is so evident as that I suppose a man shall hardly meete with any man so grosse but will confesse it. But this doth not cleare the witches at all; for their sinne is in dealing with divels, and that they imagine that their spirits do those harmes, requested and hired by them; when as indeed the Divel where he hath power given him to hurt, or where he knoweth death or grievous diseases will follow either in man or beast, setteth the witch in a rage, and moveth her to send him. Concerning your other question, I say, we shall find by the Scriptures, that if there were no witches at all, yet men shold be plagued by the divels in their bodies and goods. For, touching the godly, the Lord doth use Satan to afflict them in their bodies and in their goods, for to trie their faith and patience; as the example of holie Job doth testifie in ample manner. It were vile folly and brutish to affirme, that witches did set on the divels to kil his children, and to plague his body. And I hold it no small folly, for any man to thinke that the Lord doth not now scourge his children, at the least some of them, for their good, by the divel. There is no doubt, but the divel having power given him to afflict, useth all the craft he can, and will seeke to be sent by the witch, and so he will make it knowne, because it may seeme not to be from God, but from the anger of a poore woman. And now, touching the wicked, which provoke God by their wicked sinnes and unbeleefe, may we not read in the Scriptures that an evil spirit was sent of God unto king Saul, which did haunt and vexe him? Was this spirit sent by a witch? Or the divels in the Gospel, which entred into the herd of swine and drowned them: did the Lord give them power, and send them, and shall we be so sottish as to thinke, that he sendeth not the divel now against ungodly men, to plague and to destroy them? As I said before, here is the deepe craft of Sathan, that he will covet to be sent by witches, whereas, indeed, God hath set him, seeing none can send him but God. Againe, we must consider, that there be naturall causes in the bodies of men and beastes of grievous torments and diseases, yea even causes of death. Now they cannot be so secret, but the divell knoweth them, and even when they are like to take effect. Then doth he ply it with the witch, setteth her in a fury, she sendeth him; even upon this sending the man or the beast suddenly and strangely are tormented, fall lame, or dye. Then the witch is suspected, examined, and confesseth that she killed such a man, or such a mans cattell, or made them lame. Here the people are set in a wonderfull maze and astonishment, as if witches could plague men in their wrath, by sending their spirits, because they confesse they did it, when their spirits do lye and had no power, but the torments came by naturall causes. And to drive the people into a deeper madnesse in this, and to make them beleeve, that strange and sudden torments and languishing diseases come by witches, he hath his other sort of witches, the cunning men and women, which tell even upon his word, which you know is to be trusted, that they be bewitched, that they be haunted with fairies, and that there be thus many witches thereabout, in every towne some.

M. B. That is most true, no doubt, which you speake, I do not for my part know how to gainesay any one point thereof. Only I wonder at the craftiness of the divels in these things, that where they have power graunted unto them to hurt, they will be sent by the witches, as if they did it hired by them, and that you say where harmes do follow men upon natural causes, that they can make shew as though they did them. But are you of this mind, that there should be as many or all those harmes done by divels, if there were no witches, as there be now? Although I must needs confesse, that the witches can give the devill no power, nor can he take none by their sending: yet may it not be that God giveth them power oftener because of those witches dealing with them, then if there were no witches at all?

Dan. The craftiness of divels is such, as without the light of Gods word, the wisest men under heaven must needs be deceived thereby. We see there be some men so deepe in subtilties, and can carry matters so close, that men cannot discerne them: how much more the divels, which are exceedingly subtill, and crafty above the subtillest men? The question which you aske is (in my judgment) somewhat hard: but this is undoubted, that if the Lord God do give unto the divels oftener power to hurt because of the witches, I meane because the divels do deale by such instruments, it is in his heavy judgment against the wickednesse of the people, which despise the true and heavenly light of his word. As S. Paule (prophecying of the comming of the great Antichrist) sheweth, that because men did not receive the love of the truth, God gave the divell power by Antichrist and his ministers, to seduce by lying signes and wonders. Indeed, I will not say that for the witch the divell hath power given him, but for the wickednesse of the people, which deserve that by witches the divell should have power to seduce them further. Here yet we must take heed of the common errour which a multitude are carried so headlong withall, that they can by no meanes see, that God is provoked by their sinnes to give the divell such instruments to worke withall, but rage against the witch, even as if she could do all.

M. B. Surely, I should be a wretch to deny, that God giveth the divels power to plague and seduce because of mens wickednesse: but yet I would know, whether a godly faithfull man or woman may not be bewitched? We see the divell had power given him over Job.

Dan. This example of Job is not fit to proove that a godly man may be bewitched, seeing the divell is not said to deal by witches against him; but it doth proove, that not only the godly, but even the most godly (as holy Job, who had none like him upon earth), may for their triall be given into the hands of Satan to be afflicted and tempted. And, as I said, where Satan hath power granted him of God, to strike with bodily plagues any of the godly, for the triall of their faith and patience, he will covet if he can bring it about, to be sent by some witch, and to have it knowne that he was sent. But the faithful are to turne their eies from the witch, and to deale with God, for from him the matter commeth. When they be tried, the Lord in his good time will deliver them depending upon him, to their great praise and glory, even as valiant souldiers. It is therefore of no great force, whether Satan come from the witch against the godly, or whether he have no witch to deale by: overcome thou the Divell, and thou overcommest all. Indeed, among the more ignorant sort he prevaileth much, when he toucheth those which embrace the lively word as sent from a witch. For many nowe doe even quake and tremble, and their faith doth stagger. Hath he power (thinke they) over such as be cunning in the Scriptures, then what are they the better for their profession? the witch is on their bones as well as upon others. By this it might seeme, and so they take it, that other helpes and remedies are to be sought then by the Scriptures: and so they run and seeke helpe where they ought not.

M. B. Then I pray you, though I be already perswaded it is naught to seeke to these cunning men for helpe against witches, yet let us conferre a little of that. There be divers things which have perswaded me to think marvellous wel of them, and even as of such as God hath given wisedome and skill unto, even for to do much good. For we see many receive helpe by them, and are delivered from the plagues which come by divels. And first, I would know how they can be so earnest against witches: if they deale with the divel, and so be indeed witches themselves, how can they have any mind in charity to do good, to take pity upon such as be in misery? Or how will Satan drive forth Satan? for they no doubt, drive out divels out of some.

Dan. I would come to answer your questions touching the seeking helpe at the hands of cunning men or women: but tell me first, are you resolved touching the sending of the spirits, and touching the harmes that are done? Me thinke you slip too suddenly from these points?

M. B. I cannot tell whether I understand your meaning in every thing, but sure, I have been in error greatly, I must needs confesse. And if you please, we may stand somewhat longer in these questions.

Sam. Indeed, it is my desire that you would speake a little plainer of these points: for I have marked well al your talke, and cannot well conceive of the last things you dealt in. With your leave, M. B., I would aske two or three questions of my friend. Here was, but seven miles hence, at W. H., one M., the man was of good wealth, and well accounted of among his neighbours. He pined away with sicknesse half a yeare, and at last died. After he was dead, his wife suspected ill dealing: she went to a cunning man, I know not where, and desired to know whereof her husband died. He told her that her husband died of witchery: he asked her if she did not suspect any thereabout. She sayd there was one woman which she did not like, one Mother W.; her husband and she fell out, and he fell sicke within two dayes after, and never recovered againe. He shewed her the woman as plaine in a glasse, as we see one another, and in the very apparell she went in that houre, for she ware an old red cap with corners, such as women were wont to weare: and in that she appeared in the glasse. He taught her how she might bring her to confesse. Well, she followed his counsell, went home, caused her to be apprehended and carried before a justice of peace. He examined her so wisely, that in the end she confessed she killed the man. She was sent to prison, she was arraigned, condemned, and executed: and upon the ladder she seemed very penitent, desiring all the world to forgive her. She sayd she had a spirit in the likenesse of a yellow dun cat. This cat came unto her, as she sayd, as she sat by her fire, when she was fallen out with a neighbour of hers, and wished that the vengeance of God might light upon him and his. The cat bad her not be afraid, she would do her no harme, she had served a dame five years in Kent, that was now dead, and if she would, she would be her servant. And wheras, sayd the cat, such a man hath misused thee, if thou wilt I will plague him in his cattell. She sent the cat; she killed three hogs and one cow. The man suspecting, burnt a pig alive, and as she sayd, her cat would never go thither any more. Afterward she fell out with that M.: she sent her cat, who told her, that she had given him that which he should never recover: and indeed the man died. Now, do you not thinke the woman spake the truth in all this? Would the woman accuse her selfe falsly at her death? Did not the cat become her servant? Did not she send her? Did she not plague and kill both man and beast? What should a man thinke of this?

Dan. You propound a particular example, and let us examine every thing in it touching the witch, for the womans fact that went to the wise man, we are not yet come to that point. You say the cat came to her when she was in a great rage with one of her neighbours, and did curse, wishing the vengeance of God to fall upon him and his.

Sam. She sayd so, indeed; I heard her with my owne eares, for I was at the execution.

Dan. Then tell me who set her in such a devilish rage, so to curse and ban, as to wish that the vengeance of God might light upon him and his? Did not the cat?

Sam. Truly, I thinke that the divell wrought that in her.

Dan. Very well, then you see the cat is the beginner of this play.

Sam. Call you it a play? It was no play to some.

Dan. Indeed the witch at last had better have wrought hard, then, bene at her play. But I meane Satan did play the jugler: for doth he not offer his service? Doth he not move her to send him to plague the man? Tel me, is she so forward to send, as he is to be sent? Or do you not take it that he ruleth in her heart, and even wholly directeth it to this matter?

Sam. I am fully perswaded he ruleth her heart.

Dan. Then was she his drudge, and not he her servant: he needeth not to be hired and intreated, for if her hart were to send him anywhere, unto such as he knoweth he cannot hurt, nor seeth how to make any shew that he hurteth them, he can quickly turne her from that. Wel, the cat goeth and killeth the man, certaine hogs, and a cow: how could she tell that the cat did it?

Sam. How could she tell? why he told her, man, and she saw and heard that he lost his cattell.

Dan. The cat would lye, would she not? for they say such cats are lyers.

Sam. I do not trust the cats words, but because the thing fell out so.

Dan. Because the hogs and the cow died, are you sure the cat did kill them? might they not die of some naturall causes, as you see both men and beasts are well, and die suddenly?

Sam. That were strange, if they should die of naturall causes, and fall out so fit at the time after he was sent.

Dan. It is not strange at all, as marke what I tell you, and you shall easily see. There be naturall causes of tortures and griefe, of lamenesse, and of death in the bodies of men and of beastes, which lie so hid and secret, that the learnedest physitians cannot espie them, but the divell seeth them, and can conjecture very neare the time when they will take effect. Then doeth he plie it, to bring the matter about that it may seeme he did it. If he have anie witch to deale by, he stirreth up some occasion to set her in a rage with that party: and then he will be sent, and telleth her he doth it. If he have no witch to deale by, yet he will set debate betweene the partie and some other, whom he may bring into suspition, as his greatest desire is to have innocent bloud shed.

Sam. Here is a matter brought about indeed: how could the cat do all this?

Dan. I told you before, that the divels worke together, and can speedily and most craftily compasse things, which are farre beyond the reach of mans capacitie. But sometime the divell hath power given him to plague and doth the harme. Admit he had power given him, and did kill the cattell of this man: let us come now to that, who thinke you gave him the power for to strike and kill? Did the witch give him the power, or the Lord God?

Sam. Nay, surely the witch cannot give him power.

Dan. Did he receive power after she sent him?

Sam. That cannot I tell.

Dan. Then marke a litle: he hath power given him to plague this man in his goods: he will do it, but he will do it craftily. The Lord gave him power over the goods of holy Job: he worketh by instruments, for he stirreth up the Sabeis, and they take away his oxen and his asses: he raiseth up also the Chaldeis, and they cary away his camels. (Job i.) Even so, having power to strike, he will be sent by a witch, he could do it without her, but he gaineth much that way, as we shall see when we come to speake of the remedies which men seeke.

Sam. I wonder then that the man never had more hurt after he had burnt his pig alive.

Dan. O man, the divell can abide no roast meate, nor no fire, he is afraid, if they fall a rosting, that they will rost him. If they run at him with a spit red hote, they gaster him so sore, that his dame shall go her selfe, if she will, he will come no more there. But of these things we are to speake afterwards in their place.

Sam. You make the divell wonderfull subtill.

Dan. He is so subtill and full of craft and sleight, that no earthly creature can escape from being seduced by him, without the light of Gods heavenly word. But let us come now to the other man, whom the witch confessed she killed by her cat.

Sam. Yea, that me thinketh is more than the other: the woman was told by the cunning man that her husband was killed by witchery. The witch confessed so much at her death. The cat told the witch that she killed him.

Dan. Here be a company of credible persons to be beleeved: the cunning man saith the man was bewitched to death. Who told him that?

Sam. His spirit that maketh the witch appeare in the glasse.

Dan. That same spirit, what do you take him to be, an angell or a divell?

Sam. Some of the cunning men say, they have Moses or Elias, or the spirit of some holy man.

Dan. The divell can turne himselfe into the likenesse of an angell of light. For they that do think the cunning men and women deale with any other spirit then Satan, have no understanding. Satan saith, the man was witched to death.

Sam. Satan saith so, he is not to be beleeved, but the witch confesseth it was so.

Dan. Who told the witch?

Sam. Her cat that she sent.

Dan. What is the cat, a divell? then remember the proverbe, Aske his fellow if he be a theefe. All the matter resteth upon the testimony of divels, and they not put to their oath. We will not ground upon mans testimonie without an oath, and must we beleeve the bare word of divels?

Sam. Do you thinke then that the man was not killed by witcherie?

Dan. It may be the Lord had given Satan power to plague the man in his bodie, and then he under a colour would be sent by a witch. But it is most like that his body did languish and pine off naturall causes, which the divell did know, and so would be sent, and seeme to do all, when as indeed he had no power to touch him. For although the Lord give the divell power to strike some in their bodies, for their haynous sinnes, yet the most which the witches thinke their spirits do kill at their request, do die of naturall diseases.

Sam. Then it seemeth the witches are deceived and mocked, when he maketh them beleeve he doth kill and plague when he doth not. And againe in this, where he hath power given him of God, to strike man or beast, hee could do it, and would without the witch, and so useth the witch for a colour to draw on worse matters.

Dan. I am glad you take my meaning so right: for thinke deepely of the matters, and you shall see it must needs be so.

Sam. I interrupted M. B. I pray you go forward now to the rest.

Dan. Our matter which we come unto now, is the helpe and remedie that is sought for against witches at the hands of cunning men. And now if it please you to propound your questions, I will answer to them the best I can.

M. B. Nay truly, I see alreadie all is naught, but yet I will object those things which have carried me awry. I take it a man is to seeke remedy against evils, and I thought it was even a gift that God gave unto those whom we call cunning men, that they did very much good by. When a thing is lost, when a thing is stolen, many go to them, and they helpe them to it. I did know where the communion cup was stolen: the churchwardens rode to a wise man, he gave them direction what night, and where they should stand, and the party that had stolen it should come thither, and confesse he had it: and certainly they had it againe. I did know one that had a child of five years old, a girle, it was taken pitiously: the father was in great heavinesse, and knew not what to do: some gave him counsel to go to a woman which dwelt ten miles from him, and to cary some of the clothes which the child lay in: he did so, the woman told him that his child was bewitched, and if he did not seeke remedie in time, the child would be lost: she bad him take some old clothes, and let the child lye in them all night, and then take and burne them: and he should see by the burning, for if they did burne black, that shewed the child was bewitched: and she said further, that doubtlesse the witch would come thither. He followed her advice, and sure as we be here, there came an old woman in, which he suspected, even while they were burning, and made an errand: the man made no more ado, but even laid his clowches upon her and clawed her until the blood ran downe her cheeks, and the child was well within two days after. I could tell you of a stranger thing, but I have it but by report, but yet indeed by very credible report. There was a butcher by his trade that had a boy to his sonne, his name was John, grievous sores did breake foorth upon him: they layed salves, and none would cleave for to drawe or to ease them. The father making his moane to a friend of his, he told him whither he should goe to a very skilfull man: he did go, and being demaunded whome he suspected, she was shewed him in a glasse, an old woman that dwelt not far from him in an house alone: he told the cunning man, that the woman had shut up her doore, and was gone from home out of the shire, and so he could not tell how to come by her: he told him a way how he should fetch her home. Cut off the haire (said he) of the boyes head, and put in a cloth and burne it, and I warrant you she will come home with all the speed she can. Burne it abroad, burne it not in a chimney, for if you do, it will make you all afraid. The man went home and did this. The woman came home with all speed, came to his house, came to the boy, and said: John, scratch me; he scratched her untill the bloud followed, and whereas before nothing would draw his sores, they healed of themselves. What should a man thinke of such things?

Dan. You tell of some which have received helpe from the hands of cunning men: and no doubt there may infinit examples be brought. Some have lost, some have things stolen from them, some are vexed in their bodies: they come by the things again which were lost or stolen, they are taught to do certaine things, and are eased from their griefes. But this we must first know, they receive their helpe, if it deserve the name to be called helpe, from the divell. And do you thinke a man may lawfully seeke helpe at the hands of the divell?

M. B. Some are perswaded that they do not seeke helpe at the hand of divels, when they go to the wise men: but that it is a gift which God hath given them, even to do good withall.

Dan. I do verily thinke that many of the people are so perswaded: but what reason is there for it? Doth God by his Spirit tell where the thing is which is lost or stolen? Is it an angell from heaven, or the soule of some man that is dead, which appeareth in the christall, or in the glasse, and sheweth the image of the partie which hath stolen, or that is a witch.

M. B. I had rather heare what you thinke touching these things, then shew what I have thought.

Dan. The divels did make the heathen people beleeve that they were goddes, and so procured that they should worship them with divine worship. Through their craftines they had many waies to establish this: they conveyed themselves into images, and out of them gave answers, when they were demanded, herein they used great craft, for whereas they could not tell what should fall out, they framed the oracle in such sort as it was doubtfull, and might be taken both waies: and so looke which part it fell out on, that seemed and was taken to be the meaning of the gods If they did know how things should fall out indeed, as they did know sundry things touching the kingdoms and monarchies of the world by the writings of the prophets, and divers things by conjectures, as the divell could tell Saul he should be slaine, because he saw God had cast him off, and the hearts of the Israelites fainted, and the Philistines were full of courage, those they would tell plainely. Also they did convey themselves into the bodies of men and women, and utter things which seemed very divine, such (as I am persuaded) were the prophetisses the Sibylles among the heathen. Such was the maide at Philippos, which is mentioned in the Actes of the Apostles, which brought great gaine unto her masters by divining, out of whom Paul cast the divell. This maid could tell of things lost, of things stolen, and such like, and great resort there was unto her, as men had neede, or desired to see the strangenesse of the matter.

M. B. Let me interrupt you a litle: The divell cannot be in all places at once: how could he then, remaining in the maide, tell what was done in places farre off? how can the divell tell where the thing lost or stolen is, which is not only farre off but hidden? how can he shew the image of the theefe or witch? Can he sit and behold all things a farre off, and in secret?

Dan. We may not ascribe unto divels that they can be in all places at once, or sit in one place and behold all things done a farre off. But they joyne together in this speciall worke, to set up their kingdome, and to draw the people after them, to seeke helpe at their handes, and so to worship them. Some of them be in one place, and some in another, and from all places do stirre up the faithlesse people to run for helpe to those cunning men, and then they make the relation, for they go thither also; they know the theefe whom they mooved to the theft, and can make resemblance of his face and apparell: they can tell where things be that are hid, having had a finger in the matter. And thus one spirit (as it doth seeme) telleth things spoken and done far off, but it is otherwise, there be many that do it, which resort from all the places where the things are done.

M. B. I am satisfied touching this point. You were shewing how the divels did deale among the heathen out of the idols, and out of men and women.

Dan. Yea, and they have subtillie wound themselves in againe among Christians. For using witches as their instruments, they make them beleeve that they do many harms sent by them which they do not; and whereas they have power given them by God to afflict, they will seeme to do it at the wrath and displeasure of the witch. She must send him. The matter must one way or other appeare, either he will seeme even compelled by force of such as do adjure him, to confesse that such a woman or such a man sent him, or els the witch must confesse so much. Then the people devise how they may be safe against the witch: there is running to the wizards to learne what they should do, to withstand the fury of the witch, that she send not to them, or if she have sent, how they may expell her spirit, and keepe her from sending him again: this is it which the divell would have: for now he uttereth all his wares: he teacheth by these cunning men and women many horrible abhominations, and foule abuses of the name of God, by which they are made beleeve, that they have remedy against the divels sent by the witches, and that they are cured from their harmes.

M. B. I do not see how any man can indeed justifie, or maintain, that the spirits which appeare unto them in the christall, or in the glasse, or water, or that any way do speake, and shew matters unto them, be holy angels, or the soules of excellent men, as of Moses, Samuel, David, and others, though I have heard that the cunning men take them to be such, and thinke they deale by them against divels.

Dan. It is no matter what Satan's vassals are made to beleeve by his subtill sleights: it is most abhominable for any Christian man, ever to let it enter into his thought, that they do anything by the power or wisdome of the Holy Ghost, by any angell or good spirit, or that they do any thing against the divell, which worke by the intelligence which they have from evil spirits: therefore hold this, that they seeke unto divels, which run unto those soothsayers.

M. B. I am perswaded indeed that they seeke unto divels, but I would see some reason for it out of Gods word.

Dan. Touching all spirituall matters, as to be armed with power against divels, and to know how to avoide the daungers which they bring, we are no where to seeke and to learne but of our most blessed Lord God. And if him we cannot learne, but by his holy word, for in it he hath opened unto us all his whole will. And therefore where the Lord commaundeth the people of Israell by Moses, (Deut. xviii.) that they should not when they came into the land, learne to do according to the abhominations of those heathen, reckoning up sundrie kinds of such as were Satans instruments which he used to seduce the multitude, by devinations, by observing of times, by augurie by juglings with the helpe of the devill, by using familiar spirits, spirits of devination, and seeking to the dead: he setteth down also the remedie, shewing first, that he would cast out those nations because they hearkened unto the soothsayers and deviners, pronouncing that everie one which doth those things is an abhomination to the Lord, willing his people that they should not hearken to such, but that they should hearken unto him: and then Moses saith, *A Prophet shall the Lord thy God raise up unto thee from among you of thy brethren like unto me, him shall ye heare.*

M. B. Then you proove by that place, that we must seeke onely to God, and not such as worke by meanes beside his wordes.

Dan. If you reade that place (Deut. xviii.) and marke everie thing well, you shall see it doth not onely proove that they seeke unto divels, which runne to these cunning men and women: because the prophets which God hath raised up to declare the Lords will commaund us not to do such things: but also declareth that they be an abhomination to the Lord that use them, or that seeke unto them.

M. B. I see then it is not onely a sinne, but a most horrible sinne, to seeke unto them. Alas, many do not thinke that they seeke unto divels, when they go for helpe unto them for things stolen, or for helpe and remedie against witches.

Dan. No doubt many refuse to heare the voice of God, to be instructed by him: they despise his word, and therfore they be given up to hearken unto divels. Such as have sought unto any of these that work by the divel, and now come to see their offence, ought to shew repentance for the same, not as for a light sinne. It is no small abhomination to go for helpe unto the divel: it is to set him in Gods place, and to honour him as God. It riseth of infidelitie and distrust of help from God, as we may see in the example of King Saule, who finding no answer nor comfort from God, whom he had so wickedly disobeyed, went to a witch. The heathen man said, *Flectere si nequeo Superos, Acheronta movebo. If I cannot intreat the gods, I will downe among the divels.*

M. B. Nay doubtlesse there can be no defence made for such seeking helpe at their hands, which deale with familiar spirits: but I muse at diverse things, as this for one, how the cunning men, if they deale by the power of the divell, should use such good words, and will them that come unto them to do all in the name of Christ, teaching them to use words and sentences of the Scriptures.

Dan. O sir, here lyeth the deepe subtilty of Satan: how should the people be seduced to follow him, if he shold not use great cunning to cover matters, as if divels were driven out, and harmes cured that are done by them, even through the name and mighty power of God. Herein also lyeth a more foule abhomination, and that is the abusing and horrible prophaning of the most blessed name of God, and the Holy Scriptures unto witcheries, charmes, and conjurations, and unto all divellish arts. Such an one is haunted with a fayrie, or a spirit: he must learne a charme compounded of some strange speeches, and the names of God intermingled, or weare some part of S. Johns Gospell or such like. So against the theefe, against the divell sent by the witch, the like is practised. What can Satan desire more, then that holy things should be thus abused? There is ado to get him into the glasse, to get him into the chrystall, to get him into the basin of water: there is ado to bind him as it were by the name and power of Christ to tel this thing or that thing. The conjurer he bindeth him with the names of God, and by the vertue of Christs passion and resurrection, and so maketh him serve his turne: and all his owne worke, for he is not constrained nor bound, but seeketh thus to have God blasphemed. O (sayth the simple man) this is a good woman, she speaketh of God and of Christ, and doth all in his name: they be good words which she hath taught me to use: and what hurt can there be in using good words? Alas, poore man, what case are they in which must learne good words of the divell? It is not the speaking of good words, or the wearing of some part of the Scriptures, that defendeth from divels, therein lieth the craft of Satan, to have those holy things so fouly abused, and that men may put trust in words and sentences pronounced; but the divels are withstood only by the power of faith, where the holy Scriptures are written in the heart, and the soule armed with the power of them. From this Satan draweth men by his soothsayers, teaching them other helpes: For the naming of God, or the sentences of Scriptures bindeth not Satan, when we reade he can utter them.

M. B. Then how can the divell beare such a pittifull mind, as to helpe those that be in misery? For many have helpe by these cunning men. The divell is cruell and bent wholly to do hurt, and that is it that perswadeth many that things are done even by the power of God.

Dan. The divels be as pitifull as a greedy hungrie lyon that roareth after his pray, and as a fierce dragon all burning with wrath and bloudy malice: they make shew of doing good unto men, only of a most cruell and murtherous purpose, even to draw men deeper into the pit of hell with them. For if they can helpe the body a litle, it is to win both body and soule unto eternall damnation. Where Satan offereth his helpe, it is more to be feared, then when he manifestly impugneth and seeketh apparently to hurt.

M. B. But this then is more straunge, if they do not deal by the power of God, but by the power of the divell, when they drive out divels from hurting, how one divell should drive out another. Our Saviour saith, that Satan doth not drive out Satan, for then his kingdome should be divided and could not stand.

Dan. It is most certaine that Satan doth not drive out Satan: for our Saviour hath shewed the reason of the contrary. One divell is ready to further the worke of another: but in no wise to expell or to hinder one another.

M. B. There is it which maketh me to muse: we see the divell driven out, and doth not return againe, and if it be not wrought by the power of divels, as you say it cannot, then must it needs be by the power of God.

Dan. The divell is driven out, neither by the power of the divell, nor yet by the power of God, in these that are healed by cunning men.

M. B. I like this worst of all the speech which I heard you utter yet: for if Satan be not driven out neither by the power of Satan, nor by the power of God, what other power is there to drive him out? If you can shew a third power to expell him, it is more than ever I heard of.

Dan. There needeth not a third power to expell him, for he is not driven out at all.

M. B. I told you before, if you deny that to be, which all experience doth shew, then is it no reasoning. There be examples in many places, and daily it is seene, that the divell is driven out of some possessed, that where he did vexe and torment men in their bodies and in their cattell, they have remedy against him.

Dan. I do not denie but that some which are possessed and tormented by Satan, have release: but yet the divell is not cast forth by those meanes, but ceaseth willingly even to establish men in errour, and in most wicked prophaning of the name of God, and worshipping of himself and so entreth deeper into them.

M. B. I beseech you let me heare how that is, that you say he ceaseth of his owne accord. Will he let go his hold willingly and of his owne accord, where he hath it upon any man? Doth he not desire to do hurt?

Dan. He doeth not let go his hold which he hath upon any man, but indeed taketh faster hold when he seemeth to be cast foorth, and doth greater hurt: for tell me whose devise is the conjuration?

M. B. I am out of doubt that conjuration is the device of the divell.

Dan. Then tell me, hath the divell devised and taught a way to bind himselfe or to cast forth himselfe?

M. B. That I suppose he would never do.

Dan. Indeede if we will imagine that the divell is become an old foole, we may thinke he would teach that which should bind and cast forth himselfe: but the Scripture calleth him the old serpent: he devised and taught conjuration, therefore conjuration doth not cast him forth. Yet he seemeth to be bound by the conjurer, yea even by the name of God, and by the power of the passion of Christ. The conjurer seemeth by the same power to drive him out of the man possessed, whose bodie he doth vexe and torment. And he ceaseth willingly to torment the bodie, to establish conjuration, and to draw men quite from God, even to worship and to follow himselfe, and seeke all helpes at his hands. Even so when men are tormented in their bodies, or plagued in their cattell by the divell, and seeke unto the cunning men and women, following the way that they prescribe unto them, and have ease in their bodies, and no more harme among their cattell, Satan doth not give place as forced, but ceaseth to do those bodily harmes, that he may fully win unto himself both body and soule. If they should not seeme to be expelled, how should men be drawne to seeke helpe at their hands which deale by him? how should witches and conjurers be drawne on most horribly to pollute and blaspheme the glorious name of God?

M. B. Then I see they buy their helpe deere which have it at the hands of these cunning men.

Dan. Yea, what can be bought more deere than that which is with the losse of soule and body for ever, by running from God after divels?

M. B. What should a man thinke then touching all other which deale not with the divell, and yet have certaine wayes to find out witches, and to unwitch that which they have done?

Dan. Although they deale not directly by the divell, I meane they have no familiar spirits that speake unto them, yet they deale by divellish devices, which are also an abhomination to the Lord. For all those severall sorts of witches which the Lord rehearseth (Deut. xviii) did not deale directly with divels. For some were observers of times, which had their lucky dayes and their unlucky dayes, and so their houres. If they go to buy or sell, they chuse their hower to set foorth in. Some dealt by the intrailes of beasts, and by the flying of birds, by meeting with an hare or foxe, and on which hand, and a thousand such like. Some deale with the sive and a paire of sheeres, useing certaine words: some use a charme for the toothach, another for the ague, and for stopping the bleeding at the nose, also their spell for the theefe, and a thousand such like, when butter will not come, when cheese will not runne, nor ale worke in the fat: these would seeme of all others to have witches in the greatest detestation, and in the meane time worke by the divell themselves, and may be termed witches.

M. B. We doe count them witches which have their spirits, we doe not take them to be witches which doe but use those things which the cunning men have taught. For they doe not meane to doe any thing by the divell. Me thinketh therefore it is hard to call them witches.

Dan. Take the name of witchcraft for all that dealeth by the power and devices of the divell. No doubt some are more horrible than other of the severall sortes of witches, yet the lightest of them be abhominations before the Lord, as we are taught (Deut. xviii.) and the ignorance doeth not excuse. For what though the witch suppose it is the soule of Moses which appeareth in his chrystall, is he not therefore a witch? your neighbour, whose butter would not come, which heat a spit red hoat and thrust into the creame, using certaine wordes, doth thinke she did by the power of God fray away the devill; is she not therefore a witch, dealing with that which the divel and not God hath taught? is she not a witch also in seeking helpe at devils? they which did burne the cloths which their child lay in, to know by the burning blacke whether it were bewitched, and to bring the witch thither, dealt altogether by the power and direction of the devill, and so in scratching, for God hath taught no such things; then are they not witches? by whose instruction and by whose power was the witch fetched home at the burning of the haire of the butchers sonne you spake of? was not all done by the power of Satan and by his instruction? are not they then which practize these things the disciples of witches, and so indeede very witches? those which have their charmes and their night spels, what can they be but witches? I might recken up her that dealeth with the sieve and the sheares, and a number of such trumperies, in all which the most holie name of God is polluted, and if any thing be done, it is done wholly by the effectuall working of Satan. God hath given naturall helps, and those we may use, as from his hande against naturall diseases, but things besides nature he hath not appointed, especiallie they bee rediculous to drive away devilles and diseases.

M. B. Now you speake of naturall things, we see there be great secretes in nature: the adamant draweth iron unto it. And why may there not be some force in these naturall things then?

Dan. No doubt there be great secrets in nature, which the skilfull physitians and naturall philosophers do find out. As the hanging of some thing about the necke, may have force to drive away an ague, the wearing of something may have such vertu to deliver from the cramp, and such like. And from these Satan doeth take occasion to bring in his trumperies and curious devises. As because there be secrets in nature, a ring is curiouslie framed according to the signes in the firmament, this is tied to a thread, and let downe into a basin or cup of water, and wil show great things. Because there be secrets in nature, a horshoo must be heat red hot, and then put into a kettle seething upon the fire to drive away the witches spirit. Also he that hath his cattle bewitched, burneth some live thing, as hogge or henne, to drive out the divell. Can these naturall thinges expell devils? Nay, they play the rancke witches, which burne anything for to expell devils: for hath God taught to doe anie such thing? Doe they burne the thing to God, or is it as a verie burnt sacrifice to the devill? In the time of the law burnt sacrifices were offred to God: the devill among the heathen drewe the like to himself: And now by his sleight he doth after some sort procure the same at their hands, which professe to be Christians, and thus worshipping him, he ceaseth from hurting their bodies, or their cattell, as gaining a greater matter.

M. B. If it be so (as I am not able to gainsay it), then be there multitudes in all places which are guiltie of sorcerie and witchcraft. For I see many deale in matters by the helpe and power of the devill, which are perswaded otherwise. But I mervaile much at divers things touching the helpe which men have by devils. Let us conferre a little about them. The devill doeth know things past, and things present, but God onelie doth know what shall be done in the time to come. If these cunning men doe deale with no further power, than the power of the divell, how can they tell so right what shall come to passe?

Dan. It is peculiar to God alone, to know what shall come to passe hereafter. But the Lord God hath revealed by his prophets and apostles many thinges that after should be fulfilled. Satan can give a neere conjecture when these come to be fulfilled. He is a most subtill observer of thinges, and will guesse at many, but especially where he hath power given him to work and to bring any matter about, he can and will tell it aforehand. Finally, God in his just judgment giveth him power to seduce the wicked.

M. B. I pray you open your meaning more fully.

Dan. Very well: In which have you any doubt.

M. B. I take the devill gesseth at things which are prophecied, and is a sharpe observer of causes. But you said he telleth what shall be, where he worketh that which he foretelleth: give some example for this.

Dan. There needeth no better example, than that which you tolde of the churchwardens, that went to the cunning man, to knowe the theefe which had stolen their communion cuppe. It may be sayd, where the cunning man bad them to go to such a place, such a night, and at such an hower, and thither shall come he that stole the cup, how could the divell tell, if it were a night or two after, that he should come to that place, and at that hower? You must note what power the divell hath in the mind of a theefe. He stirred him up to steale the cup. He stirred up the churchwardens to seeke the cunning witch. He nameth the place and the time, whether and when he would move the heart of the theefe to come: and at the time appointed he bringeth him thither; for he that could move him to steale, could also, by secret suggestion, moove him to goe thither. The divel told that the witch shuld come home with speed that had bewitched the butchers son: he that had power in her heart to make her become a witch, did know he should have power to make her with haste to come home. One carieth somewhat which a sick person hath lien in to the cunning man. He can tell, it seemeth, by the smell of the cloath, whether the divell hath been in it (if it smell like his divel), and so telleth the partie is bewitched. Take the cloathes which the sicke partie hath lien in, and burne them; if they burne blacke, then may you see it is so, and the witch shall come in while they be a burning. Now, if the Lord gave him power, and he hath striken and tormented the bodie of the sicke person; and if hee have colourably stirred up a witch to send him; is it not an easie matter for him to make the fire burne blacke, and to moove the witch to come at that present: or if he have power for to torment, and hath no witch to send him, his great desire being to have men guiltie of innocent bloud, is it not as easie by the permission of God, which in his just judgment giveth him power to seduce such people as will hearken unto divels, for him to make the fire burne blacke, or at least to seeme so to them, and to moove some forward suspected woman or other to come in, though she be no witch? A thousand such things he worketh in, and as a cunning juggler can compasse and bring them about.

M. B. Indeed, an innocent person may come in at such a time: but I have heard, I cannot tell how true it is, that therefore there is a further thing which they observe. And that is this, the cunning man biddeth set on a posnet, or some pan with nayles, and seeth them, and the witch shal come in while they be in seething, and within a fewe daies after her face will be all bescratched with the nayles. And I have heard that some olde woman comming in, her face hath indeed been as it were scratched within a few dayes after, for the shingles or such like brake forth.

Dan. O, the depth of Satans illusions, to make blinde people become witches, and to deale by him. He doth know the corrupted humours in the bodie, which will breake out into the small pockes, or such like, and if he can procure one to come in which is even ready to have them, what a show doth he make, as if the nailes did it?

M. B. This were great subtiltie of Satan.

Dan. Nay, we are not able to imagine the depth of his sleights, neither can we see the secret force wherewith he moveth the minds of ignorant people, and so bringeth about his enterprises. There doth not lie the greatest cunning of Satan.

M. B. Indeed it seemeth strange and incredible, that the divell should so move the minds of men, and leade them unto this thing and that thing, and in the meane time they doe not know it, but thinke they goe against the divell. But now I have a further doubt. I confesse it is an easie thing for the divell to tell where a thing is that is lost or stollen, but what power hath he to heale that which is sicke or sore? Out of question they be innumerable which receive helpe by going to the cunning men. You say, he helpeth the bodie that he may destroy the soule. He helpeth that men may seeke unto him, and so set him, as it were, in the place of God. Me thinketh it should not be in the power of divels for to helpe.

Dan. Indeed that is well mooved, there lieth a great sleight of the divell in it. You say that innumerable doe receive help by going unto cunning men. I warrant you not so many as you are perswaded.

M. B. O very many: there be a number which doe never make it knowne, because it is misliked by some.

Dan. Yea, and there be many which come home againe with a flea in their eare, they receive an answere as good as a flim flam.

M. B. It may be they come too late, the matter is over farre spent, and if they had come sooner they could have holpen them.

Dan. Yea, a number of such cosoning answers the devill maketh, which satisfie ignorant people, which are ready to beleeve all that he telleth, and to dance after his pipe. One cometh to him for his childe; if he know the disease be deadly, hee will say it is bewitched, but so farre spent, that there is no help, the childe will hardlie live two daies: the father commeth home and findeth his child deade, or it dieth within two or three dayes after; here the devill getteth credit. Another is sicke and grievously tormented, hee sendeth: Satan doth see (for he sendeth them), that the disease is even spent, and that the cause of it begins to fail, and so that the partie in a few dayes will recover, here he prescribeth one paltrie or other, they use it, the man is recovered, and so should have bene without the divels medicine, but now Satan hath gotten further credite. Another is sicke and languisheth, his neighbours tell him he may bee bewitched, it is good to send, and then he shal know. He sendeth, the devill doth not know whether the sicke man can escape and recover, or not. He saith, it is like he is bewitched: and teacheth what to doe, if there bee any helpe at all, but doubteth, and so whether the man live or die, Satan saveth his credite whole and sound. And many of these answeres he giveth. Againe, we must note that mans imagination is of great force, either to continue a disease, or to diminish and take away some diseases. And in this also Satan deludeth some, for his medicine seemeth to do somewhat when it is but the parties conceit.

M. B. These be sleightes indeede: but mee thinketh you goe farre in the last. I do not see how a mans conceit can helpe him.

Dan. Imagination is a strong thing to hurt, all men doe finde, and why should it not then be strong also to help, when the parties mind is cheared, by beleeving fully that he receiveth ease?

M. B. But yet it is hard to shewe that ever anie such cure hath beene wrought.

Dan. It is not hard to shew, for that which men doe, it is presumed the divell can doe the like. And I have heard of a mery companion that wrought such a cure. There was one in London (as report goeth), which was acquainted with Feats. Now this Feats had a blacke dogge, whome he called Bomelius. This partie afterward had a conceit that Bomelius was a devill, and that hee felt him within him. He was in heavinesse, and made his moane to one of his acquaintance, who had a merie head, hee tolde him hee had a friend could remoove Bomelius. Hee bad him prepare a breakfast, and he would bring him. Then this was the cure: he made him be stripped naked and stand by a good fire, and though he were fatte ynough of himselfe, basted him all over with butter against the fire, and made him weare a sleeke stone next his skin under his bellie, and the man had present remedie, and gave him afterward greate thankes.

M. B. I know men have many foolish imaginations: but though one imagination may drive out another, which is not the curing of any disease in deed, but of an imagination: yet it doth not followe, that where there is an apparant griefe, that a mans conceit can help to cure it.

Dan. Yes, the conceit doth much, even where there is an apparant disease. A man feareth hee is bewitched, it troubleth all the powers of his mind, and that distempereth his bodie, maketh great alterations in it, and bringeth sundrie griefes. Now, when his mind is freed from such imaginations, his bodily griefe which grew from the same is eased. And a multitude of Satans cures are but such.

M. B. Nay, there bee also evils which be apparant in the bodie, and bee cured, which come not of anie feare or imagination: how can these be cured by any conceit? There is great reason that such griefes may bee cured indeede by quieting the minde, as did growe from the disturbance of the same.

Dan. Yea, and that falleth out sometimes in griefes of the body, which doth not growe from imagination, but from some other passions. As I can give you an example, which is written and reported by a very reverend learned physitian. The cure was done by a lewde cosening knave in Germanie. A woman had bleare eies that were watery. The knave lodging there, promised for certaintie that hee would heale them: hee did hang a little writing about her necke, charging strictly that it should not be taken from thence, nor read, nor opened: for if any of these were done, she could have no helpe at all by it. The woman had such a confidence in the thing, and was so merrie and glad, that she left weeping (for her often weeping and teares had spoiled her eyes), and so by little and little, the moysture stayed, and her eyes were whole. It fell out that shee lost the writing, whereat she was in such griefe and sorrowe and weeping, that her eyes were sore againe. Another found the writing, opened it, and read it. It was written in the Germane tongue, to this effect, translated into English:— *The divell pluck out thine eyes, and fill their holes with his dung.* Was not this, thinke you, a proper salve for to cure her eyes? If this medicine had taken effect, her eyes should not have bin healed, but plucked quite out. We may not think but that Satan hath mor cousening tricks then al men in the world, for men are but his schollers. Againe, where men faile, he can worke somewhat in the affections of the parties mindes. And you shall heare them say, when any charme is used, you must beleeve it will helpe, or else it will do you no good at all. Thus, if it were well seene into, the greatest part of your innumerable cures come to bee meere cousonages.

M. B. Well, let all this be true as you have sayd: yet there be many things wherein the divels doe helpe. What say you to the boy which healed within few daies after he had scratched the witch, whereas his sores were most grievous before, and could not be cured? What say you to that which they doe, when butter will not come, or when drink will not worke in the fat? What say you to the burning of some live thing, as hogge or henne, and the harme ceassing? And, finally, what say you to the helping of them where the divell is, and doth torment their bodies?

Dan. All these are answered in few words, that where he hath power to hurt either man or beast, drink or butter, he helpeth only by giving place, and ceasing to hurt, which, as I shewed you before, he doth most willingly, to bring to pass that men may seeke to him, and become even very witches. If a man be vexed and tormented by a divel, and men seeke by fasting and praier to cast him foorth, even instantly intreating the Lord, then he goeth out with much adoe, and unwillingly, as overcome and expelled by the power of God. But when he hurteth, as you say he did the butchers sonne, and they seeke to him, and will follow his prescriptions, as to draw bloud of the witch, he goeth out willingly, I meane he ceaseth from hurting the bodie: for he goeth not out indeede, but rather goeth further in, and seateth himselfe deeper in the soule. And so is it in all the rest. How gladly will he cease to hurt the hennes, so that to please him, a henne may be burnt alive? his helping is no more but a ceasing from doing harme, if he had power given him to hurt.

Sam. This is a strange thing, if it be so. There be thousands in the land deceived. The woman at R. H. by report hath some weeke fourtie come unto her, and many of them not of the meaner sort. But I doe but hinder, I pray you goe forward.

Dan. The divell can deceive thousand thousands, and even the wisest of this world: for when they will not bee taught of God, but despise his doctrine, then are they justly given over to be the disciples of the divell.

M. B. If there be such deceit in all these things, and that the witches do not kill nor hurt, but the divell craftily seemeth to kill and to hurt when the diseases be natural, and maketh the witch beleeve that hee hath done all at her request. Or where God hath given him power, he stirreth her up to send him, as if either he could not, or would not meddle, unless he had been sent. Seeing all lieth upon Satan, it should seeme, there is no reason that witches should be put to death; but the Scripture doth command that they should be put to death.

Dan. The Holy Scriptures doe command that witches should be put to death: therein you say right: but if you did take it, that the word of God commaundeth they shall not be suffered to live, because they kill men and beasts, or because they send their spirits which possesse men, and torment their bodies, you are much deceived. For you shal never finde, of all that have been tormented and plagued by evill spirits, that the Holie Ghost layeth it upon the witches. The causes why they should be put to death are, that they have familiaritie with divels, which are the blasphemous enemies of God: and that they seduce the people into errour, to runne after divels, and divelish practises, and that they have such wicked mindes. Although they never mind to kill or to hurt any, but to doe them good, as they imagine; yet if they deale with divels they ought to dye for it.

M. B. Then you take it, that these cunning men and women, unto whom so many runne for helpe, which are thought to do very much good, and no hurt at all, ought to be rooted out, and destroyed. Let us know what Scripture there is for it.

Dan. Yea, of all other they ought to dye, because they doe the greatest harme. Other witches that have spirits are thought to doe harme, because the divell at the appointment of God doth harme, and he beareth in hand hee doth it at the request of the witch: but these that seeme to doe good, doe harme indeed, and that many waies, as every one that light in him may easily see. And for the Scriptures which shew that they ought to dye, reade first in the 22 chapter of Exodus, verse 18, and there it is said, *Thou shalt not suffer a witch to live.*

M. B. That place we take to be meant of those witches which send their spirits to do harme: the other be not called witches.

Dan. It is that witch that is there commanded to bee put to death, that is called Mecasshephah: such were they and so called, which before Pharaoh did withstand Moses, and made in shew rods turned into serpents. So that in one kinde the Lord doth include all such as worke by the divell. For there be divers other sorts named in Deut. xviii., and they be all called an abomination to the Lord: and no abomination is to bee suffered to remaine among the Lords people. Also in the same place, when hee saith, Let there not be found in thee any such or such, as he there reckoneth them up: it is not alone to will that none should practise such things, but also that they should bee rooted out.

M. B. I must needes agree unto that which the word of God doth set downe. But this is the hardest matter of all, how they shall be convicted.

Dan. Why doe you take it to bee the hardest matter, how a witch shall be convicted? how is a theef or a murtherer convicted but by proofe? If there be vehement suspition, and the partie upon examination confesse the fact, that is a sufficient proofe. If the partie doe denie, and two or three of credit doe testifie upon their knowledge with a solemne oath, that he is guiltie of the fact, that is also a sufficient proofe. And touching this, God commanded by Moses, that none should dye, unlesse the matter were prooved against them by two witnesses at the least. (Deutronom. xix., vers. 15.)

M. B. I graunt, if the partie doe denie, and especially, if the matter touch life, that there ought, by the word of God, to be due proofe by two witnesses at the least. This may be for murtherers, this may be for theeves: but for witches I see not how. They deale so secretly with their spirits, that very seldome they can be convinced by flat testimonies of men, as to say directly they have heard or seen them send their spirits. And againe, it is a rare thing to have a witch confesse. For it is generally thought the divel hath such power over them, that he will not suffer them to confesse.

Dan. O then, I perceive why you account it the hardest matter of all to convict a witch, if both testimony and confession doe faile; but what would you have further?

M. B. I have been of this opinion, that if there were any likelihood, and suspition, and common fame, that it was even proofe enough, and the best deede that could be done was for to hang them up, and so ridde the countrey of them.

Dan. Then you thought that their spirits were hanged with them, and so the countrie being rid of the witches and their spirits, mens bodies and their cattell should bee safe.

M. B. I had a little more wit then to thinke so: but in truth it was but a little more. For I thought if al the witches were hanged, that then their spirits should not have any to hire them, nor to send them to hurt either man or beast: but I see mine owne follie, and that onely God giveth the power unto the divells to afflict and trie the godly, and to vexe, torment, and plague the wicked, and that they shall do this though al the witches in the world were hanged. I know they neede none to cherish them, or to set them a worke.

Dan. But did you not feare, if all suspected should bee hanged, then some guiltles persons might be put to death: as you see many that have been executed as witches, have taken it upon their death that they were innocent.

M. B. I will tell you my thought touching that poynt, which was this. The witches raise tempestes, and hurt corne and fruites upon the trees, the witches bring the pestilence among men, and murraine among cattell: the witches send their spirits and make men lame, kill their children and their cattell: their spirits cannot bee taken heede of, nor kept out with doores and wals, as theeves and murtherers, but come in when they be sent, and doe so many harmes: for this cause I thought it a marveilous good worke to put all suspected to death, though some of them were innocent, that so sure work might bee made to have not one left.

Dan. Did you not thinke it a fearfull thing to shead innocent bloud?

M. B. Yea, but I thought it much better that some should bee put to death wrongfully, then to leave any one witch, which might kill and destroy many.

Dan. Then I perceive that this was the reason which did perswade you that it was very good to put all to death that were suspected, (although it might fall out that some of them were innocent), to avoyde greater inconvenience, and that is, if some few witches should escape, which might plague and kill many. Better a few should be put wrongfully to death, then many should be tormented and killed, or lamed by the divels. But are you still of that mind?

M. B. No, verily. For you have put me in minde that the wicked spirits receive their power to plague both men and beasts only from God. They seeke about, they watch when and where hee will give them leave to touch; where God will trie the faith and patience of the just by him, as he did in Job, he sendeth him, if he will be sent by a witch, it is but under a colour, shee giveth him not the power, hee would touch though she were not. Where God wil strike and plague the wicked by him, he giveth him leave, it is not the anger of the witch that bringeth it, but their owne wickednes, whereby they have provoked God to displeasure, and so give this enemy power over them.

Dan. Then so long as these two things stand, that God by Satan will afflict in some sort and trie his children (as you alleage hee did Job), and that hee will use him as his executioner, to plague and torment the wicked, as he sent an evill spirite to vex King Saule: so long the harmes done by wicked spirites shall not cease, although all the witches and conjurers in the worlde were hanged up. Looke then to the causes, if wee will remoove the effects. As if thou feare God, and Satan afflict thee, stand fast in faith and patience, and waite upon God for thy deliverance. If thou endure temptation, thou art blessed, and shalt be crowned. (Jam. i. ver. 12). If thy sinnes have provoked God, and the enemie doth touch thy bodie or thy goods, fall downe and humble thy selfe with fasting and prayer, intreate the Lord to turne away his displeasure: looke not upon the witch, lay not the cause where it is not, seeke not helpe at the hands of devils, be not a disciple of witches, to commit thinges abhominable, by polluting the name of God, and honouring Satan, nor thirst not after the bloud which is innocent, as it falleth out in many.

M. B. I do assent unto al this: and surely it is a great fault to shead innocent blood.

Dan. We may learne in the holie Scriptures, that the sheading of innocent blood is a verie horrible thing in the eies of Almightie God: and a very grievous thing it is to have a land polluted with innocent blood: and that is one speciall cause why Satan dealeth by witches: for he laboureth to wrap in many guiltlesse persons upon suspitions, hee suggesteth by his helping witches, that there be many hurting witches in all townes and villages, that so he may set the multitude in a rage, and to suspect upon every likelihood that hee can devise or make shew of. And thus whole juries must become guiltie of innocent bloud, by condemning as guiltie, and that upon their solemne oath, such as be suspected upon vaine surmises, and imaginations and illusions, rising from blindnes and infidelitie, and feare of Satan which is in the ignorant sort.

M. B. If you take it that this is one craft of Satan, to bring many to be guiltie of innocent bloud, and even upon their oathes, which is horrible, what would you have the judges and juries to doe, when any are arraigned of suspition to be witches?

Dan. What would I have them doe? I would wish them to bee most warie and circumspect that they bee not guiltie of innocent bloud. And that is, to condemne none but upon sure ground, and infallible proofe, because presumptions shall not warrant or excuse them before God, if guiltlesse bloud be shed.

M. B. It falleth out sometimes when a theef is arraigned, or a murtherer, that direct evidence faileth, and yet such circumstances are brought, as doe even enforce the jurie in their conscience to finde them guiltie. It seemeth that this holdeth chiefly about witches, because their dealing is close and secret, and it is also thought that the divell hath so great power over them, that he will not suffer them to confesse.

Dan. You bring two reasons to proove that in convicting witches, likelihoods and presumptions ought to be of force more then about theeves or murtherers. The first, because their dealing is secret: the other, because the divell will not let them confesse. Indeede men imagining that witches doe worke strange mischiefes, burne in desire to have them hanged, as hoping then to be free, and then upon such perswasions as you mention, they suppose it is a verie good worke to put to death all which are suspected. But, touching theeves and murtherers, let men take heede how they deale upon presumptions, unles they be very strong for we see that juries sometimes doe condemne such as be guiltlesse, which is an hard thing, especially being upon their oath. And in witches, above all other, the proofes had need to be strong, because there is greater sleight of Satan to pursue the guiltles unto death, than in the other. Here is speciall care and wisdome to be used. And so likewise for their confessing, Satan doth gaine more by their confession than by their deniall, and therefore rather bewrayeth them himselfe, and forceth them to confession, oftner than unto deniall.

M. B. These things are beyond my reach, I cannot conceive of them. I pray you open it so that I may perceive your meaning, and see some ground of reason for that which you shall affirme.

Dan. Then is it requisite to stand upon them more at large. And let us begin with the latter.

M. B. If you goe first to the latter, then shew some reason or experience that Satan bewrayeth the witches, and draweth them to confesse, and to disclose themselves, rather then to conceale and hide their doings. I can tell you this before hand, that the common opinion is otherwise, which seemeth to be grounded both upon reason and experience.

Dan. I know the common opinion is as you say: but I do much marveile at it, seeing reason and experience doe prove the contrarie, as I will shew. As first, touching reason, you will graunt that the divels dealing altogether by sleight and subtilties, do that which doth most further their purposes and desires.

M. B. That is the verie reason why the divell would by no meanes have the witches bewrayed, as it is thought, because he would lurke secretly to doe mischief.

Dan. Indeed it were a good reason to prove that part, if Satan received his power from the witch, or could doe nothing but by her sending, or needed to bee harboured by her, or had no minde to meddle, but as it were hired to satisfie her wrath. But seeing all these be absurd, and he useth the witch and conjurer but under a colour to bring in further evils, it must needes followe, that the disclosing is fitter for his purpose than the keeping secret, for if they should be kept secrete: how should he make men think that he doth so many harmes at the request of the witch? howe should he drawe so many to runne after devils, to seek help at their hands? how should he procure so many to use wicked and blasphemous charms and sorceries, and in so horrible manner to abuse the blessed name of God, and his most sacred word? Or how should he draw the people into manifold errours, and to thirst even in rage after innocent blood? All these, and a number such like hee procureth and furthereth, by disclosing witches.

M. B. But how shall this reason be confirmed by experience? No doubt in shew he is loathe to have his dame (as some speake) disclosed.

Dan. You say well, that in shew he is loath to have the witch bewrayed: for indeede it is onely in shew, seeing he would make her and others also beleeve, even when he doth bewray her by one meanes or other, that it is sore against his liking.

M. B. I pray you make that evident.

Dan. When one feeleth himselfe plagued any way, and doeth take it to be by Satan, admit it be so: he goeth to a cunning man, and he sheweth him in a glasse or in a chrystall the shape of the witch. Who now bewrayeth her?

M. B. That is the cunning mans spirite which bewrayeth her, and not her spirit which she dealeth withall.

Dan. You are not sure of that: for it may bee the same devill that she dealeth withall, that resembleth her in the glasse: none can doe it better.

M. B. I doe not thinke that hee departeth away from her.

Dan. Yea, but you must remember, that she which dealeth with a spirit, dealeth not with a devill, but with devils: for manie doe joyn together. When one of them departeth, and carieth the matter to the cunning man, they do not all depart. But what if it be as you said, that som other spirits do bewray, doe you thinke he doeth it against the liking of the witches spirite? Is Satan devided against Satan? Will Satan bewray Satan to his hindrance? Remember what our Saviour hath taught touching that.

M. B. Then if it be so, doe you not take it a sufficient proofe against a witch, even for a jurie to finde guilty upon their oath, if a cunning man by his spirite do bewray anie.

Dan. It is the most insufficient proofe that can be, for although he doe tell true in bewraying many, as their owne confessions do witnes, yet he doeth it of an evill purpose, he is a lyer, and the father of lies, he desireth chiefly to accuse the innocent, that he may bring men to bee guilty of innocent blood, to make the people beleeve there be multitudes of witches, to set them a worke to learne charmes and sorceries, and chiefly, that they may be brought to seeke unto him, as the bewrayer even in pitie of such bad people. Now because he craftily bewrayeth some, to get credite, shall mens verdict by oath, even unto bloud, be grounded upon his testimony? If a divel should come in unto a jurie, and say the partie about whom you enquire is a witch, should they beleeve him, or wold they say, let him be sworne, and witnesse upon his oath? If not, why should they beleeve that which he hath spoken to the cunning man?

M. B. Surely I am out of doubt hee doth all in craft unto a most bad purpose, and that no credit out to bee given unto his testimony, when it is voluntary. But what say you to his testimonie, when it is even charged and forced in the name and power of God to tell the trueth? It seemeth then he would conceale, but cannot.

Dan. The conjurer which supposeth that hee doeth bind by the name and power of God to tell him the trueth, is utterlie deluded. For he is not bound, but is glad that the most glorious name of God is so horriblie abused, and that he can drawe men into such a gulfe of all abhomination.

M. B. Nay, I doe not meane the conjurer, but when such as be godlie go about to cast him foorth by prayer.

Dan. This I take to bee your meaning, a man or a woman is possessed with a divell: put case it bee so indeede (to distinguish them from so many counterfaits, as have bene), and men assemble together where the possessed is, and call upon God, and then charge Satan in the name of Christ, to tell how hee came there and who sent him.

M. B. I meane so indeede. And some being possessed, the divell being charged to tell who sent him, he hath confessed, that such a man did conjure him in thither, or such a witch did send him. Shall not this be of force to convince?

Dan. When any is possessed by the fiend, mens compassion, their love and pity are to be shewed, even to helpe what they can in such a distresse. They ought with all instant suit to intreat the Lord to shew mercy, and to expell him. The doctrin of the holy Scriptures doth warrant this: but for men to talke and question with him, I see no warrant at all by Gods word, much lesse to commaund and adjure him to depart. He is the Lords executioner, he hath sent him; wee may intreat the Lord to remoove him, but what authority have we to command him to depart, where God hath sent him?

M. B. Men have no authority, I grant, but they command and adjure him in the name and power of the Lord for to depart.

Dan. That I take ought not to be, for mark this comparison: the prince is displeased with a subject for some disloyaltie: an officer is sent from the prince to attach and imprison him: shall hee or any other charge this officer in the princes name to let him alone, and not to meddle? Is not their way only to pacifie the prince, and so the prince wil command the officer to cease? Even so, where God sendeth Satan his executioner, the only way is to intreat the Lord to be pacified, for then shall the tormentor no longer remaine.

M. B. How doeth this which you speake agree with that which we read in the Acts of the Apostles, how Sainte Paule commaunded the divell to come out of a mayde at Philippos?

Dan. The holy apostles and others in the primitive Church, had an extraordinary power given them to caste foorth divels, and to heale diseases, and they did execute the same power by the direction and instinct of the Holy Ghost. We may not draw a patterne from that.

M. B. We see that divels are sometimes expelled.

Dan. They are when the Lord is intreated, otherwise they but seeme to be bound by adjuration and expelled. But how can it be prooved that the father of lies may be bound, and forced through charge and adjuration in the name and power of God to tell the truth? And what warrant have wee to learne any trueth from his mouth? As to say, wee command thee in the name of God, that thou tel us who sent thee. Who sent thee? who sent thee? Mother Joan, mother Joan, saith he. Also we command thee to tell us, who sent thee? L. B. conjured me in hither (saith hee). Shall wee thinke he doeth this even compelled? Or shall we ground upon it for certaine that he telleth no lie?

M. B. The devill in a partie possessed hath said, such a man conjured me in hither. The conjurer hath bene put to death for it, and hath confessed so much. The divell in another hath said, such a woman sent me: it hath likewise bin confessed by the woman.

Dan. All this maketh for that which I affirme. The Lord giveth him power to possesse a man. He under a colour will be sent by a conjurer, or by a witch: and the one thinketh the devill entreth at her intreaty: the other supposeth he doeth even bind him thereto, whereas he ruleth both their mindes, and setteth them a worke. Then doeth hee willingly bewray them, even for many subtell purposes: but chiefly that he may establish conjurations, witchcrafts, and charmes, that hee may be sought unto, that he may set the people a worke in their calamities to be troubled about witches and conjurers, as though they could plague, and never looke to God, and that bewraying some witches and conjurers, hee may winne credite, and bee beleeved, even when he accuseth falslie, that he may bring innocent blood upon the land. Let all men take heed how upon their oath they give a verdict, especially touching life, upon his word, howsoever he seeme to be forced thereunto: al is most deepe craft and subtilty in him.

Sam. I pray you give me leave to speake a little. You say the devil willinglie bewrayeth witches and conjurers, and that for many subtill purposes. I have heard of divers things done of late which seeme quite contrarie, and that he taketh it grievously when they doe confesse and bewray matters.

Dan. Hee will seeme to take it in evill part, but let us heare the matters, and you shall see plainely that hee juggleth and maketh shewe of that which is contrary to his practise.

Sam. Well, I have heard very credibly, that a woman of late, suspected another woman to be a witch, and that she had hurt her some way. She procured a gentleman to send for the partie suspected, and charging her in his presence, she left her to the gentleman, who taking her aside, and walking alone with her, began to admonish and perswade her to renounce the divell, and to forsake such wicked waies. While he was thus perswading, and she denying stifly that she was any such woman, suddenly there appeared some distance from them, a weasill or lobsterre looking even upon them. Looke (said the gentleman) yonder same is thy spirit. Ah, master (said she) that is a vermine, there be many of them every where. Well, as they went towards it, it was vanished out of sight: by and by it appeared againe, and looked upon them. Surely (said the gentleman) it is thy spirit: but she still denied, and with that her mouth was drawne awrie. Then hee pressed her further, and she confessed all. She confessed she had hurt and killed by sending her spirit. The gentleman being no justice, let her goe home, and did minde to open the matter unto some justice. When she was come home, another witch meeteth her, and saith: Ah thou beast, what hast thou done? thou hast bewrayed us all. What remedie now (said she): what remedy? said the other, send thy spirit and touch him: she sent her spirit, and of a suddaine the gentleman had as it were a flash of fire about him: he lifted up his hart to God, and felt no hurt. The spirit returneth, and tolde he coulde not hurt him, because he had faith: what then, said the other witch, hath he nothing that thou maist touch? he hath a childe, said the other. Send thy spirit, said she, and touch the child: she sent her spirit, the childe was in great paine and died. The witches were hanged and confessed.

Dan. What is the chiefe thing which you alleadge this for?

Sam. To shew how unwilling the divell was that the witch should confesse and bewray things. No doubt it should seeme, that when the gentleman was talking with her, he appeared to call her away, for feare least she should confesse: and when she would not come away, he drew her mouth awry: and when she had confessed, the divell complained unto the other witch, and made her chide her.

Dan. The thing is as cleere as may be, that he willinglie bewrayed them: and will you imagine the contrarie? Why did he appeare in a likenesse, but even to enforce her for to confesse, both by abashing, and giving the gentleman evident notice, especially, when he drew her mouth awrie? And why did he set on the other witch to moove her that had confessed to send her spirit, but that he would have the matter more open, and bring them both to light?

Sam. What should moove him to bewray the witches? what could he gaine by it?

Dan. Nay, what almost doth he not gaine by it? Now all the countrie rings of the matter. As if the witches set on their spirits to lame and to kill: and that they doe not meddle, but sent by them. He did know what power he had from God to afflict any, he will deale by witches: hee maketh others afraide of them, that so they may accuse them. He findeth meanes to have all disclosed. Hee mooveth the witches to send him against the gentleman: hee knoweth what he can doe: he returneth and saith there is faith. As though God did not give him power sometimes to afflict the faithfull? Or as if he could touch all that have no faith? If he could, the greatest part of the world should be destroied by him. For they be very few in the world in comparison which have the true faith. Then must he be sent to the child that hath no faith: doth not the faith of the parents holde Gods protection over their infants as over themselves? Here is Satans craft: either hee did know by things breeding in the bodie of the child that it would at such time fall sicke and die: and he would be taken to be the killer of the child, to beare in hand that he hath such power and will doe when hee is requested. Or els he had power given him of

121

God, and would bring it about this way. If hee did strike the child, do you imagine he doth it at her pleasure? Or doe you thinke he would never have thought of any such thing, but moved by her. Doe not all the armies of divels goe about continually, seeking whom they may devour? Do they not waite where God will give them power to strike? Shal we still be so simple as to thinke that women neede to hire or to intreat them to doe harme. Looke unto God, for those wicked spirits play all parts in the play, and delude both the witches and others.

Sam. I will tell you another thing which was done of late. A woman being suspected to be a witch, and to have done some hurt among the cattell, was examined, and confessed indeed, that she had a spirit which did abide in a hollow tree, where there was an hole, out of which hee spake unto her. And ever when she was offended with any, she went to that tree, and sent him to kill their cattell. She was perswaded to confesse her fault openly, and to promise that she would utterly forsake such ungodly waies: after she had made this open confession, the spirit came unto her being alone. Ah, said he, thou hast confessed and bewrayed all, I could teeme it to rend thee in peeces: with that she was afraid, and wound away, and got her into companie. Within some few weekes after, she fell out greatly into anger against one man. Towards the tree she goeth, and before she came at it, Ah, said the spirit, wherefore commest thou? who hath angred thee? Such a man, said the witch. And what wouldest thou have me doe? said the spirit. Hee hath (saith she) two horses going yonder, touch them, or one of them. Well, I think even that night one of the horses died, and the other was little better. Indeed they recovered that one again which was not dead, but in very evill case. Here me thinketh it is plaine: he was angrie that she had bewrayed all. And yet when she came to the tree, he let goe all displeasure and went readily.

Dan. Doe you thinke all is plaine here? Indeede here is that plaine dealing which divels doe use. First, doe you thinke Satan lodgeth in an hollow tree? Is hee become so lazie and idle? hath he left off to be as a roaring lion, seeking whom he may devour? hath he put off the bloodie and cruell nature of the firie dragon, so that hee mindeth no harme, but when an angrie woman intreate him to goe kill a cow or a horse? Is he become so doting with age, that men shall espie his craft: yea, be found craftier then he is? Alas, may there not be deep subtiltie in these things?

Sam. Doe you thinke there is nothing but subtiltie in these things?

Dan. Doe I thinke there is nothing but subtiltie? Tell me what you thinke. What other end can there be but subtiltie?

Sam. He may have this purpose (as I thinke the divels studie nothing els) to doe harme.

Dan. I doe not denie that: for all his craft tendeth unto harme. But what harme meane you?

Sam. You see here he killed mens cattell.

Dan. It may be he did: but how know you that?

Sam. You see he went at her request and killed one horse, and almost killed the other.

Dan. I would be loth to adventure my hand upon that: for who told you that he killed the one, and almost killed the other?

Sam. The witch her selfe hath confessed the whole matter.

Dan. Who told the witch so?

Sam. Her spirit told her that he did it at her request.

Dan. He is a credible person, and kind he was unto her as it seemeth.

Sam. Nay, but we see all things fell out according as she confessed.

Dan. How doe you meane?

Sam. Why, she confessed her fault, the spirit was angrie with her; afterward she fel our wirh that man, and upon this his horse died; she confessed she sent the spirit, how could all things fall out so fit?

Dan. The spirit when she came towards the tree, asked her, wherefore commest thou? who hath angred thee?

Sam. He did so.

Dan. And doe you imagine that the divell did lie there, and knew nothing untill she came and told him?

Sam. Why needed he to aske her if he did know?

Dan. Because he is subtill: for hee wrought in her heart, and kindled her wrath, and procured the falling out betweene her and that man: hee did know either that the horses at that time had some what in them which would bring death, or els that the Lord had given him power for to strike them: he moved and wrought in her heart to have her come againe to the tree: he seemed to be angrie that she had confessed before, but was not, but sought to have things knowne. If he had not knowne that the horse should dye, either by some naturall cause, which would then breake foorth, or by some power given to him, he would not at this time have mooved her heart to goe to the tree. And if her wrath had without his suggestion caried her so farre, hee could quickly have turned her: for great is the efficacie of Satans working in the hearts of such.

Sam. But I marked one thing which you said before, as that it might bee that God giveth sometimes power to the divell, even at the sending of the witch.

Dan. I say that God in justice giveth power unto Satan to delude, because men refuse to love his trueth: but that maketh not that the divell obtaineth any power to hurt because the witch sendeth, but the fault is in men, the sinnes of the people give power to the divell: for God is offended, and sendeth (as S. Paul saith) strong delusion. But have you any moe examples to proove that the divell is not willing to have witches bewrayed?

Sam. I have heard of many such like, but you say all is but craft, and that he would have men thinke hee doth all harmes that are done.

Dan. The divell would have men beeleeve that hee doth all, if he could bring it about: and therefore it is for his advantage if he doe hurt, to have it not kept secret, but openly to be made knowne.

M. B. What say you then unto this: a witch is apprehended upon vehement suspition, and caried before a justice: he handleth the matter in such sort that she confesseth, as I heard of one not long since: her confession was to this effect: She had two spirits, one like a weasill, the other like a mouse. These, she said, did many things for her. Now, she accused a woman about ten or twelve miles off, whom (it may be) she did not know, and yet could name, and not onely that, but said the woman had, as it were, a little bigge in her mouth, where the spirit did sucke bloud.

Dan. It is a most easie thing for the divell to tell witches, that such a man or such a woman is a witch, and hath this or that secret mark upon them. And within these few yeares hee hath by witches and cunning men, accused such as were very religious and godly. Men must beware that they proceed not upon his testimony: he is not to be medled withall, nor any medling which he useth, is to be taken in good part, seeing he doth all in deepe subtilties.

M. B. I doe take it, that the testimonie of the divell ought not of itselfe to have any force with a jurie, unles it can be prooved by some other firme proofes. But what say you unto this: a witch is condemned, and telleth at the gallows not only what she hath done, but also of whom she first had her spirit. She doth this in repentance, and even readie to depart out of the world. It is to bee presumed that she will not in this case lie, nor accuse falsly. Let it be some woman in another towne, whom she saith, brought her the spirit. This woman is also suspected by some of her neighbours, apprehended and brought to judgement, and stifly denieth that she is any witch, or that she ever delivered any spirit unto the other which accused her. Now here is the question: Is not the testimonie of the woman upon her death, a sufficient warrant for a jurie to find this woman guiltie? Here they have now the testimonie not of the divell to proceede by, but of a woman, and though not upon her oath, yet upon her death, which is no lesse.

Dan. This testimonie may seeme to be sufficient even to warrant a jurie to finde guiltie, though it touch life: but if we looke well into it, we shall see it is not.

M. B. It may be you take it to be infirme, because it is the testimonie but of one.

Dan. Nay, not onely in respect that it is the testimonie but of one, but that it is the testimonie of such a one.

M. B. I put the case of such an one as doth shew repentance, who though she had been bad, yet now may bee beleeved.

Dan. I doe not meane in that respect, as to say she was a witch, and therefore not to be credited: but if she repent never so much, yet her testimonie in this is weake, because she may be utterly deceived, and think she telleth the truth, when it was nothing so, but she utterly deluded.

M. B. Doe you meane, that he may make the other woman thinke, that such a woman delivered her the spirit, and never so much matter?

Dan. Yea, that is my meaning.

M. B. It is farre beyond my reach to see how that can be.

Dan. You must consider that the divell doth many waies delude witches, and make them beleeve things which are nothing so. In Germany and other countries, the divels have so deluded the witches, as to make them beleeve that they raise tempests of lightnings and thunders. For the divels do know when these things be comming, tempests of winds, and thunders, and faine would they make the blinde world beleeve that those great works of God, be not Gods but his: and that is the cause why he coveteth to appeare in them. These divels make the witches beleeve, that at their request they kill both men and beasts, and many waies afflict, when as many of the things fal out naturally, which they would seeme to doe, and the rest in which they have power given to worke, they stirre up the witch but under a colour for to send them. These divels make the witches in some places beleeve, that they are turned into the likenesse of wolves, that they rend and teare sheepe, that they meet together and banquet, that sometimes they flie or ride in the ayre, which things indeede are nothing so, but they strongly delude the fantasies of the witches. Even so the divell can delude a poore woman with the likenesse of another woman delivering a mouse or a cat unto her, by appearing in such a likenes. Or he can set a strong fantasie in the minde that is oppressed with melancholie, that such or such a matter was, which indeed was never so. Men must be wise in these causes, or els may they soone be circumvented by the crafts of Satan and drawne into great sinne.

M. B. If it be thus, then how should a jurie condemne by their verdict any witch? For she hath not killed, nor the devill at her request, but maketh her beleeve he did it at her request.

Dan. A witch by the word of God ought to die the death, not because she killeth men, for that she cannot (unless it be those witches which kill by poyson, which either they receive from the divell, or hee teacheth them to make) but because she dealeth with divels. And so if a jurie doe finde proofe that she hath dealt with divels, they may and ought to finde them guiltie of witchcraft.

M. B. If they finde them guiltie to have dealt with divels, and cannot say they have murdered men, the law doth not put them to death.

Dan. It were to be wished that the law were more perfect in that respect, even to cut off all such abhominations. These cunning men and women which deale with spirites and charmes seeming to doe good, and draw the people into manifold impieties, with all other which have familiarity with divels, or use conjurations, ought to bee rooted out, that others might see and feare.

M. B. You will not have the testimony of devils to be of any credit with a jury, what say you then unto men, there be some which die, and take it upon their death, that they are bewitched, and will say precisely such or such have done it. For that is in the other point touching likelihoods.

Dan. They are bewitched indeed, for the devill doth delude their minds: for you shall finde them able to render no reason but onelie this, in their conscience the partie is naught and they are out of doubt it is so.

M. B. That may bee as you say in some, but I have knowne a woman my selfe which many have counted to be a witch, and many things have fallen out where she hath taken displeasure. Do you not thinke that is a firm proofe? She denieth, but the things which fall out doe manifest her to be naught.

Dan. you must shew the things, and thereby it will appear.

M. B. She fell out, or els at the least seemed to be displeased with one, and he had an hogge died suddainlie. Another thought she was displeased with him, and his horse fell sicke. And a third could not sit upon his stoole at worke. And within nine or ten yeares space divers others. One saw the divell bigger than a cat with great eies. An other was haunted with a spirite. An other brewing, the drinke would not worke in the fatte. An other sawe a thing in her house as big as lambe, playing in the window. An other in her grievous torment saw the woman stand by her all the night, whom she suspected to bewitch her, and divers such like, which were too long to recken up. If she were not a witch, how should all these fall out so fit?

Dan. I have shewed alreadie, that where Satan hath a witch to deale by, hee bringeth it about, that in all such things as he hath power given him of God, he will seeme to do nothing but requested and sent by the witch. In those things which fall out in sicknesses, lamenes, and death, upon naturall causes, he worketh in such sort, as that he maketh the witch beleeve she doeth them. And this he coveteth to have breake forth by hir confession. Now, where he hath no witch to deale by, he gaineth exceedingly, if he can worke in the minds of any a strong suspition of any man or woman. For if it bee once begun, he pursueth it with all his power and cunning. If one be visited with grievous torment of sicknes, and be so ignorant, and voyde of the faith in Gods providence, that he imagine the divell doeth it at the sending by a witch, the divell will delude him, and make him beleeve that the witch standeth by him. The man or woman suspected cannot come there: who then worketh that illusion but Satan? Another is affraide of the divell to be sent unto him, by that partie whom he suspecteth to be a witch: and thus through want of faith in God, giveth the devill the more power over him, either to hurt or to appeare unto him. For Sathan haunteth all men continually, seeking all occasions, and needeth not to be sent by man or woman. They be exceeding blind which will reason thus: an evill spirit came and appeared unto me, after I had angred such a woman, therefore she sent him. Satan, if he had power to doe harme, or knowe where somewhat will follow, is he not cunning to make the partie which shall receive the harme, to fall out with some that he may suspect, and so the harme may seeme to come from that partie? Againe, in feare, in the darke, men take some little cat or dog to be an uglie devill. As not long since a rugged water spaniell having a chaine, came to a mans doore that had a saut bitch, and some espied him in the darke, and said it was a thing as bigge as a colt, and had eyes as great as saucers. Hereupon some came to charge to him, and did charge him in the name of the Father, the Sonne, and the Holy Ghost, to tell what he was. The dogge at the last told them, for he spake in his language, and said, bowgh, and thereby they did know what he was. If hee doe know where harmes doe follow upon naturall causes in men or beasts, hee laboureth either to make them offended, and to fall out with the partie that is suspected, or at the least to perswade them of such displeasure conceived, that the harms may seeme to come from the same. If he do torment indeede, having power to possesse the bodie, hee will not sticke to lie, and to say such a woman sent him.

M. B. And doth it not fall out sometimes, that as hee said such a woman sent him, so the woman upon examination confesseth so much.

Dan. Yea, but I speak where he hath no witch to deale by, but pursueth the innocent with suspition upon suspition, that men may bee guiltie of innocent blood. Hee telleth the truth sometimes, to the end he may be credited when he doth lie. For let no man be so simple as to thinke, that he will ever tell truth but for some wicked purpose.

M. B. Yet this of all the rest seemeth most strange unto me, how so many things should fall out, as it seemeth, after the displeasure of a suspected person, and some of them such as apparantly are done by Sathan, as in drinke not working, or in creame, when butter will not come, and yet the partie suspected is not a witch.

Dan. Oh sir, the sleights of Satan in compassing such matters bee marveilous. I know it is taken (as they say) to bee dead sure that the partie is a witch, if sundrie such shewes of matters doe concurre. But how easie a thing is it for craftie divels to compasse such matters?

M. B. Then you doe not thinke that common fame is sufficient to warrant the conscience of the juror, to condemne any.

Dan. Experience doth teach how headie many people are in judging men or women to bee witches upon every surmise. And the power imagined to be in witches, which breedeth a feare in many, causeth them to be credulous. Many goe so farre, that if they can intice children to accuse their parents, they thinke it a good worke.

M. B. You say the testimonie of the divell is not to bee taken, although it be manifest that he doth many times tell the truth, because when he speaketh the truth, he doth it of a bad purpose. And you hold it the testimonie of the divell, not onely which he speaketh when any charge him, but also which the cunning men and women give, in as much as they can say nothing but upon his word. Moreover, unles I mistake you, the testimony of a witch in many things at her death is not (as you say) any other then the testimonie of the divell, because the divell hath deceived her, and made her beleeve things which were nothing so. Besides al this, you wil have likelihoods and suspitions to be of no waight, nor common fame and opinion to move the conscience of a jurie, because Sathan is exceeding subtill in all these. Then how shall a jurie finde a witch? What proofes will you have?

Dan. Men are upon their oath to deale, and it doth touch life, if they doe finde any guiltie of witchcraft. This is a most waightie matter, whereupon it followeth, that there must be either due proofe by sufficient witnesses, or els the confession of the witch. For if the testimony be such as may be false, as all that commeth from divels is to be suspected: or if it be but upon rumours, and likelihoods, in which there may be exceeding sleights of Sathan, as for the most part there be: how can that jurie answere before God, which upon their oath are not sure, but that so proceeding they may condemne the innocent as often it commeth to passe.

M. B. You mistake one point, for the finding of a witch guilty by a jury doeth not in all causes touch blood.

Dan. I am not deceived, for where the jurie having but likelihoods doth find a man or a woman guilty but for killing a beast, it casteth them into prison, setteth them upon the pillorie, and not only confirms them for ever, but also if suspition follow againe and arraignment, it is death; you see then how neere a way they have made unto blood. But if it touch not blood, but the party escape with the imprisonment and pillory, and never againe fall into suspition, how grievous an infamie is it, to have been condemned by jury to be a witch? I speake it where it is onely upon suspition, or such testimonie as is onelie from Satan, and the partie may be cleere.

M. B. It falleth out sometimes that upon suspition and common fame they hitte right, and the partie which would not confesse any witchery upon examination, and arraignment, being condemned doth confesse it.

Dan. Let it be graunted that the jury upon Satans testimony, or suspitions and common fame, sometimes hitteth right, which yet I feare is very seldome, that is no warrant before God for men that are sworne, for are they sworne to indict upon likelihoods, or upon knowledge in the which upon sound testimony or confession they shall finde? If the party be a witch which is suspected, and yet no proofe, the jury doeth more rightly in acquitting, than in condemning, for what warrant have they upon their oath to goe by gesse, or to find that which they know not?

M. B. I doe take it men offend grievously, if upon insufficient proofe they condemne the innocent, and especially, because they are solemnly sworne: but if they hit right, though it be only by conjectures and likelihoods, I cannot see how they should therein offend: they condemne not the innocent, they doe the party no wrong.

Dan. I doe not say they are to bee charged with any innocent blood, or wrong to the partie: but I aske what warrant they have before God upon oath to touch blood by suspitions? Admit one be arraigned upon felony, the likelihoods are great that he is guiltie of the same, but yet it may be hee is cleere. What is a jurie nowe to do? Are they to venture upon the life of a man by their oath by suspitions. Let it be he is one that God knoweth to bee guiltie, but no man can disclose the same, and therefore they cleare him, doe they commit anie offence? Are they bound to find that which they cannot know? What innocent person then may not be condemned.

Sam. I pray you give me leave a little. I do not well conceive this matter about finding out and condemning of witches. It is somwhat strange unto me which you speak: I have my selfe sundry times beene of the jurie when witches have beene arraigned, we have found them guilty upon common fame, upon likelihoods, and upon such testimonie as you disallow. They have indeed taken it upon their deaths that they were innocent, but that never made me to doubt but that they were witches: for it is sayde, the devill hath such power over them, that he will not suffer them to confesse.

Dan. What should moove you to thinke that the devil will not have them to confesse? you see some doe confesse when they be examined, and when they be executed: the devill hath power over the most desperat theeves and murtherers?

Sam. Yea, but he careth not so much though the theeves and the murtherers doe confesse, it maketh not so much against him, as when witches bewray all.

Dan. What, doe you take it hee is loath to be diffamed or hardly thought off? Otherwise what should it make against him when witches confesse? It is some step to repentance when theeves and murtherers acknowledge their sinnes, and if he can hinder them, or holde them desperate from confessing, he will. It is apparant that hee coveteth to have witches to confesse, it maketh so much for him. He would have men judge that there bee an hundred folde more witches then there be. He discloseth by his cunning men and women, and otherwise. He coveteth greatly to have it thought that hee doth all, in tempests, in straunge plagues and diseases which light upon man or beast. And for this cause hee maketh the witch beleeve and confesse more then all, that is, that at her request he did that which he never did nor could doe: unlesse we will denie the soveraigntie and providence of God over all.

Sam. If Satan gaine so much by disclosing them, what should be the reason that men are generally perswaded, that he coveteth to have the things kept secret, and so will not let the witch confesse.

Dan. It ariseth from false perswasions, and from a false feare that witches doe so many harmes, and that at their sending and request the spirits worke all. If Sathan be so kind and serviceable to the witch, how is it that he doth not fetch her some money? for hee knoweth where it is lost, or where it lieth in mens houses. Hee telleth the witch he can make a man lame. Hee saith hee can kill an horse. Yea, at sometime he will say he can and will (if she will have it so) kill a man. As if it were in his power to doe many great things, and will not but requested. Let us see if all the divels can fetch one penny out of a mans house whose horse or cow they say they have killed. The conjurer, saith he, can conjure him into a man, or out of a man: let him conjure him but into a mans chest if he can, to fetch somewhat from thence. If the divels cannot doe these things, then be assured that either they make but a shew of killing and laming, as they do in the most of such harmes, or else where they do hurt, it is upon speciall leave from God, and not from the witches pleasure. And to what purpose then should all such juggling and shewes serve, if they should be kept close and not confessed.

Sam. Yet for my better satisfaction give me leave without offense to lay open some particulars which I have seen. I was of a jurie not many years past, when there was an old woman arrained for a witch. There came in eight or ten which gave evidence against her. I doe not remember every particular; but the chiefe, for some things were of small value. One woman came in and testified uppon her oath, that her husband upon his death-bed, took it upon his death, that he was bewitched, for he pined a long time. And hee sayd further, hee was sure that woman had bewitched him. He tooke her to be naught, and thought she was angry with him, because she would have borrowed five shillings of him, and he denied to lend it her. The woman tooke her oath also, that she thought in her conscience that the old woman was a witch, and that she killed her husband. There came in a man that halted, he tolde a shrewde tale. I once, sayd he, had both my legges sound. This old woman and I fell out and did chide. She sayd she would be even with me. Within three daies after I had such a paine in my knee that I could not stand. And ever since I goe haulting of it, and now and then feele some paine. There came in another, a little fellow that was very earnest, me thinkes I see him yet. He tooke his oath directly that she was a witch: I did once anger her (sayd he) but I did repent me: for I was afeared what would follow. And the next night I saw the ugliest sight that ever I saw: I awaked suddenly out of my sleepe, and there was me thought a great face, as bigge as they use to set up in the signe of the Saracens head, looked full in my face. I was scarce mine owne man two dayes after. Another came in, a woman, and her child dyed with grievous paine, and she tooke her oath, that in her conscience she killed her child. Then followed a man, and he sayd hee could not tell, but he thought she was once angry with him because she came to begge a few pot-hearbes, and he denied her: and presently after he heard a thing as he thought to whisper in his care, thou shalt be bewitched. The next day he had such a paine in his backe, that he could not sit upright: he said hee sent to a cunning woman, she tolde hee was bewitched, and by a woman that came for pot-hearbes. But she said he should recour of it, and so he said hee did within some tenne daies. Then came in two or three grave honest men, which testified that she was by common fame accounted a witch. Wee found her guiltie, for what could we doe lesse, she was condemned and executed: and upon the ladder she made her prayer, and took it upon her death she was innocent and free from all such dealings. Do you think we did not well?

Dan. Nay, what thinke you? Are you sure she was a witch? May it not be she was innocent, and you upon your oathes shed innocent blood?

Sam. If she were innocent what could we doe lesse? we went according to the evidence of such as were sworne, they swore that they in their conscience tooke her to bee a witch, and that she did those things.

Dan. If other take their oath that in their conscience they think so, is that sufficient to warrant me upon mine oath to say it is so?

Sam. Nay, but you see what matters they brought, which perswaded them to thinke so.

Dan. Might not both you and they be deceived in your thinking, or may you upon matters which may induce you to thinke so, present uppon your oath that you know it is so?

Sam. If witnesses come in and sweare falsely, the jury proceeding according, their testimony is cleere from blame, for they goe but by testimonie of men sworne.

Dan. If witnesses doe sweare directly that in their knowledge a matter was so or so, and sweare falsely, the jurie is cleere which proceedeth according to their evidence: unlesse the jurie do perceive that their oth cannot be true. But what is that to make the testimonie sufficient where men doe but thinke, and can shew no necessarie reason to ground their thought upon? As let us see in al these which one could proove that she must needes be a witch. One saith her husband tooke it upon his death that she killed him, because hee would not lend her five shillings: does this prove she bewitched him? Can the divell kill a man at his pleasure, to gratifie the witch? Is it not rather to be judged he dyed of som pining sicknesse growing from an evill constitution of bodie, which the divel did know, and would set him at some variance with one old woman or other, that so it might breed suspition of witchcraft?

Sam. You see there were some things which could not be done but by the divell.

Dan. Indeed the great face which the man thought he saw, was the illusion of the divell. But is this a good proofe, the divel appeareth to a man after he hath displeased a woman, therefore she sent him? Doth not Sathan haunt all men continually, and would if he could get leave from God terrific them with such illusions? when men are affraid and have strong imaginations. What reason did the woman shew which toke it upon her conscience that the old woman killed her childe, to proove that it was so? If shee thought so in her conscience, and tenne thousand more with her upon bare imagination, was that a warrant for you to sweare solemnly that it was so? As for the testimonie of the cunning woman that he was bewitched which had the paine in his backe, upon the deniall of pot-hearbes, it was the testimonie but of the divell, as I shewed before. And what is common fame grounded upon imaginations?

Sam. Then you thinke we did amisse, doe you?

Dan. I would not upon mine oath doe such a thing for to gaine a kingdome.

Sam. It may be she was a witch, although she tooke it upon her death that she was not.

Dan. It is rather to be thought she was not a witch: for what should make her denie it upon her death? The divell had accused her to be a witch, for no direct testimony against her but his.

Sam. You say it was the divell that told by the cunning woman that she was a witch.

Dan. And doe you thinke it was any other but Satan?

Sam. I did not at that time thinke it was the divell: but now I see it could be none other.

Dan. Then be wiser hereafter, and sorie for that which you have done.

Sam. Indeed I have cause to be grieved if she were not a witch.

Dan. If she were a witch your warrant was small: but she being no witch, you have taken away both her life, and covered her with infamie.

Sam. I was of another jurie since, and there was a woman indicted for a witch, but not for killing any man or childe. There came in five or sixe against her: the first was an old woman, and she sayd she had displeased her, as shee thought, and within two or three nights after as she sate by her fire, there was a thing like a toad, or like some little crabbe fish which did creepe upon the harth, she tooke a beesome and swept it away, and suddenly her bodie was griped. Another fel out with her, as she said, and her hennes began to die up, untill she burnt one hen alive. A third man came in, and hee said she was once angrie with him, he had a dun cow which was tyed up in a house, for it was in winter, he feared that some evill would follow, and for his life he could not come in where she was, but he must needs take up her tayle and kisse under it. Two or three other came in and said she was by common fame accounted a witch. Wee found her guiltie, and she was condemned to prison, and to the pillorie, but stood stiffe in it that she was no witch.

Dan. And are you sure she was one?

Sam. I thinke verily shee was one, although there bee many of her neighbors which thinke she is none: for how could those thinges followe so upon her anger? It seemeth they were all done by the devill.

Dan. Hee is cunning that can tell that: let it be that it was the devil which appeared to the old woman like a toad, or like a crabbe fish, and that he did gripe her bodie: doth it follow therefore of necessitie that the other woman sent him? He can not turne him selfe into any likenesse unlesse God give him leave, as he doth in justice permit that so he may delude ignorant persons. No witch can give him power to appeare unto any in a visible shape. He had this

133

graunted him from God, and Satan by and by will set anger, and then appeare, that it might seeme it grew from that.

Sam. Wee see hee appeareth unto witches and conjurers.

Dan. Yea, but wee may not thinke hee can at his pleasure take a likeness for to appeare in. That he doth appeare unto witches and conjurers, it is granted in Gods wrath, to the ende he may strongly delude such wicked people as will not heare and obey the voyce of the Lord God. For the devils are chained up by Gods most mightie power and providence, and in all things so farre as he letteth foorth their chaine, so farre they proceede, one inch further they can not proceede. Where men love darkenes more then light, hee hath leave given him to do many thinges. Some he terrifieth with ugly shapes, some he intiseth with faire shewes: others he playeth withall in likenes of a weasell, or mouse, or some such small vermine.

Sam. I thought Satan could appeare in what likenesse he would, and to whom he would, if the witch sent him.

Dan. Therein you were much deceived: for the sending by the witch can give him no power, and if hee had power, he would no doubt in all places appeare unto many as far and in such sort, as should best serve his turne. Therefore if he appeare unto any man, let him thinke, God hath given him leave to goe thus farre with mee, and let him call for faith to resist him, and for true wisedome that he may not be deceived nor deluded by him.

Sam. But doth hee not appeare sometimes when the witches send him?

Dan. Where he findeth it is graunted unto him for to appeare, he mooveth witches to send him, if he have any to deale by: but if there be none, yet will he appeare, and deale so farre as he hath power given him.

Sam. But what say you to the womans hens?

Dan. What should one say to them when they be dead?

Sam. I meane doe you not thinke they were bewitched?

Dan. Christ saith, a sparrow cannot fall without the will of your heavenly Father: and is not a henne as good as a sparrow?

Sam. Nay, I am fully perswaded by that which you have sayd, that the divell cannot touch any thing to kill or to hurt it, but upon speciall leave from God. They can give him no power, she thinketh she setteth him on, and it is hee that setteth her on worke. Let these things be no more called in question: but was it not evident that the divell killed those hennes? because after the burning of one henne the woman had no more that died. If Satan did it not, how could they cease dying for that? You sayd that he, where he hath power to hurt in such bodily harmes, is willing to cease, that such wickednesse may bee practised. And then if this hurt were done by the divell, is it not to bee thought that the woman was a witch, seeing it followed after she was angrie? Let it be that Satan having power to do that he did, would be sent by the witch for a colour, and to make it evident did set anger between her and that other woman, to make men thinke that he would not deale, but intreated by her being angrie. And so we could doe no lesse but finde her a witch.

Dan. These be weake foundations to set such a weightie building upon. For first it is not certaine that the divell killed those hens. Might it not be they had some infection which he did know would kill them, and he craftily bringeth the matter about, making two women fall out (which is the easiest matter of an hundred) even upon the dying of the hennes, that so it might seeme they were bewitched. But you say then, how could it bee that upon the burning of an henne, they dyed no more, if the divell did not kill them? Nay how can you tell but that there should no more have dyed, although the live hen had not been burned? What if hee saw there should no more dye, and thereupon mooved the heart of that woman to use that witchcraft in burning a henne, that it might seeme that was a present remedie to drive away divels? Or put case he had the power to kill the womans hens, either he is a weake killer, or els he goeth to his worke but lazily. He could kill a great heard of swine quickly when Christ gave him leave: could he not, if the woman had five thousand hens, have killed them all at once? Why did the foole then but nibble, killing now one and then one, and so was scared away before he had killed all? If he had power before the henne was burnt for to kil, why did hee not then when they went about to burne an henne kill the rest? It may be he did not know what they went about, he was laid soft in his pot of wooll: and comming to kill another henne, he was met withall, he smelt the roastmeat, and was scared.

Sam. Then you thinke he did not kill those hennes.

Dan. What certaintie had you that hee did kill them? You found it upon your oath that he killed them, and that such a woman sent him and set him a worke, and yet it is an hundred to one hee never had power for to touch them.

Sam. But what can you say to the other: the man which could not chuse but kisse under his cowes tayle?

Dan. I say he was farre in love with his cow. Let such men learne to know God, and to expell fantasies out of their mindes, that the devil may not have such power over them, for he worketh in the fantasies of mans mind, and the more strongly where they feare him, as it appeareth this man did. Satan did worke in this mans minde many foolish imaginations, and to make him beleeve he was bewitched he maketh him fall out with one that may bee suspected. And thus you jurie men take your oath and condemne many innocent persons because you beleeve the devill, and imagine that witches do that which they cannot do.

M. B. I have heard of many that have beene condemned for witches which have taken it upon their death that they were innocent. And sundry of them have had farre weaker proofes brought against them then these that have bin mentioned.

Dan. Yea, that is it which I say, men do so little consider the high soveraignety and providence of God over all things: they ascribe so much to the power of the devill and to the anger of witches, and are in such feare of them, that the least shew that can be made by the sleights of Satan deceives them. The only way for men that will eschew the snares and subtilties of the devill and all harmes by him, is this, even to heare the voyce of God, to be taught of him by his lively word which is full of pure light to discover and expel the darke mistes of Satan, in which he leadeth men out of the way: and to be armed with faith to resist him, as the holy Apostle S. Peter willeth, so such as doe forsake this way are seduced into grosse errors and into many abominable sinnes, which carrie men to destruction. I must now bidde you farewell.

M. B. I could bee content to heare more in these matters, I see how fondly I have erred. But seeing you must be gone, I hope we shall meete here againe at some other time; God keepe you!

Sam. I am bound to give you great thankes. And I pray you, when occasion serveth, that you come this way, let us see you at my house.

M. B. I thought there had not been such subtill practises of the divell, nor so great sinnes as he leadeth men into.

Sam. It is strange to see how many thousands are caried awry and deceived, yea many that are very wise men.

M. B. The divell is too craftie for the wisest, unlesse they have the light of Gods word.

The wife of Sam. Husband, yonder commeth the goodwife R.

Sam. I would she had come sooner.

The goodwife R. Ho, who is within, by your leave?

The wife of Sam. I would you had come a little sooner, here was one even now that said you are a witch.

The goodwife R. Was there one said I am a witch? you doe but jest.

The wife of Sam. Nay, I promise you hee was in good earnest.

The goodwife R. I a witch? I defie him that saith it, though he be a lord. I would all the witches in the land were hanged, and their spirits by them.

M. B. Would not you be glad if their spirits were hanged up with them to have a gowne furred with some of their skinnes?

The goodwife R. Out upon them, there were furre!

Sam. Wife, why diddest thou say that hee said the goodwife R. is a witch? he did not say so.

The wife of Sam. Husband, I did marke his words well enough, he said she is a witch.

Sam. He doth not know her, and how could he say she is a witch?

The wife of Sam. What though he did not know her? did hee not say she played the witch that het the spit red hot, and thrust it into her creame, when the butter would not come?

Sam. Indeede, wife, thou saist true, he said that was a thing taught by the divell, as also the burning of an henne, or of an hogge alive, and all such like devices.

The goodwife R. Is that witchcraft? Some Scripture man hath tolde you so. Did the divell teach it? Nay, the good woman at R. H. taught it my husband: she doth more good in one yeere then all these Scripture men will doe so long as they live.

M. B. Who doe you thinke taught it the cunning woman at R. H.?

The goodwife R. It is a gift which God hath given her. I thinke the Holy Spirit of God doth teach her.

M. B. You doe not think then that the divell doth teach her.

The goodwife R. How should I thinke that the divell doth teach her? Did you ever heare that the devill did teach any good thing?

M. B. Doe you know that was a good thing?

The goodwife R. Was it not a good thing to drive the evill spirit out of my creame?

M. B. Do you thinke the divell was afraid of your spit?

The goodwife R. I know he was driven away, and we have been rid of him ever since.

M. B. Can a spit hurt him?

The goodwife R. It doth hurt him, or it hurteth the witch: one of them I am sure: for he commeth no more. Either she can get him come no more, because it hurteth him: or els she will let him come no more, because it hurteth her.

M. B. It is certaine that spirits cannot be hurt but with spirituall weapons: therefore your spit cannot fray nor hurt the divell. And how can it hurt the witch, you did not thinke she was in your creame, did you?

The goodwife R. Some thinke she is there, and therefore when they thrust in the spit they say: If thou beest here have at thine eye!

M. B. If she were in your creame, your butter was not very cleanly.

The goodwife R. You are merrily disposed, M. B., I know you are of my mind, though you put these questions to me. For I am sure none hath counselled more to goe to the cunning folke then you.

M. B. I was of your minde, but I am not now, for I see how foolish I was. I am sorie that ever I offended so grievously as to counsaile any for to seeke unto divels.

The goodwife R. Why, M. B., who hath schooled you to day? I am sure you were of another mind no longer agone then yesterday.

The wife of Sam. Truly, goodwife R., I thinke my husband is turned also: here hath been one reasoning with them three or foure houres.

The goodwife R. Is your husband turned to? I would you might lose all your hens one after another, and then I would she would set her spirit upon your ducks and your geese, and leave you not one alive. Will you come to defend witches?

M. B. We doe not defend witches.

The goodwife R. Yes, yes, there be too many that take their part; I would they might witch some of them even into hell, to teach others to defend them. And you, M. B., I would your nagge might hault a little one of these daies: see whether you would not be glad to seeke helpe.

M. B. I would seeke helpe, I would carrie him to the smith to search if he were not pricked or graveld.

The goodwife R. Tush, you laugh: if you were plagued as some are, you would not make so light account of it.

M. B. You thinke the divell can kill mens cattell, and lame both man and beast at his pleasure: you thinke if the witch intreate him and send him he will goe, and if she will not have him go, he will not meddle. And you thinke when he doth come, you can drive him away with an hot spitte, or with burning a live henne or a pigge.

The goodwife R. Never tell me I thinke so, for you your selfe have thought so: and let them say what they can, all the Scripture men in the world shall never perswade me otherwise.

M. B. I doe wonder, not so much at your ignorance as at this, that I was ever of the same minde that you are, and could not see mine owne follie.

The goodwife R. Follie? how wise you are become of a sudden? I know that their spirits lie lurking, for they foster them: and when any bodie hath angred them, then they call them foorth and send them. And looke what they bid them do, or hire them to do, that shall be done: as when she is angrie, the spirit will aske her what shall I doe? Such a man hath misused me, saith she, goe kill his cow; by and by he goeth and doth it. Go kill such a womans hens; downe goe they. And some of them are not content to do these lesser harmes, but they will say, goe make such a man lame, kill him, or kill his child. Then are they readie and will doe any thing: and I thinke they be happie that can learne to drive them away.

M. B. If I should reason with you out of the worde of God, you should see that al this is false which you say. The divell cannot kill nor hurt any thing, no not so much as a poore henne. If he had power, who can escape him? Would he tarrie to be sent or intreated by a woman? he is a stirrer up unto al harmes and mischiefs.

The goodwife R. What tell you me of Gods word? Doth not Gods word say there bee witches, and doe not you thinke God doth suffer bad people? Are you a turne coate? Fare you well, I will no longer talke with you.

M. B. She is wilfull indeede. I will leave you also.

Sam. I thanke you for your good companie.

on the punishment of witches

by Thomas Pickering and William Perkins

The year 1603 saw a new ruler, James I, on the English throne. He had previously been James VI of Scotland but became sole ruler of the united kingdoms of England and Scotland on Elizabeth's death. James was much more bitterly opposed to witchcraft than the late queen had been.

The king's hatred for witchcraft had had a personal origin, for when he was twenty-four he believed he had been the target of a group of Scottish witches from North Berwick who had tried to raise a storm to wreck the ship on which he was journeying to Norway.

The conspirators were subsequently brought to trial, but when one woman, of noble birth, was acquitted by the jury, the young king was so incensed that he took over the trial personally. "Witchcraft," he declared, "which is a thing grown very common among us, is a most abominable sin." He then reversed the jury's decision, "to make men be more wary, how they give false verdicts."

The king's antiwitchcraft fervor was also stimulated by the publication of Reginald Scot's *The Discovery of Witchcraft* in 1584, and he worked for several years on a book to refute its claims, *Demonology*, which eventually appeared in Edinburgh in 1597.

Once James came to the English throne, however, his anger was turned into more concrete action. He immediately gave orders for

Scot's book to be burned, brought out a new edition of his own work to prove that "The assaults of Satan are most certainly practised and the instruments thereof merit most severely to be punished," and in the following year had parliament pass a new witchcraft act that was considerably more severe than that of Elizabeth, widening the range of offenses for which death was the penalty, and undoubtedly contributed to the increasing number of accusations being made against supposed witches.

If the king needed approbation for his work from his new English subjects, he did not have long to wait, for not only did the persecution of witches redouble, but a new and important book was published, attacking those of Scot and Gifford and coming out passionately on the side of the king.

This book, *A Discourse of the Damned Art of Witchcraft*, had actually been written before the king came to the throne, but it now finally emerged under the auspices of the vicar of the small Essex village of Finchingfield, the Reverend Thomas Pickering. The book was the work of the late William Perkins (1555–1602), a demonologist and Puritan preacher, who had risen from obscurity to a position of preeminence in the English religious fraternity. He divided the work into seven chapters, in which he discussed miracles, the alliance between witches and the devil, the art of divination, the white, or good, witch ("the worse of the two," he maintained), and the discovery and punishment of witches, advocating torture and automatic execution.

The climate of opinion at the end of Elizabeth's reign would probably not have permitted a wholehearted welcome of such a virulent book, but under King James's new, harsher strictures the Reverend Pickering, who had inherited the manuscript, saw no reason to delay its appearance any longer. The Reverend Pickering, a scholar and historian, published the work himself and introduced it with an impassioned affirmation of all that Perkins had to say, obviously sharing his viewpoint down to the last word.

Of this Essex clergyman little is known except that he commenced his ministry in Finchingfield in 1605 and died there in 1625.

The book's author, William Perkins, had been educated at Cambridge and thereafter lived a somewhat dissolute life until he overheard someone holding him up as a bad example to a child and calling him "drunken Perkins." After this he resolved to mend his ways and turn to God. In time his dedication to the church led him to be described as "the greatest Calvinist preacher, theologian and controversialist that England has produced." His book was to prove one of the most important authorities consulted by the witch hunters in the next half century, far surpassing that of King James, whose own witchcraft hysteria was to be gradually tempered until, on his death, he had become a complete skeptic on the whole issue.

Here is Thomas Pickering's introduction to Perkins's book and a section from it dealing with the punishment of witches. In these two items is much of the thinking that could whip smoldering intolerance in simple minds into the raging fires of indiscriminate persecution.

I

The Work of the Devil

The Word of God, that Only Oracle of truth, has pointed out the Enemy of mankind, by his proper Characters, in sundry places. Our Saviour terms him, the "Prince of this World" and "a Murderer from the beginning." Peter compares him to a "roaring lion", that rangeth abroad in the earth, "seeking whom he may devour".

The Power of this Prince of Darkness, being above the might of all sensible Creatures, and every way seconded by the greatness of his knowledge and experience, manifests itself herein, for the most part, by works of wonder, transcendent in both sexes; sometime in matter of Divination, sometime by Enchantment, sometime by rare sleights and delusions; otherwhiles by hurting, by curing, by raising of Tempests, by speedy conveyance and transportation from place to place, &c. and all to purchase unto himself admiration, fear, and faith of the credulous world, which is usually carried away with affectation and applause of signs and wonders. His policy appears in a wise and exquisite manner of framing and conceiving both his practises and grounds; the one to procure credit and entertainment; the other that he may not fail in his purpose, but proceed upon certainties.

Touching the manner of his practise. He stands resolved, that the world hath taken notice of him to be "a liar, and the father thereof": and therefore if he should offer to speak in his own language, or inform an Art by rules of his own devising, he might happily incur suspicion of falsehood. Hereupon he composes his courses, by way of counterfeit and imitation, not of the actions and dealings of men, but of the order of God's own will proceeding with his Church; holding it a sure principle in policy, that actions will be much more effectual, when they be framed after the best presidents, than when they are suited to the direction of meaner examples. To this purpose, as God hath made a Covenant with his Church, binding himself by promise to be their God, and requiring of them the condition of faith and obedience; so doth Satan indent with his Subjects by mutual confederacy, either solemnly or secretly; whereby they bind themselves on the one part to observe his Rules, and he on the other to accomplish their desires. Again, God gives his Word, the Interpreter of his Will, and his Sacraments, the Seales of his promises, to which being rightly administered and received, he hath tied his own preference, and the work of his grace in them that believe. Answerably to this, the Devil gives a word of direction to his instruments, and addeth unto it, Charmes, Figures, Characters, and other outward Ceremonies, at the use whereof he hath bound himself to be present and to manifest his power in effecting the thing desired. Furthermore, God hath revealed his will to the Patriarchs, Prophets, and Apostles, by familiar conference, by dreams, by inspiration, by trances: In the same manner, Satan hath his Diviners, and Soothsayers, his Sybilles, to whome he maketh known things to come, by familiar presence, by dreams, &c. To conclude, God had in the Old Testament his Temple at Jerusalem, yea his Oracle, from whence he spake, and gave the answer unto Moses: So of ancient times, the Devil erected his Temple at Dodona, and Delphos, whence he gave his answers, for the satisfaction of the superstitious Heathen. Yea and at this day, as the Minsters of God do give resolution to the conscience, in matters doubtful and difficult: so the Ministers of Satan under the name of wise men and wise women, are at hand by his appointment, to resolve, direct, and help ignorant persons, in cases of distraction, loss or other outward calamities.

Now from the consideration of the premises, we believe it a necessary thing for the Church and people of God, to be acquainted with the dealing of Satan in this kind, that knowing his subtle devices, they may learn to avoid them. For which purpose this Treatise was first framed, and is now exhibited. The just commendation whereof, above others formerly divulged touching this Argument, that it serveth to the full opening and declaration of Satan's Method in the ground and practises of Witchcraft. Wherein among many other remarkable points it may please you to take special notice of these particulars.

1. That they do grossly err, who either in express terms deny that there be Witches, or in effect, and by consequence avow that there is no league between them and the Devil; or affirming they can do no such miraculous works as are ascribed to them. That there is a covenant between them, either explicit in manner and form or implicit by degrees of superstitious proceeding in the use of means insufficient in themselves; is plainly taught and confirmed. That Witches may and do work wonders is evidently proved: howbeit not by an omnipotent power, (as the gainsayer[1] hath unlearnedly and improperly termed it) but by the assistance of Satan, their Prince, who is a powerful spirit, but yet a Creature as well as they. And the wonders wrought by them, are not properly and simply miracles, but works of wonder; because they exceed the ordinary power and capacity of men, especially such as are ignorant of Satan's abilities and the hidden causes in nature, whereby things are brought to pass.

2. That the Witch truely convicted, is to be punished with death, the highest degree of punishment; and that by the Law of Moses, the equity whereof is perpetual. Yea, even the better Witch of the two in common reputation, because both are equally enemies to God, and true religion: and it is well known by true experience, that all professed Sorcerers are guilty of many monstrous impieties.

3. That the Miracles of the Popish Church at this day are indeed either no miracles, or false and deceitful works. Touching corporal presence in the Sacrament, which they affirm to be by miracle. If it were true, then miracles were not yet ceased, but should still be as ordinary in the Church as are the Sacraments.

4. That the light of the Gospel purely preached, is a Sovereign means to discover, confound the power and policy of Satan in Witchcraft and Sorcery. The word of God preached, is the weapon of the Christian's warfare, and is mighty through God to cast down strongholds. At the dispensation of it by the Disciples of Christ, Satan fell from heaven as lightning. After the ascension of Christ into Heaven, in the times of Claudius Caesar, the Devil stirred up sundry persons, who in regard of the admirable works which they did, by the help of Magic and Sorcery were accounted as Gods, and their Statues erected and worshipped with great reverence. Amongst the rest one Simon, called Magus, practising his trade with success, to the admiration of the multitude, was holden to be the great power of God: Whose dealing was first discovered by the light of the word, shining in the Ministry of the

1 Reginald Scot, *The Discovery of Witchcraft*, (Reginald Scot, 1584; London: Nicholson, 1886.)

Apostles, and himself convicted with such evidence of truth, to be an instrument of Satan, that he was forced at length to fly out of Samaria into the Western parts. By this, Christ the true Angel of the Covenant, locked and bound up Satan for a 1000 years after his ascension, that he might not be so generally powerful in seducing the Gentiles, as he had been before his incarnation. But towards the expiration of those years, when corruption began to creep into the Papacie, when the Bishops affected that Sea, and aspired unto it by Diabolical Arts; when the Canons, Decrees, Sentences, Synodals, Decretals, Clementines, Extravagants, with other Lawes and Constitutions, prevailed above the Scriptures, then began Satan again to erect his kingdom, and these works of iniquity to be set abroad.

These points I humbly commend to your attention along with the argument of the author which follows. I trust that they may now freely pass the common view of the world, and humbly take my leave commending you to the grace of God, who does rule all the Judges of the Earth.

Thomas Pickering
Finchingfield, October 26, 1608.

II

The Punishment of his Servants

Hitherto I have treated of the nature of Witchcraft, both in general and particular, and have also shown what Witches are, both good and bad. And now I proceed to the second point considered in this Text—the Punishment of a Witch, and that is Death.

In the Judicial lawes of Moses (whereof this is one) the Lord appointed sundry penalties, which in qualities and degree differed one from another, so as according to the nature of the offence, was the proportion and measure of the punishment ordained. And of all sins, as those were the most heinous in account, which tended directly to the dishonour of God, so to them was assigned death, the greatest and highest degree of punishment. 'He that despiseth the Law of Moses died without mercy under two or three witnesses.' (Hebr.10.28); 'The punishment of the thief, was restitution fourfold.' (Exod.22.1); 'But the murderer must be put to death.' (Num.35.31) 'The Blasphemer must be stoned.' (Levit.29.19); and the Witch is numbered amongst these grievous offenders; therefore his punishment is as great as any other. For the text saith, he might not be suffered to live (Exod.22.18).

But why should the Witch be so sharply censured? and what should move the Lord to allot so high a degree of punishment to that sort of offenders?

Answer. The cause was not the hurt, which they brought upon men in body, goods, or outward estate. For there be sundry that never did harm, but good only. We read not of any great hurt that was done by the Enchanters of Egypt, or by Simon Magus in Samaria. And those divining witches which have taken upon them to foretell things to come, hurt not any, but themselves, yet they must die. This therefore is not the cause. But what if these do hurt, or kill, must they not then die? Yes verily, but by another law, the law of murder, and not by the law of Witchcraft; for in this case, he dieth as a murderer, and not as a witch, and so he should die, though he were no Witch.

The cause then of this sharpe punishment, is the very making of a league with the Devil, either secret, or open, whereby they covenant to use his help for the working of wonder. For by virtue of this alone it cometh to pass, that Witches can do strange things, in Divining, Enchanting, and Juggling. Now let it be observed, of what horrible impietie they stand guilty before God, who join in confederacy with Satan. Hereby they renounce the Lord that made them, they make no more account of his favour and protection, they do quite cut themselves off from the communion of the Saints, from the true worship and Service of God. And on the contrary they give themselves unto Satan, as their god, whom they continually fear and serve. Thus are they become the most detestable enemies to God, and his people, that can be. For this cause Samuel told Saul, that rebellion was as the Sin of Witchcraft: that is, a most heinous and detestable sin in the Sight of God. The traitor that doth no hurt to his neighbour, but is willing and ready to do him the best services that can be desired, is notwithstanding by the law of Nations, no better than a dead man, because he betrays his Sovereign and consequently cannot be a friend unto the Commonwealth. In like manner, though the Witch were in many respects profitable, and did not hurt, but procured much good; yet because he hath renounced his God his king and governor, and hath bound himself by other laws to the service of the enemy of God, and his Church, death is his portion justly assigned him by God; he may not live.

Thus having delivered the true sense and interpretation of this Judicial Law, both concerning the sin of Witchcraft and the persons by whom this sin is practised, it remaineth now that I should make some use thereof, by way of application to the Witches of our times.
Question: Whether the Witches of our times, be the same with those that are here condemned by Moses' Law?
Answer: If we do well consider the quality and condition of the witches of our days, we shall easily see, that they be the same. For experience showeth, that whether they be men or women, but especially aged women, they be such

persons, as do renounce God, and their Baptism, and make a league with the devil, either secretly or openly, in which the devil binds himself to teach them certain rites and ceremonies, whereby they may be able to work wonders, or to stir up tempests, to reveal secrets, to kill or hurt men, and cattle, or to cure and do good, according to the tenour of their covenant.

The confessions of Witches recorded in the Chronicles of countries through all Europe, do with common consent declare and manifest this point. So that howsoever our Witches may differ in some circumstances from those in the time of Moses, as either in the instruments, and means used, or in the manner and form, or in some particular ends of their practises; yet in the substance and foundation of Witchcraft, they agree with them. For both of them have made a covenant with the Devil one way or other, and by virtue thereof have wrought wonders above the order of nature. Agreeing therefore in the very foundation, and form of Witchcraft, which is the league, and in the proper end, the working of wonders; they must need be in substance and effect the same with the Witches mentioned by Moses. And yet this point is denied by some, and the Witches of these days have their patrons, who use reasons to prove that now we have none such as we speak of. Their reasons are specially three.

First, they labour to take away the form of Witchcraft, affirming that there can be no confederacy made between the Witch and the Devil and that for four causes.

1. In every league and contract, the parties must be mutually bound each to other: now between man or woman and the Devil, there can be no bond made, and though there could, yet man is bound in conscience to God, to renounce the bond of obedience to Satan, and to breake the covenant. Answer. There be two sorts of leagues; lawful, and unlawful: in all lawful leagues it is true, that there must be a mutual bond of both parties each to other, which may not be dissolved; but in unlawful compacts it is otherwise. And no man can say that this league between a Witch and the Devil is lawful, but wicked and damnable; yet being once made, howsoever unlawfully, it is a league and compact. This therefore proveth not, that there can be no covenant at all, but that there can be no lawful covenant betwixt them, which no man will deny.

2. Satan and the Witch are of divers natures: he is spiritual, they are corporal substances; therefore there can be no league made between them. Answer. The reason is not good. For even God himself, who is of nature most simple and spiritual, made a covenant with Adam, renewed the same unto Abraham, Isaac, Jacob: and continued it with his Church on earth, from age to

age. Hence it appears that diversity of nature in the parties, cannot hinder the making of a covenant. And therefore if man may make covenant with God himself, who is most spiritual then may he likewise come in league with the Devil, whose substance is not so pure and spiritual. Again, we must remember, that in making of a covenant, it is sufficient, that the parties consent and agree in will and understanding, though other circumstances and rites, which are but signs of confirmation, be wanting.

3. Whatsoever the devil doth in this compact, he doth it in fraud and deceit, never meaning in his promises, as man do: and when both parties mean not one and the same thing, how can they grow to agreement in any kind? Answer. Suppose this be true, yet it only proveth, that the covenant made between them was deceitful and unlawful. But what of that? Still it remaineth a bargain howsoever: for it faileth only in the circumstance, the substance, which is the consent of the parties was not wanting.

4. Witches of our times (say they) are aged persons, of weak brains, and troubled with the abundance of melancholy, and the devil taketh advantage of the humour, and so deludes them, persuading them that they have made a league with him, when they have not, and consequently moving them to imagine that they do, and may do strange things, which indeed are done by himself, and not by them. Answer. This reason is a mere melancholy conceit, without ground. And the contrary is a manifest truth, that they are not so, as is affirmed, parties deceived by reason of their humours. For first, our Witches are as wise and clever, yea as crafty and cunning in all other matters, as other men be; whereas brainsick persons troubled with melancholy, if their understanding be distempered in one action, it will be faulty likewise in others more or less. Again, our Witches know that they sin in the practises of Witchcraft, and therefore they use subtle means to cover them; and he that would convict them, must have great dexterity to go beyond them. Now if they were persons deluded, through corruption of any humours; look what humour caused them to do a thing, the same would urge them to disclose it. Thirdly, they are also of the same stamp, they take the same courses in all their practises; their consent in word and action is universal. Men of learning have observed, that all Witches through Europe, are of like carriage and behaviour, in their examinations and convictions; they use the same answers, refuges, defenses, protestations. In a word, look what be the practises and courses of the Witches in England, in any of these particulars, the same be the practises of the Witches in Spain, France, Italy, Germany, &c. Wherefore the case is clear, they are not deluded by Satan, through the force of Humour, as is avouched; for such persons, accordingly as they are diversely taken, would

shew themselves diversly affected; and vary in their speeches, actions, and conceits, both public and private. Fourthly, our Witches are wont to communicate their skill to others by tradition, to teach and instruct their children and posterity, and to initiate them in the grounds, and practises of their own trade, while they live, as may appear by the confessions recorded in the courts of all countries. But if they were persons troubled with melancholy, their conceits would die with them. For conceits, and imaginary fancies which rise of any humour, cannot be conveyed from party to party, no more than the humour itself. Lastly, if this slight might serve to defend witches under pretence of delusion thorough corrupted humours, then here were a cover for all manner of sins.

Therefore howsoever the patrons of Witches be learned men, yet they are greatly deceived in fathering the practises of Sorcery upon a melancholy humour.

But for the further ratifying of their assertion, they proceed, and use this argument: They which confess of themselves things false and impossible, must need be parties deluded: but our Witches do this, when they be examined or consulted with: as that they can raise tempests that they are carried through the air in a moment from place to place, that they pass through key-holes, that they be sometimes turned into cats, hares, and other creatures; lastly that they are brought into far countries, to meet with Herodias, Diana, and the Devil, and suchlike; all which are mere fables, and things impossible.

Answer. We must make a difference of Witches in regard of time. There is a time, when they first begin to make a league with Satan, and a time also after the league is made and confirmed.

When they first begin to grow in confederacy with the Devil, they are sober, and their understanding found, they make their match waking, and as they think wisely enough knowing both what they promise the Devil and upon what conditions, and therefore all the while it is no delusion. But after they be once in the league, and have been intangled in compact with the Devil (considerately as they think, for their own good and advantage) the case may be otherwise. For then reason and understanding may be deprived, memory weakened, and all the powers of their Soul blemished. Thus becoming his vassals, they are deluded, and so intoxicated by him, that they will run into thousands of fantastical imaginations, holding themselves to be transformed into the shapes of other creatures, to be transported in the air into other countries, yea to do many strange things which in truth they do not.

I come now to their second reason. The Witches of our age (say they) were not known in the days of Moses, nor of Christ, therefore the law concerneth them not.

Again, I answer, that our Witches are the same that were in Moses' time: and therefore by their own reason must needs be condemned by this Judicial law. For by the records of ancient writers it is proved, that about 1200 years before Christ's birth, shortly after the Trojan war, which was 100 years and upward before the building of the Temple by Solomon, there were the same Witches that are now, as the Circes and Syrenes, and such like mentioned in the narration of that war, as is manifest to them that know the story.

The third and last reason is this: Christ at his coming abolished all sin, and therefore miracles and Witchcraft then ceased also. The Apostle saith, "that he spoiled principalities and powers, and triumphed over them upon the cross". (Col.2.15)

Answer. This argument is frivolous, serving as well to justify the traitor, the thief, and the murderer, as the witch. For whereas it is alleged, that Christ abolished all sin: we must understand how? Not simply, so as sin should be no more, but only in part, in this life, reserving the final destruction thereof to the last judgement. Again, sin is not abolished, no not in part unto all, but only to the members of Christ. Whereupon the Apostle saith, "There is no condemnation to them, that are in Christ," (Rom.8.1.) because no sin is imputed unto them. But unto Witches, and all the enemies of Christ, sin is imputed, and not abolished.

To conclude, howsoever much is said in their defence, yet the first part is clear affirmatively, that the Witches of our time, are the same with the Witches that were in Moses' time, in truth and substance.

Question. Whether the Witches of our age are to be punished with death, and that by virtue of this law of Moses?

I doubt not, but in this last age of the world, among us also, this sin of Witchcraft ought as sharply to be punished as in the former times; and all Witches being thoroughly convicted by the Magistrate, ought according to the Law of Moses to be put to death.

This Law of Moses flatly enjoyneth all men, in all ages, without limitation of circumstances, not to suffer the Witch to live; and hereupon I gather, that it must stand the same both now and for ever to the worlds end.

Patrons of Witches except against this, holding that it was a Judicial Law which continued but for a time, and concerned only the Nation of the Jews, and is now ceased. But I take the contrary to be the truth, and that upon these grounds.

Every Judicial Law, that hath in it the equity of the Law of nature, is perpetual; and this Law of punishing the Witch by death, is such. For it is a principle of the Law of nature, held for a grounded truth in all Countries and

Kingdoms, among all people in every age; that the traitor who is an enemy to the State, and rebelleth against his lawful Prince, should be put to death; now the most notorious traitor and rebel that can be, is the Witch. For she renounceth God himself, the King of Kings, she leaves the society of his Church and people, she bindeth herself in league with the devil: and therefore if any offender among men, ought to suffer death for his fact, much more ought she, and that of due desert.

The second reason for the proof of the point in hand is this: According to Moses' law, every Idolater was to be stoned to death: (Deut.17.ver.3,4,5.) "If there be found any among you, that hath gone and served other gods, as the Sun, the Moon, or any of the host of heaven: if the thing upon enquiring be found to be true and certain, thou shalt bring them forth unto thy gates, whether it be man or woman, and shalt stone them with stones till they die." Now this is the very case of a Witch, she renounceth the true God, and maketh choice to serve the devil, she is therefore a gross Idolater, and her punishment must be suitable.

The third reason. Every Seducer in the Church, whose practise was to draw men from the true God to the worship of Idols, though it were a man's own son or daughter, wife or friend, by the peremptory decree and commandment of God, was at no hand to be spared or pitied, but the hand of the witness first, and then the hands of all the people must be upon him, to kill him. (Deut.13.6.9.) If this be so, no Witches convicted ought to escape the Sword of the Magistrate; for they are the most notorious seducers of all others. When they be once entangled with the Devil's league, they labour to inure their dearest friends and posterity, in their cursed and abominable practises: that they may be the more easily drawn into the same confederacy wherewith they themselves are united unto Satan.

I might here allege that they deserve death because many of them be murderers, but I stand not upon that instance, because I hold in the general that Witches are not to be suffered to live, though they do no hurt either to man or other creatures, and that by virtue of Moses' law, only for their league's Sake, whereby they become rebels to God, Idolaters and Seducers, as now hath been shown. Yet notwithstanding all that hath been said, many things are brought in defence of them, by such as be their friends and well wishers.

First, it is said, that the hurt that is done comes not from the Witch, but from the devil; he deserves the balm because it is his work, and she is not to die for his sin.

Answer. Let it be granted that the Witch is not the author of the evil that is done, yet she is a confederate and partner with the devil in the fact, and so the law takes hold on her. See it in a familiar comparison. A company of men conspire together in a robbery, by common consent some stand in open place to spy the booty, and to give the watchword, others are set about the passage, to rush upon the man, and to rob him of his goods. In this case what saith the law? The Parties that gave the watchword, though they did nothing to the man, yet being accessories and abettors to the robbery by consent, they are thieves, and liable to condemnation and execution, as well as the principals. Even so stands the case with the Witch. In the workings of wonders, and in all mischievous practises, he or she is partaker with the devil by consent of covenant: the Witch only uses the watchword in some charm or otherwise, and doth no more; the devil upon notice given by the Charm, takes his opportunity, and works the mischief. He is the principal agent, but the other gave help, and is rightly liable to punishment.

Again, they object, that Witches convicted either repent, or repent not: If they repent, then God pardoneth their sin and why should not the Magistrate as well save their bodies, and let them live, as God doth their souls? If they do not repent, then it is a dangerous thing for the Magistrate to put them to death: for by this means he kills the body, and casts the soul to hell.

Answer. All Witches judicially and lawfully convicted, ought to have space of repentance granted unto them, wherein they may be instructed and exhorted, and then afterward executed. For it is possible for them to be saved by God's mercy, though they have denied him. Secondly, the Magistrate must execute justice upon Malefactors lawfully convicted, whether they repent or not. For God approves the just execution of judgment upon men without respect to their repentance, neither must their impenitence hinder the execution of Justice. When the people of Israel had committed Idolatry in worshipping the Golden Calf, Moses did not expect their repentance, and in the meanwhile forbade the punishment, but he and the Levites presently took their swords and slew them, and the Lord approved their course of proceeding, (Exod.32.28).

And whereas they say that by executing an impenitent Witch, the Magistrate casteth away the soul; we must know that the end of execution by the Magistrate is not the damnation of the malefactor's soul, but that sin may be punished that others may beware of the like crimes and offences, and that the wicked might be taken away from among God's people.

But some Witches there be that cannot be convicted of killing any: what shall become of them?

Answer. As the killing Witch must die by another law, though he were no

Witch: so the healing and harmless Witch must die by this Law, though he kill not, only for the covenant made with Satan. For this must always be remembered as a conclusion, that by Witches we understand not only those which kill and torment; but all Diviners, Charmers, Jugglers, all Wizzards commonly called wise-men and wise-women; yea, whosoever do anything (knowing what they do) which cannnot be effected by nature or art; and in the same number we reckon all good Witches, which do no hurt but good, which do not spoil and destroy, but save and deliver. All these come under this sentence of Moses, because they deny God and are confederates with Satan. By the laws of England, the thief is executed for stealing, and we think it just and profitable; but it were a thousand times better for the land, if all Witches, but especially the blessing witch, might suffer death. For the thief by his stealing, and the hurtful Enchanter by charming, bring hindrance and hurt to the bodies and goods of men; but these are the right hand of the Devil, by which he takes and destroys the Souls of men. Men do most commonly hate and spit at the damnifying Sorcerer, as unworthy to live among them; whereas the other is so dear unto them, that they hold themselves and their country blessed, that have him among them; they fly unto him in necessity, they depend upon him as their God, and by this means thousands are carried away to their final confusion. Death therefore is the just and deserved portion of the good Witch.

William Perkins.
1602.

how a witch served a fellow in an alehouse

Anonymous

Few written records better illustrate the prejudice and intolerance that began to rage against all suspected of witchcraft in the early years of King James's reign than the pamphlet on the Royston witch Joan Harrison. Here are crystallized all the familiar elements of malice directed against an ugly old woman who, for no other crime than having addressed herself to a drunk in a public house, is accused of witchcraft and hurried to the gallows.

Although Royston, where the event occurred, was on the border between Essex and the neighboring county of Hertfordshire (and the trial was held in the town of Hertford), it was known throughout Essex and was similar in many respects to several Essex prosecutions of this period that are not so graphically recorded. For instance, only the indictment still exists in the case against John Banckes, of Newport, who allegedly bewitched to death the daughter of a neighbor, Henry Nicholls, because she spurned his advances (1603). A similar document four years later accuses Blanche Worman, of Moulsham in Chelmsford, of bewitching two men and three women to death "all of them being decrepit, but carried off too soon to their Maker by this Witch." Both Banckes and Worman were found guilty and hanged.

Joan Harrison, the woman in the Royston case, was an elderly widow who lived in a tumbledown cottage on the outskirts of the small farming community. It was said that she kept ointments and potions that could cure all manner of illness, but at the trial no one could produce any evidence of ever having seen the widow using them. The complaint laid against her followed an encounter in a public house, and her trial was held in August 1606 at the Hertford summer sessions.

The case was recorded in an anonymous little pamphlet printed in London a few days after the trial by William Firebrand. It is written in a light and easy manner unlike the heavy-handed, moralistic style that was then so popular; but for all this there is no disguising the bigotry and prejudice it reveals.

There was an honest fellow, and as boon a companion dwelling in Royston, one that loved the pot with the long neck almost as well as his prayers. For (quoth he) as I know one is medicinable for the soul, I am sure the other's physic for the body.

It was this Fuddle-cap's chance with three or four as good malt-worms as himself, and as sure, where the best lap was to be found, together as four knaves in a pack of cards, to be drinking, when this Witch came in and stood gloating upon them.

Now this good fellow (not enduring to look upon a bad face, but his own especially when he is cup-shot) called aloud to her, "Do you hear, Witch, look the other way, I cannot abide a nose of that fashion, or else turn your face the wrong side outward, it may look like raw flesh to blow maggots in."

Still as the Witch was ready to reply, he would cross her with one scurvy jest, and between every jest drink to her, yet swear, God damn him, she should starve ere she should have a drop of it, since the pot was sweet he'd keep it so, for should but her lips once look into the lid on it, her breath's so strong, and would so stick in the cup, that all the water that runs in the river would not wash it out again.

At last the Witch got so much time to call to him, "Dost thou hear good friend?" (quoth she).

"What sayest thou ill-face?" (quoth he).

"Listen I say" (quoth she) "that thou throwest in thy drink apace, but shall not find it so easy coming out."

"Nay, as for the coming out" (answered the fellow) "I throwed it in above, and it shall come out beneath, and then thou shalt have some of it, if thou wilt, because I am in hope it will poison thee."

Then with this greeting, away goes the Witch in a chafe and the fellow sits down to follow his drink, but as the end of all drunkards is either to piss or to sleep.

So out goes this fellow, and drawing his Gentleman Usher against a fence side, finds on top of his nose a red lump as big as a cherry. And in his belly felt such a rumbling, as if the Tower of Babel had fallen about his ears.

Oh! the sight thereof drove his heart to an ague, and his tongue to an alarm, and out he cries, "The Witch! The Witch! I am undone! I am undone! Oh God, men of Royston, help, help. The Witch! The Witch! I am a man spoiled, help, I am undone."

At the words, "Help! The Witch!" out comes one of his fellows, running in haste, and asking him what they should help, the witch?

"Oh!" (quoth he) "to the gallows, for I am undone by her."

Well, yet out he runs for that night she could not be found. But the next morning meeting her in a lane, his pain rather increased than lessened, and there he fatened his ten commandments on her.

He almost scratched out her eyes. Nay, left her not till he brought her to the town, where for this and the rest she was apprehended.

And she was brought before the justice, and the story given, and she worthily suffered death on the gallows the 4 of August.

a child possessed by the devil

Anonymous

King James, as mentioned earlier, began his reign as a confirmed believer in witches and witchcraft, yet ended it as just as firm a skeptic. Several elements led to this change of heart, and it is to the king's credit that he allowed himself to be persuaded that his initial hysteria was ill founded.

The first seeds of unease were undoubtedly sown in the second decade of the seventeenth century when several cases collapsed because witnesses either contradicted each other or broke down under examination and admitted they were lying. The king became personally interested in such instances and either called for reports of the proceedings or examined the witnesses himself. He was particularly concerned where children appeared as the main witnesses, and in 1618 he interposed in the notorious case of John Smith, a Leicestershire child who had already condemned nine witches to the gallows and was busy accusing more. The king found the evidence inconclusive and the boy vindictive and untrustworthy; he dismissed the accusations and stopped the trial.

In 1621 another similar case came to the king's attention, and several authorities have asserted that this event, more than any other, finally severed his belief in the probability of witchcraft. More amazing still, this case came from Essex, the county that had so eagerly supported his early zeal in both word and action. The case concerned a young girl, Katherine Malpas, from Westham (now West Ham), who claimed to be possessed by the devil and allowed herself to be visited by people who took pity on her and made donations for her "relief." It was shown eventually that the whole thing was a tissue of lies invented by the girl's mother to make money and that the accusations against two old women who were said to have bewitched the girl were without any foundation whatsoever.

So fascinated was the king by the case that he summoned Katherine Malpas and her family to his residence in Hertfordshire and there examined her himself. There is no record that any punishment was inflicted on either the child or her parents once the deceit was revealed.

According to Dr. Thomas Fuller, this case was the final straw for the king. "The frequency of forged possessions wrought such an alteration upon the judgment of King James," he wrote, "that he finally grew diffident of, and then flatly to deny, the workings of witches and devils as but falsehoods and delusions." This is reflected by the fact that in the last nine years of King James's reign, only five people were executed for witchcraft. It is only to be regretted that his change of heart did not spur him to remove from the statute books the savage witchcraft laws he had enacted.

Unfortunately, no complete contemporary account of the bizarre Royston case exists, but the noted witchcraft expert C. L'Estrange Ewen has paraphrased it in his work *Witchcraft in the Star Chamber* (1933), and this is quoted here.

A bill of the Attorney-General (Sir Thomas Coventry), endorsed on 11th February 1622 alleges that, notwithstanding the laws against deceit, Thomas Saunders of Upton in the parish of Westham, Essex, and Elizabeth, his wife, and Katherine Malpas, her elder daughter, wife of John Malpas of St. Mary Maudlin, near Old Fish Street, London on December 18th 1621, procured Katherine Malpas, younger daughter of the said Katherine Malpas and grandchild of Thomas and Elizabeth, to counterfeit herself to be bewitched and possessed with an evil spirit, and to feign strange fits and trances, etc., so that people would be drawn to the house and money be given in pity, etc.

They procured preachers to pray with the said Katherine Malpas the younger, and that the fits and trances might be more colourable and appear to be the work of witches, they directed her to fling away bibles and prayer books etc., whereby it might be thought that some evil spirit possessed her and hindered her devotions.

Having conceived malice towards Goodwives Hedlyn and White, and to cause them to be taken for witches, they also persuaded Katherine their grandchild to accuse them, and accordingly she declared that they appeared to her in the shape of cats and dogs. They also endeavoured to make one Anne Godfrey believe that her illness resulted from the witchcraft of Goodwife Hedlyn, and persuaded her likewise to perform tricks and fits.

Thomas Saunders, sworn on 18th February 1622, denied the charge saying that a licence having been procured from the Lord Bishop of London's Chancellor for preachers, Mr. Jennings, vicar of Westham, and Master Holbrooke, the preacher there, came to see the young girl, and read "divers godlie and comfortable prayers."

Elizabeth Saunders, in her answer sworn on 19th May 1622 admitted the truth of the accusation, taking the whole blame. She explained that desiring to obtain money for the keep of Katherine Malpas the younger, she taught her various tricks, and in three weeks or so she became expert in heaving up her stomach, writhing her hands, making her backbones crackle, leaping and skipping, and such 'antic gestures'.

More particularly she "would have a rising up in her stomach to the bignes of a halfe penny loafe and woulde beat her heade against the wainscotte and would shrugge up her shoulders and woulde make her bones to crackle within her skin and some tymes her mouth would be drawne on one side."

Further, without receiving instruction, "she would beat the walls of her roome where she laye and would call upon her neyghbors and crye out 'Gammer Dawes bringe hether a sallet for puffene and Elias.' " Both she and Anne Godfrey used a squeaking voice.

Thomas Saunders, knowing nothing of the deception, employed one Dr. Francklin of Ratcliffe, and one Gouldman. To Francklin a dealer in "sawcerie," he gave 20s., whereupon one said: "God's bread, Tom Saunders, whie wouldest thou give this fellowe money being thou knowest shee counterfeites?"

There being no decree issued, the said Elizabeth Saunders was taken to Theobald's Manor, Herts., the royal residence, to be examined by His Majesty, King James, at his command, and he was much affected in his views by the admission of deception on the part of the child and her parents.

a poem of witchcraft

by Sir Francis Hubert

From the end of King James's reign, with his change of heart, and throughout much of the reign of Charles I (1625–1649), the number of prosecutions for witchcraft dropped noticeably in both Essex and England as a whole. Predictably, there were the occasional cases of old women brought to trial for bewitching cattle or old men charged with conjuring, but for the most part a climate of rationality seemed to have settled over the country.

Unfortunately, this was not to be a permanent state, for the most terrible era of all—that of Matthew Hopkins and the witch finders—was almost on the horizon. During Charles's reign only one specific study of witchcraft was published, Richard Bernard's *Guide to Grand-Jurymen in Cases of Witchcraft* (1627). This work attempted to reflect all shades of opinion, and although it is not much consulted today, it does demonstrate the questioning attitude of the time toward devilry and superstition.

In fiction, however, the supernatural was slowly starting to attract the attention of writers, and several books of the time include it as a feature of the plot or an incidental. One such use is to be found in the work of an Essex scholar and poet, Sir Francis Hubert. Hubert, who had begun writing during Queen Elizabeth's reign, was a freethinker by nature. His open questioning of various topics, including witchcraft, had resulted in the banning of much of his work until the closing years of his life. Born in 1568, he was the son of a family of wealthy landowners in Birchanger near Maldon. As a very young man he followed the pursuits of his station by hunting, hawking, and gambling voraciously. In 1584, at the tender age of 15, he matriculated at Oxford.

In 1587, Francis qualified as a lawyer in London, but in 1590 he left the capital and returned to Essex to avoid the plague, which had just broken out. There he married and quietly began to compose poetry and raise a family. Despite the earnestness and sincerity of his prose, he suffered in company with numerous other poets, authors, and playwrights of the time in having his work banned by Queen Elizabeth, who felt that the slightest spark of freethinking might ignite civil unrest.

Francis's father, a clever and ambitious man, had steadily increased his holdings in Essex by astute buying and had bought the manor of Stansted Mountfichet as an inheritance for his son so that he might become a nobleman. In 1602, following the death of his father, Sir Francis (as he now was) became embroiled in a number of business transactions, all of which proved disastrous, and he was forced to sell much of his property in Essex to pay off his debts. He spent the remainder of his life in retirement, writing prose occasionally and assisting in the publication of what little of his work was permitted to appear before the public.

On his death in 1629 it was learned that only two of his major prose poems, *Egypt's Favourite* and *The Historie of Edward II* (which Elizabeth had specifically banned) had survived. In the second of these he displays his personal knowledge of witchcraft. The following verses have been extracted from the *Historie* and superbly reflect the author, his attitude, and the times. They are also unique as the only piece of poetry written specifically about Essex witchcraft during the entire period of our study.

> Witchcraft may work upon the Body much
> But there's no fascination of the mind.

The Soule is free from any Magic touch,
  Nor can inchanting charmes loose or bind
The powers and faculties thereto assign'd.
    Spirits may suggest, they may persuade to ill,
    But all their power cannot compell the will.

It is the sole Prerogative of Heaven,
  'Tis Gods peculiar command to the heart.
That damned Imposter had his power given
  From the most high ere he with all his Art
Could work on him in whom he had most part.
    Seduced by *Ahab* falls by his persuasion,
    But it is God that first grants the Commission.

The Prince of Darkness may corrupt the brain
  And so work strongly upon the imagination,
Which being abused oft becomes most vain
  In the conceiting a strange transmutation
Of its own self into some wolvish fashion,
    Which is no other (As our Doctors say)
    Than the disease called Lycantropia.

He may (and doth oft times) delude the sight
  By offering strange Phantasmacs to our Eyes,
And then the Judgement is perverted quite
  When 'tis seduced by such erronious Spies
As brings us no Intelligence but lyes.
    A thousand like devises he hath got
    To make us think he doth what he doth not.

Besides, when any Error is committed
  Whereby we may incur of loss or shame
That we ourselves thereof may be acquitted
  We are too ready to transfer the blame
Upon some Witch: That made us do the same.
    It is the vulgar Plea that weak ones use:
    I was bewitched: I could nor will: nor choose.

the witches' meeting

by Martha Hurrell

The conditions and attitudes that culminated in the bloody civil war in England in 1645 have been so widely and fully discussed that they need no more than passing mention here. Basically, the king's "divine right" to rule the country came into conflict with the rights of Parliament, which sought to govern by legal right rather than by favor. Also, the Catholicism of the king and his nobleman clashed strongly with the Puritanism of many of the lower-class people. Consequently, as the two sides drew further apart and the king attempted to overrule all that Parliament did, civil war became inevitable.

After some indecisive campaigns, the Puritan leader Oliver Cromwell won two major victories at Marston Moor and Naseby and King Charles surrendered.

Barely had the Puritans time to effect control of the state, however, before Charles escaped from prison and the second phase of the war began. This quickly failed, however, and when Charles was recaptured, he was swiftly charged with treason and beheaded in 1649. The "Puritan Revolution" went far in ensuring a fair government for all the people establishing a better climate of religious tolerance. But it also generated the intractible attitudes toward good and evil, the devil and God, that were again to set alight the fires of witchcraft hysteria, culminating with the rise of Matthew Hopkins and the witchfinders.

Before we come to Hopkins, however, there is another instance that reveals an aspect of witchcraft in Essex that we have not so far encountered. It shows that witchcraft was not considered solely the prerogative of poor and simple-minded old men and women (ignoring for the moment the fact that many of them were innocent of the charges brought against them) and that there were among the nobility and the wealthy those who actually sought out witchcraft and sorcery for personal gain or as a new pleasure for their perverted tastes.

"Superstition was rife from the highest circles downwards," C. L'Estrange Ewen has commented in his *Witch Hunting and Witch Trials*, "and many noble dames consulted the wizards and astrologers, or even themselves dabbled in the forbidden arts. Necromancy, heresy and treason were largely bound up with one another, and an accusation of witchcraft or heterodoxy often served to remove a hated opponent in a political sphere. The public records name numerous great personages who were accused officially and unofficially of using sorcery to attain their desire."

The most famous of these people at the period of this study was Robert Devereux, the Third Earl of Essex, who was the subject of a famous divorce action brought against him by his wife in 1613. During the case the countess accused her husband of practicing witchcraft and said that because of this he had become impotent and unable to consummate the marriage. An account of this fascinating action, complete with its undertones of witchcraft, is to be found in *State Trials*, Volume II.

A less important, though perhaps more fascinating, case concerns a group of Essex men and women who were said to meet together for "conjuration, lechery and magic." The background to the accusation is a little obscure, but the allegations were made in the form of a deposition by a servant, Martha Hurrell, to the Chelmsford magistrates in 1645. The document is now lodged in the Essex records office and further inquiries have failed to discover whether the practitioners were brought to trial. Nonetheless, it is a remarkable story, and students of witchcraft will note the similarities between what the group is said to have done and practices of modern black-magic devotees.

Martha Hurrell deposes that, between Easter and Michaelmas 1643, being the last summer but one, those that she now names did meet together for the purpose of conjuration, lechery and magic.

They were Robert and Thomas Aylett, James Richardson, Sarah Fletcher, Abraham Rich, John Drake, John Dier, William Drake and his wife, all of Stisted, three men servants and two maids from the family of Sir William Maxie, Lambert Smith, Ellen Warren, Elizabeth Waite and Edward Mott, all of Bocking and "a conjuror that went in black apparrel with brown hair and blackish beard."

During this time she sayeth they had two meetings at her master's house, half a score at William Drake's and also at Sir William Maxie's house, and my Lady Eden's and Sir Robert Lumley's once or twice.

She said that these meetings were always in the night and when they met they went into the bed chambers of those persons at whose house they met. When they were at her (Hurrell's) house, they took Mistress Drurie out of her bed and carried her into the hall chamber and there the Conjuror and others had the use of her body.

And they fetched her (Hurrell's) husband and laid him by her and then Elizabeth Waite and Sarah Fletcher kissed him and pulled up his shirt, and took up their coats, and lay down on top of him, and they said that he did them some good.

And further she saith that Sir William Maxie's servants did conjure by making a circle in her master's hall, and setting up three candles which burned blue, and when they put them out they did it with milk and soot.

She said that they also feasted and had fiddlers from Coggeshall, and Sir William Maxie's maid played on the virginals. Also that she took a bushel of wheat out of the malt chamber and give it to one Robert Wibrook and Elizabeth Waite also stole two bushels of malt and sent to young Samuel's to be brewed for a merry meeting.

She finally saith that they rode in Sir William Maxie's coach to the meetings and all of high and low order mingled together.

the labors of satan

The Witch Trial of 1645
Anonymous

In 1645, onto the stage of witchcraft persecution came perhaps the
most notorious name in the whole history of demonology, the
self-styled Witch Finder General, Matthew Hopkins. This small,
hard-eyed, ruthless man blazoned his name and reputation across
England in a matter of a few months and became the most hated and
feared man throughout the eastern counties. "In fourteen months,"
remarks one modern commentator, Wallace Notestein, "he sent to the
gallows more witches than all the other witch hunters hung in the 160
years during which this persecution flourished in England."

Hopkins was utterly dedicated to his task; he used fear and torture to
get confessions and suffered not a seemingly quirk of conscience for all
his bloodletting and cruelty. We shall come to personal details about
the man in the next section, when we deal with his writing, but here
we are more concerned with the climate that allowed him freedom for
such unbridled savagery.

Essex had, of course, its traditional reputation of the "witch county"
and shared with the other eastern counties a fervent support of
Cromwell and the Roundheads and a burning desire to rout out heresy.
With the uncertainty of the war during its early months, everyone was
on the lookout for subversives—and who could be more subversive

than a witch? Of course, witches were easier to find than supporters of the king, so the climate was ideal for someone like Hopkins to point the finger of accusation at any poor old soul who happened to cross his path. This was the manner in which he addressed himself to his self-appointed task, and in March 1645 he began his work by seizing a one-legged old woman named Elizabeth Clarke and torturing her for information—taking particular care not to leave any tell-tale marks on her body. Soon he had incriminating evidence not only against Mother Clarke, but also against six of her friends.

At this point another single-minded despot named John Stearne joined Hopkins to help him in his examinations, and soon the two men had gathered thirty-two suspects to parade before the court in Chelmsford in July. Hopkins believed the most important evidence that could be presented against a witch was that she kept familiars and that she suckled them by way of a witch mark to be found somewhere on her body. (He had learned this from King James's *Demonology*, the book the unfortunate king came to disown at the end of his life.)

The remarkable prosecution of Elizabeth Clarke was carefully documented by a pamphlet writer. About half a dozen original copies of the pamphlet survive. It is here reprinted in full, portraying what is without doubt both the most savage of Hopkins's forays and one of the worst witch trials of the seventeenth century. At the end of the proceedings, nineteen of the accused were hanged, five were found guilty but reprieved, and eight were remanded to the next assizes. Of these, only one was found not guilty.

A True and Exact Relation of the several Informations, Examinations and Confessions of the late Witches, arraigned and executed in the County of Essex; who were arraigned and condemned at the late sessions, holden in Chelmsford, before the right hon. Robert, Earl of Warwick, and several of his majesty's justices of the peace, the 29th July A.D. 1645. Wherein the several murders, and devilish witchcrafts, committed on the bodies of men, women and children and divers cattle, are fully discovered. Published by authority. London, printed by M.S. for Henry Overton and Benj. Allen, and are to be sold at their shops in Pope's-head-alley. 1645.

THE PREFACE

Ingenuous reader, thou has here presented to thee a sad emblem of the strange sleights and cunning subtilties, whereby Satan labours to ensnare souls, and at last to bring them to utter ruin; who being that grand impostor, soon began this work, even in the morning of the creation, in the body of a serpent miraculously, to reason, dispute, speake and conferre with Adam and Eve; and never ceased till he had laid the honour of those glorious creatures in the dust: and therefore is called that old serpent, that deceiveth all the world, by whose deceitful promises and subtle devices, for his own end, and desire of their destruction, hath ensnared and drawn these poor silly creatures, into these horrid and detestable practices of renouncing God and Christ, and entering into a solemn league and contract with the Devil: the thought whereof is sufficient to cause a man to be filled with horror and astonishment. The law and expresse command of God doth allow of no familiarity or inquiry of any other spirit, but from himself; as Isaiah, Chapter 8.19. 'And when they shall say unto you, seek ye unto them that have familiar spirits, and unto wizards that peep and that mutter, should not a people seeke unto their God,' &c. Under this interrogative is understood this affirmative, a people should inquire of no other spirit, but of their God only. By which also it is evident, that all spirits that do suffer themselves to be inquired at, are evill spirits, and therefore devills. And although these devillish practises were frequent and common amongst heathens and infidels who usually held familiarity with these spirits, and many inquired of them in their oracles; and therefore called those spirits that gave answer by them, Daemons, of their skill and knowledge in foretelling things to come: yet now when the light of the gospel shineth so gloriously, that such a generation of poor deluded soules, and to such a number as hath of late been discovered should be found amongst us, is much more matter of admiration and astonishment. I doubt not but these things may seem as incredible unto some, as they are matter of admiration to others. *Nolle nimis sapere*, saith the poet, it is true wisdom not to be too wise; that is not to know or desire to know more than is allowed or needfull; needfull not in our desires, but in Gods decree: Here then let reasonable men be persuaded not too much, as is usual to swell with indignation, or to be puffed with impatience, where God doth not appertly reveal and plainly, as they desire and thinke needfull the subtile engines and mysticall craft of the devill in the machinations of witches and sorcerers; but soberly, modestly, and discreetly so far forth be contented to pursue the triall and just way of their discoverie, as with sense, with reason, with religion, is just and righteous; knowing that whatsoever is beyond these lists, is reasonlesse, senseless and impious.

The Information of John Rivet, of Mannintree, Taylor, taken before Sir Harbottell Grimston, Knight and Baronet, one of the Members of the Honourable House of Commons; and Sir Thomas Bowes, Knight, another of his Majesties Justices of Peace for this County, the 21th of March, 1645.

This informant saith, That about Christmas last, his wife was taken sicke and lame, with such violent fits, that this informant verily conceived her sicknesse was something more than meerly naturall: whereupon this informant, about fortnight since, went to a cunning woman, the wife of one Hovye, at Hadleigh in Suffolke, who told this informant, that his wife was cursed by two women who were neer neighbours to this informant, the one dwelling a little above his house, and the other beneath his house, this informant's house standing on the side of an hill: whereupon he beleeved his said wife was bewitched by one Elizabeth Clarke, alias Bedingfield, that dwelt above this informant's house, for that the said Elizabeth's mother and some other of her kinsfolke did suffer death for witchcraft and murther.

The Information of Matthew Hopkins, of Mannintree, Gent, taken upon oath before us, the 25th day of March, 1645.

This informant saith, That the said Elizabeth Clarke (suspected for a witch as aforesaid) being by the appointment of the said justices watched certaine nights, for the better discovery of her wicked practises, this informant came into the roome where the said Elizabeth was watched, as aforesaid, the last night, being the 24th of this instant March, but intended not to have stayed long there. But the said Elizabeth forthwith told this informant and one Master Sterne there present, if they would stay and do the said Elizabeth no hurt, shee would call one of her white imps, and play with it in her lap; but this informant told her, they would not allow of it: and that staying there a while longer, the said Elizabeth confessed she had had carnall copulation with the Devill six or seven years; and that he would appeare to her three or foure times in a weeke at her bed side, and goe to bed to her, and lye with her halfe a night together in the shape of a proper gentleman, with a laced band, having the whole proportion of a man, and would say to her, 'Besse, I must lye with you;' and she did never deny him: and within a quarter of an houre after there appeared an impe like to a dog, which was white, with some sandy spots, and seemed to be very fat and plumpe, with very short legges, who forthwith vanished away: and the said Elizabeth said the name of that impe was Jarmara: and immediately there appeared another impe, which shee called Vinegar Tom, in the shape of a greyhound with long legges: and the said Elizabeth then said that the next impe should be a black impe, and should come for the said Master Sterne, which appeared, but presently vanished: and the last that appeared was in the shape of a polcat, but the head somewhat bigger. And the said Elizabeth then told this informant that shee had five impes of her owne, and two of the impes of the old beldam Weste (meaning one Anne Weste, widow) who is now also suspected to be guilty of witchcraft; and said, sometimes the impes of the old beldam sucked on the said Elizabeth, and sometimes her impes sucked on the old beldam Weste. And the said Elizabeth further told this informant, that Satan would never let her rest, or be quiet, untill shee did consent to the killing of the hogges of one Mr. Edwards of Mannintree aforesaid, and the horse of one Robert Tayler of the same towne. And this informant further saith, That going from the house of the said Mr. Edwards to his own house, about nine or ten of the clock that night, with his greyhound with him, he saw the greyhound suddenly give a jumpe, and ran as shee had been in a full course after an hare; and that when this informant made haste to see what his greyhound so eagerly pursued, he espied a white thing about the bignesse of a kitlyn, and the greyhound standing aloofe from it; and that by and by the said white impe or kitlyn daunced about the said greyhound, and by all likelihood bit off a piece of the flesh of the shoulder of the said greyhound; for the greyhound came shrieking and crying to this informant, with a piece of flesh torne from her shoulder. And this informant further saith, That coming into his own yard that night, he espied a black thing, proportioned like a cat, onely it was thrice as big, sitting on a strawberry bed, and fixing the eyes on this informant; and when he went towards it, it leaped over the pale towards this informant, as he thought, but ran quite through the yard, with his greyhound after it, to a great gate, which was underset with a paire of tumbrell strings, and did throw the said gate wide open, and then vanished; and the said greyhound returned againe to this informant, shaking and trembling exceedingly.

The Information of John Sterne, Gent. taken upon oath before us, the 25th day of March 1645.

This informant saith, That watching with Elizabeth Clarke, (suspected of witchcraft, as aforesaid) shee confessed that the Devill had had carnall copulation with her in the likenesse of a man; and that the said Elizabeth desired this informant, and the rest that were in the roome with her, to sit downe, and said, shee would shew this informant and the rest some of her impes: and within halfe an houre there appeared a white thing in the likeness of a cat, but not altogether so big: and being asked, if she would not be afraid of her impes, the said Elizabeth answered, 'What, do yee think I am afraid of my children?' And that shee called the name of that white impe, Hoult. And this informant further saith, That presently after there appeared another white impe, with red spots, as big as a small dog, which shee then called Jarmara: and that immediately after, there appeared at the threshold of the doore another impe about the bignesse of the first, but did presently vanish away. And then the said Elizabeth being asked, if any more impes would come? she answered, 'That Vinegar Tom would come by and by.' And forthwith there appeared another in the likenesse of a dumb dogge, somewhat bigger than any of the former. And the said Elizabeth also told this informant, that shee had three impes from her mother, which were of a browne colour, and two from the old beldam Weste: and that there had five impes appeared; but shee had one more, called Sack and Sugar, which had been hard at worke, and it would be long before it came, but it should teare this informant. And a while after, the said Elizabeth said, That it was well for this informant he was so quick, otherwise the said impe had soone skipped upon his face, and perchance had got into his throate, and then there would have been a feast of toades in this informant's belly. And the said Elizabeth further confessed to this informant, that shee had one impe for which she would fight up to the knees in bloud, before shee would lose it; and that her impes did commonly suck on the old beldam Weste, and that the said old beldam's impes did suck on her the said Elizabeth likewise.

The Information of Frances Milles, Grace Norman, Mary Phillips, and Mary Parsley, taken upon oath before the said Justices, the 25th of March, A. D. 1645.

These informants say jointly, That watching with the said Elizabeth Clarke, suspected as aforesaid, about twelve of the clock last night, the said Elizabeth smacked with her mouth, and beckned with her hand, and instantly there appeared a white thing about the bignesse of a cat; and that these informants saw five impes more, which the said Elizabeth named as aforesaid; and that the said Elizabeth told these informants, that the old beldam (meaning the said Anne Weste) did by witchcraft kill the wife of one Robert Oakes, of Lawford in the county aforesaid, and was the death of a clothier's childe of Dedham in the said county of Essex; both which dyed, as these informants very well know, about a weeke since. And the said Elizabeth told these informants, that the said old beldam Weste had the wife of one William Cole, of Mannintree aforesaid, in handling, who dyed not long since of a pining and languishing disease.

The Information of George Turner, taken upon oath, the 25th day of March, 1645, before the said Justices.

This informant saith, That going to the said Elizabeth Clarke alias Bedingfield, after shee was apprehended, and asking her whether shee had any hand in the drowning of one Thomas Turner, this informant's brother, who was cast away at sea about thirty moneths since; the said Elizabeth answered, That the old beldam Weste raised that winde that sunke his hoy: And that she the said Elizabeth had no hand in that businesse.

The Information of John Bankes of Mannintree, taken upon oath before the said Justices the 25th of March, 1645.

This informant saith, That watching with the said Elizabeth, he doth informe and confirme all the particulars expressed and set downe in the information of the said Mr. Sterne.

The Information of Edward Parsley of Mannintree, taken upon oath before the said Justices the 25th of March, 1645.

This informant saith, That watching with the said Elizabeth Clarke, alias Bedingfield, the last night, he asked the said Elizabeth if he should continue still in the roome with her; And the said Elizabeth desired he should, if he would fight for her with the Devills, for they would come this night, and that which shee called Hoult would come first, and then that which shee called Jarmara; which did appeare in the likenesse of a white dogge, with red spots; and presently after there appeared that impe which shee called Vinegar Tom; and then that which shee called Sack and Sugar: And the said Elizabeth then told this informant, that the Devill had had possession of her six or seven yeares. And that he had oftentimes knocked at her dore in the night time; and that shee did arise, open the dore and let him in; and that he went to bed to her three or foure times in a weeke, and had the carnall knowledge of her as a man.

The Examination of the said Elizabeth Clarke, alias Bedingfield, taken before the said Justices the 25th of March, 1645.

This examinant saith, That about six moneths since shee met with the said Anne Weste, widow, (who is now likewise apprehended) in a field neere the house of the said Elizabeth, where the said Elizabeth was picking up a few sticks; The said Anne Weste seemed much to pitie this examinant for her lamenesse (having but one leg) and her poverty; And said to this examinant, That there was wayes and meanes for her to live much better then now shee did: And said, that shee would send to this examinant a thing like a little kitlyn, which would fetch home some victualls for this examinant; and that it should doe her no hurt. And this examinant saith, that within two or three nights after there came a white thing to her in the night, and the night after a gray one, which spake to this examinant, and told her they would doe her no hurt, but would helpe her to an husband, who should maintaine her ever after: And that these two things came into this examinant's bed every night, or every other night, and sucked upon the lower parts of her body.

The Information of Robert Tayler of Mannintree, taken upon oath before the said Justices the 23rd of Aprill, 1645.

This informant saith, That about nine weekes since, Elizabeth, the wife of Edward Gooding (who is accused by the said Elizabeth Clarke to be a confederate with her) came to the shop of this informant, and desired to be trusted for half a pound of cheese, which being denyed, shee went away, muttering and mumbling to her self, and within a few houres came again with money, and bought a pound of cheese of this informant, and the same night this informant having an horse standing in his stable, the said horse was taken in a strange manner sick and lame; whereupon this informant sent for four farriers to have their best advice, who could not discover the cause of the disease; but the said horse about foure dayes after died: And this informant also saith, that it was observed by himself, and divers others who often went to see the said horse, that still upon their coming into the stable, he lay quiet, and looked cheerfully, but as soon as the door was shut, and the horse alone, hee did violently beat himself, and that the belly of the said horse would rumble and make a noyse, as a foule chimney set on fire: And this informant further saith, that hee is induced to believe, that the said Elizabeth Gooding was the cause of the death of his said horse; for that this informant hath heard, that Elizabeth Clarke and Anne Leech widow, (who stand both accused for Witchcraft, and have confessed themselves guilty) have impeached the said Elizabeth Gooding for killing of this said horse, and that the said Elizabeth Gooding is a lewd woman, and to this informant's knowledge, hath kept company with the said Elizabeth Clarke, Anne Leech, and Anne West, which Anne West hath been suspected for a witch many yeers since, and suffered imprisonment for the same.

The Examination of Elizabeth Gooding, taken before the said Justices the 11th of Aprill, 1645.

This examinant saith, That shee is not guilty of any one particular charged upon her in the information of the said Robert Tayler.

The Information of Richard Edwards of Mannintree aforesaid, taken before the said Justices the 23rd day of April, 1645.

This informant saith, That about twelve moneths since, upon a Sabbath day, after the afternoon sermon, driving his cowes home by the house of Anne Leech of Misley, widow, about forty yards from her said house, a black cowe of this informant's, (being very well to his thinking) fell down, and within two dayes after died. And the very next day driving his cowes from the same pasture, this informant had a white cowe that fell down within a rod of the same place where the other cowe fell, (being also, as this informant conceived, sound and well) and within a weak after dyed; and hee further saith, that hee caused both the said cowes to be opened, and that there could be no disease discovered, which might occasion their death: And this informant likewise saith, that about August last hee had a childe nursed by one goodwife Wyles, dwelling neer the houses of the said Elizabeth Clark and Elizabeth Gooding, and that his said childe was taken sick, and had very strange fits, extending the limbs, and rowling the eyes, and within two dayes after dyed: And this informant doth verily believe, that Anne Leech and the said Elizabeth Gooding were the death of his said child, as is confessed by the said Anne Leech in her own Confession and Examination.

The Examination of Anne Leech of Misley in the county aforesaid, widow, taken before the said Justices, April 14, 1645.

This examinant saith, That she had a grey impe sent to her, and that this examinant, together with the said Elizabeth Clark, and Elizabeth the wife of Edward Gooding, did about a yeer since, send their imps to kill a black cowe and a white cowe of Mr. Edwards, which was done accordingly: And this examinant saith, that she sent her gray imp, Elizabeth Clark a black imp, and Elizabeth Gooding a white imp: And this examinant saith, that about thirty yeeres since, shee sent a gray imp to kill two horses of one Mr. Bragge of Misley, which were killed accordingly; and that the occasion of her malice was, because Mistresse Bragge had told this examinant, that shee suspected her to be a naughty woman; and this examinant confesseth, that she and the said Elizabeth Gooding, sent either of them an imp to destroy the childe of the said Mr. Edwards; this examinant's imp being then a white one, and Elizabeth Gooding's a black imp; and that about thirty yeers since, this examinant had the said white imp and two others, a grey and a black imp of one Anne, the wife of Robert Pearce of Stoak in Suffolk, being her brother; and that these imps went commonly from one to another, and did mischief where ever they went; and that when this examinant did not send and imploy them abroad to do mischief, she had not her health, but when they were imployed, she was healthfull and well, and that these imps did usually suck those teats which were found about the privie parts of her body; and that the said imps did often speak to this examinant, and told her, she should never feele hell torments, and that they spake to her in a hollow voyce, which she plainly understood: And this examinant also confesseth, that she sent her gray imp to Elizabeth, the daughter of Robert Kirk of Mannintree, about three yeers since, to destroy her; and upon the sending of the said imp, the said Elizabeth languished by the space of one whole yeer untill shee dyed, and that the occasion of offence this examinant took against her the said Elizabeth was, for that she had asked a coife of the said Elizabeth, which shee refused to give to this examinant. And further, this examinant saith, that long since, but the exact time she cannot remember, she sent her gray imp to kill the daughter of the widow Rawlyns of Misley aforesaid; and the reason was, because this examinant was put out of her farm, and the said widow Rawlyns put in, where shee dwelleth at this present. And moreover, this examinant confesseth, that she was acquainted with the sending of an imp by the aforesaid Elizabeth Gooding, to vex and torment Mary the wife of John Tayler of Mannintree aforesaid about three years since; and this examinant being asked why she did not discover it to the said Mary, she said, the Devill would not suffer her, and that the cause of the said Elizabeth Gooding's malice against the said Mary was, because the said Mary refused to give to the said Elizabeth some beere-good. And lastly, this examinant saith, that about eight weeks since, this examinant, the said Elizabeth Gooding, and one Anne West of Lawford widow, met together at the house of the said Elizabeth Clark, where there was a book read, wherein shee thinks there was no goodnesse.

The Information of Grace the wife of Richard Glascock of Mannintree, taken upon oath before the said Justices the 11th day of April, 1645.

This informant saith, that there being some falling out between Mary the wife of Edward Parsley of Mannintree, and one Hellen Clarke, the wife of Thomas Clarke (which said Hellen is the daughter of the said Anne Leech, whose confession doth immediately precede) this informant heard the said Hellen to say, as the said Hellen passed by this informants door in the street, that Mary the daughter of the said Edward and Mary Parsley should rue for all, whereupon presently the said Mary the daughter, fell sick, and died within six weeks after.

The Information of Edward Parsley of Mannintree, taken upon oath before the said Justices, April 11, 1645.

This informant saith, that his said daughter sickned very suddenly, as the said Grace Glascock hath before informed, and died about six weeks since; and this informant doth verily believe, the said Hellen Clark was the death of his said daughter.

The Examination of Hellen Clark, taken before the said Justices the 11th of April, 1645.
This examinant confesseth, that about six weeks since, the Devill appeared to her in her house, in the likenesse of a white dog, and that she calleth that familiar Elimanzer; and that this examinant hath often fed him with milk-pottage; and that the said familiar spake to this examinant audibly, and bade her deny Christ, and shee should never want, which shee did then assent unto, but doth altogether deny the killing of the daughter of the said Edward Parsley.

The Information of Prudence Hart, the wife of Thomas Hart of Lawford, taken upon oath before us the 13 of Aprill, 1645.
This informant saith, that about eight week since, being at her parish church, on the Sabbath day, half a mile distant from her house, and being about twenty weeks gone with childe, and to her thinking, very well and healthfull, upon the sudden shee was taken with great pains, and miscarried before shee could be got home; and this examinant saith, that about two moneths since, being in her bed, in the night, something fell down upon her right side, but being dark, she cannot tell in what shape it was: and that presently she was taken lame on that side, with extraordinary pains and burning, but recovered again within a few dayes after: and this informant further saith, that she verily believeth, that Rebecca West, and Anne West her mother, were the cause of her pains; for that the said Rebecca hath in part of her confession expressed, that she had much maliced this informant, because the said Rebecca West ever thought this informant to be her greatest enemy.

The Information of John Edes, Clerke, taken upon oath before the said Justices the 28th day of Aprill, 1645.
This informant saith, That Rebecca Weste confessed unto him, that about seven yeares since, shee began to have familiaritie with the Devil, by the instigation of her mother Anne Weste; who hath appeared unto the said Rebecca at severall times, in diverse shapes: at one time in the likenesse of a proper young man, who desired of her, that he might have the same familiaritie with her, that others that appeared unto her before had had:

promising that if shee would, he would then doe for the said Rebecca what she desired, and avenge her on her enemies; but required further, that shee would deny God, and relie upon him. Now there was one Thomas Hart of Lawford, where the said Rebecca lived, with her said mother, Anne West, and the said Rebecca told this informant, that shee required of him, that hee would avenge her on the said Hart by killing his son, who not long after was taken sick, and dyed, whereupon the said Rebecca told this informant, that she conceived hee could do as God; after which time she gave entertainment to him, who lay with her as a man; and the said Rebecca further confessed to this informant, that whilest she lived at Rivenall in the said county of Essex, the said Anne her mother, came to the said Rebecca, and told her the barley corn was picked up (meaning George Frances jnr., the only son of one George Frances, one of the chief inhabitants of that town, where the said Anne West dwelt) and that his father thought the said George his son was bewitched to death; and the said Anne then said unto the said Rebecca, be it unto him according to his faith.

The Confession of Rebecca West, taken before the said Justices at Mannintree, the 21 of March, 1645.

This examinant saith, that about a moneth since, the aforesaid Anne Leech, Elizabeth Gooding, Hellen Clark, Anne West, and this examinant, met all together at the house of the aforesaid Elizabeth Clark in Mannintree, where they together spent some time in praying unto their familiars, and every one in order went to prayers; afterwards some of them read in a book, the book being Elizabeth Clarks; and this examinant saith, that forthwith their familiars appeared, and every one of them made their severall propositions to those familiars, what every one of them desired to have effected: and this examinant saith, that first of all the said Elizabeth Clark desired of her spirit, that Mr. Edwards might be met withall about the middle bridge, as hee should come riding from Eastberyhoult in Suffolk; that his horse might be scared, and he thrown down, and never rise again: and this examinant saith, that the said Elizabeth Gooding desired of her spirit, that shee might be avenged on Robert Tayler's horse, for that the said Robert suspected the said Elizabeth Gooding for the killing of an horse of the said Robert formerly; and this examinant saith, that the said Hellen Clark desired of her spirit, that shee might be revenged on two hogs in Misley street, (being the place where the said Hellen lived) one of the hogs to die presently, and the other to be taken lame; and this examinant further saith, that Anne Leech desired of her spirit, that a cowe might be taken lame of a man living in Mannintree, but the name of the man this examinant cannot remember: and this examinant further saith, that the said Anne West, this examinants mother, desired of her spirit, that shee might be freed from all her enemies, and have no trouble: and this examinant saith, that shee desired of her spirit, that shee might be revenged on Prudence the wife of Thomas Hart, and that the said Prudence might be taken lame on her right side. And lastly this examinant saith, that having thus done, this examinant, and the other five, did appoint the next meeting to be at the said Elizabeth Goodings house, and so departed all to their owne houses.

The Information of Richard Edwards of Mannintree, Gent. taken upon oath before the said Justices the 23rd of Aprill, 1645.

This informant saith, that not long since, about three moneths to his best remembrance, as he was coming from Eastberyholt in Sufflke, halfe an houre within evening; within ten score of the middle bridge (according to the desire of the said Elizabeth Clarke, as is declared in the confession of the said Rebecca Weste) this informants horse started with him, and greatly endangered him; and he heard something about his horse cry, Ah, ah; much like the shrieke of a polcat. And this informant saith, That with much difficulty he saved himselfe from being thrown off his horse. All which, this informant reported to his wife and neighbours as soone as he came home.

The Information of Matthew Hopkins, Gent. taken upon oath before the said Justices the 18th of Aprill, 1645.

This informant saith, That being lately at Colchester, he went to the castle, where the said Rebecca Weste, with the other five, are secured untill the next gaole delivery: and this informant going to Rebecca Weste, and asking her how shee came first to be a witch, the said Rebecca told this informant, that about a yeare since, or thereabouts, halfe an houre before sun-set, the said Anne Weste (her mother) carried the said Rebecca Weste towards Mannintree, (which is about a small mile from the place where the said Anne dwelt) and the said Rebecca told this informant, that as her mother and shee walked together, the said Anne told the said Rebecca, shee must keepe secret whatsoever shee saw, whither they were then going; and the said Rebecca promised so to doe; and the said Rebecca told this informant, that her mother and shee went to the house of the aforesaid Elizabeth Clarke, where at their comming in they found the aforesaid Anne Leech, widow, Elizabeth Gooding, Hellen Clarke, and the house-keeper Elizabeth Clarke, and that forthwith the Devill appeared to them in the shape of a dogge; afterwards in the shape of two kitlyns; then in the shape of two dogges; and that the said familiars did doe homage in the first place to the said Elizabeth Clarke, and skipped up into her lap, and kissed her; and then went and kissed all that were in the roome, except the said Rebecca: and the said Rebecca told this informant, that immediately one of their company asked the said Anne her mother, if shee had acquainted her daughter (the said Rebecca) with the businesse; and her mother answered shee had, and told them all, they need not feare her the said Rebecca for revealing any thing: and the said Rebecca told this informant, that forthwith the said Anne Leech pulled out a booke, and swore the said Rebecca never to reveale any thing shee saw or heard; and if shee should discover any thing, they all told the said Rebecca, shee should endure more torments on earth, than could be in hell: and the said Rebecca told this informant, that shee promised to keepe all their secrets; and moreover they all told her, that shee must never confesse any thing, although the rope were about her necke, and shee ready to be hanged: and that after she had consented to all these things, the Devill came into her lap, and kissed her, and promised to doe for her what she could desire; and that within halfe a yeare after the Devill appeared to her the said Rebecca, as shee was going to bed, and told her, he would marry her, and that shee could not deny him; shee said he kissed her, but was as cold as clayy, and married her that night, in this manner; he tooke her by the hand and lead her about the chamber, and promised to be her loving husband till death, and to avenge her of her enemies; and that then shee promised him to be his obedient wife till death, and to deny God, and Christ Jesus; and the said Rebecca told this informant, that shee sent the Devill to kill the sonne of the said Thomas Hart, which he did within one fortnight; and that after that shee tooke him for her God, and thought he could doe as God.

The Information of Susan Sparrow, taken upon oath before the said Justices the 25th day of Aprill, A. D. 1645, at Little Bentley.

This informant saith, That about thirty yeares since, living under the same roofe with Mary Greenleif of Alresford, either of them had a daughter of about thirteen or fourteen yeares of age, and being one night in bed with their children, this informant heard the childe of the said Mary Greenleif to cry out in a fearefull manner; oh mother, now it comes, it comes, oh helpe mother, it hurts me, it hurts me: whereupon this informant called to the said Mary, and said, good-wife Greenleife, good-wife Greenleife, if your childe be asleepe, awaken it, for if any body comes by, and heare it make such moane (you having an ill name already (they will say you are suckling your impes upon it: whereupon the said Mary replyed; I doe so indeed, and I will fee with them (meaning her said impes,) that they shall suck my daughter one night, and thine another: and this informant saith, that the very next night, her childe cryed out in the same manner, and clasped her arms about this informants necke, being much affrighted, sweating, and shrieking in a terrible manner, complaining that shee was nipped and pinched on her thigh; and that the next morning searching what the cause should be, shee found above the right knee of her childe, a black and blew spot, as broad and long as her hand: and this informant saith, that her childe did complaine on that leg, at least a moneth after. And this informant saith, that the house where this informant and the said Mary did dwell together, was haunted with a leveret, which did usually sit before the dore: and this informant knowing that one Anthony Sharlock had an excellent greyhound that had killed many hares; and having heard that a childe of the said Anthony was much haunted and troubled, and that the mother of the childe suspected the said Mary to be the cause of it: this informant went to the said Anthony Sharlock and acquainted him, that a leveret did usually come and sit before the dore, where this informant and the said Mary Greenleife lived, and desired the said Anthony to bring downe his greyhound to see if he could kill the said leveret; and the next day the said Anthony did accordingly bring his greyhound, and coursed it, but whether the dog killed it this informant knows not; but being a little before coursed by good-man Merrills dog, the dog ran at it, but the leveret never stirred, and just when the dog came at it, he skipped over it, and turned about and stood still, and looked on it, and shortly after that dog languished and dyed. But whether this was an impe in the shape of a leveret, or had any relation to the said Mary, this informant knows not, but does confesse she wondered very much to see a leveret, wilde by nature, to come so frequently and sit openly before the dore in such a familiar way.

The Information of Elizabeth Hunt and Priscilla Brigs, taken upon oath before the said Justices the 25th day of Aprill, 1645.

These informants say, That being by the said justices imployed to search the said Mary Greenleife, upon suspect for being a witch, these informants found that the said Mary had bigges or teates in her secret parts, not like emerods, nor in those places where women use to be troubled with them; and that they verily beleeve, these teates are suckled by her impes; for that these informants have been formerly imployed to search other women suspected for witchcraft, who have had the like bigges, and have afterwards confessed themselves to be witches.

The Examination of Mary Greenleife, taken before the said Justices, April 25, 1645.

The examinant being asked how she came by those teats which were discovered in her secret parts, she saith she knows not unlesse she were born with them: but she never knew she had any such untill this time, they were found in those parts upon the said search; And she does deny that ever she had any impe sucked on these teats; But she does confesse she hath seen a leveret once sitting before her doore within a yard of the threshold; and that she wondered much at it, being about noon time as she remembreth. And further saith, she is not guilty of any accusation charged upon her this examinant.

The Information of Elizabeth Otley of Wyvenhoe, taken upon oath before the said justices, April 25, 1645.

This informant saith, that Alice Dixon, who now stands committed for a suspected witch, did in the presence of Mary Johnson of the same town, charge and accuse the said Mary Johnson to be the death of this informant's child, saying, that the said Mary Johnson did carry an impe in her pocket to this informant's house, and put the said impe into the house, at an hole in the doore, bidding it go rock the cradle, and do the businesse she sent it about, and return to her again: And this informant saith, that upon a Monday before Michaelmas last, the said Mary Johnson came to the house of this informant, and gave her child an apple, and kissed it; And within a short time after the said child sickned and died; And the said Alice Dixon did also affirm, that the impe which the said Mary Johnson sent to this informant's house, was in shape somewhat like a rat, but without a tayl and eares. And this informant saith, that the said Mary Johnsons answer was, that if she did it, she did it, she could but receive punishment for it. And at the said time the said Mary Johnson said, the said Alice Dixon did the mischief to this informant's child herself. And this informant further saith, that after the said Alice Dixon had made this discovery, she, this informant, was taken with extreme pains in her body, and that during the time of her extremity, the said Mary Johnson did many times come to this informant's house, persuading her, that she was not the death of this informants child: But this informant could not be satisfied untill she had gotten the blood of the said Mary Johnson; And meeting with her after long scuffling, this informant made the said Mary Johnsons teeth to bleed, and immediately after, this informants extraordinary pains left her, and her stomack came to her, having eat little or nothing a fortnight before, and slept very well the night following, having been restlesse by reason of her extreme pains all the time aforesaid. And this informant further saith, that the next day after the said Mary Johnson had given this informants child the apple, the child was taken with very violent fits, and in the fits, although the child was but two yeers old, yet this informant could very hardly with all her strength hold it down in the cradle, and so continued untill it died.

The examination of Mary Johnson, taken before the said Justices the 25 of April, 1645.

This examinant saith, that she is not guilty of any one particular charged upon her in the information of the said Elizabeth Otley touching the killing of the child of the said Elizabeth.

The Information of Joseph Long, Minister of Clacton in the County of Essex, taken before the said Justices April 29, 1645.

This informant saith, that Anne the wife of John Cooper of Clacton aforesaid, being accused for a witch: Confessed unto this informant, that she the said Anne was guilty of the sin of Witchcraft; and that she hath had three black impes suckled on the lower parts of her body; called by the names of Wynowe, Jeso, and Panu: And this informant saith, that the said Anne told him, that once she cursed a colt of one William Cottingams of Clacton aforesaid, and the said colt broke his neck presently after going out of a gate: And the said Anne further confessed unto this informant, that she the said Anne offered to give unto her daughter Sarah Cooper an impe in the likeness of a gray kite, to suck on the said Sarah; which impes name the said Anne called Tom boy: and told the said Sarah, there was a cat for her; And this informant saith, that the said Anne confessed unto him, that she the said Anne about ten yeers since falling out with Johan the wife of Gregory Rous of Clacton aforesaid; the said Anne Cooper sent one of her impes to kill the daughter of the said Gregory and Johan, named Mary: And this informant saith, that to his own knowledge about the same time the said child was strangely taken sick, and languishing, within a short time died.

The Information of Roger Hempson, taken upon oath before the said Justices, April 29, 1645.

This informant doth confirm the information of the said Joseph Longe, and concurs in every particular.

The Information of Roger Hempson, taken upon oath before the said Justices, April 29, 1645.

This informant saith, that Mr. Longe telling Elizabeth Hare, that she was accused by one Mary Smith, for giving of her the said Mary two impes; And that the said Elizabeth Hare, praying to God with her hands upward, that if she were guilty of any such thing, he would shew some example upon her; And this informant saith, that presently after she shaked and quivered, and fell down to the ground backward, and tumbled up and down upon the ground, and hath continued sick ever since.

The Information of Anaball the wife of George Durrant, taken upon oath before the said Justices, April 29, 1645.

This informant saith, that about ten moneths since, going from Wivenhoe towards Fingeringhoe, in the county of Essex, by the way Mary Johnson the wife of Nicholas Johnson met with this informant, whom this informant never saw before to her knowledge; And this informant leading her child upon her hand, being about two yeers old, and perfectly well: the said Mary Johnson took occasion of her own accord to commend the said child, saying, it was a pretty child; and stroaked it upon the face, and gave it a peece of bread and butter, and so left this informant. And this informants child did eat a peece of the said bread and butter; and within half a quarter of an houre after, her said child shrieked and cried out it was lame. And this informant carried her child home, and had the advice of one Mr. Dawber a chirurgeon, who could find no naturall cause of its lamenesse; and so the said child continued for the space of eight dayes shrieking and tearing itself, and then died.

And further, this informant saith, that immediately after the death of her child, she was taken with extreme pains in her body, some times every day or at least every third day, for the space of seven or eight moneths together, as if she had been to be delivered of a child, but was not with child; and this informant saith, that setting up of broome in an out-house presently after her child was dead, she had the perfect representation of a shape, to her thinking, like the said Mary Johnson, and was struck with a lamenesse in her arms, and such a stiffnesse that three or foure that came to help her, were not able to bow her arms: and this informant continued speechlesse all that day and the night following, and had such a weaknesse in the rest of her limbes, that she was carried into her house by some of her friends, and continued by the space of a fortnight, being before untill this present (as she conceived) in perfect health and strength: and further this informant saith, that she being charged by the constable by vertue of a warrant to give this her information before the said justices against the said Mary Johnson this day; this informants husband called her up in the morning, wishing her to make her ready to go before the said justices; and presently after he gave a great shriek, and said the said Mary Johnson would be his death, and had a great swelling risen up in his breast, and now lies sweating, and in great extremity. And at this very instant a noise was heard in the roome where her husband lay like an hornet, and thereupon her husband cried out, It comes, it comes; Now goodwife Johnsons impe is come, now she hath my life: and forthwith a great part of the wall in the said roome fell down. And this informant saith, that she doth verily beleeve the said Mary Johnson was the cause of her childs death: and that she is now the cause of her husbands extremity.

The Information of Ric. Carter and Henry Cornwall of Thorp, taken upon oath before the said Justices, April 29, 1645.

These informants say, that being appointed to watch Margaret Moone, after she was accused and apprehended for a witch, the said Margaret going about the roome, these informants did see a thing drop from under her coats (as they thought) in the likenesse of a rat for bignesse and shape, but of a grayer colour; and presently there was such an extreame offensive stink in the roome, that these informants were scarce able to endure to stay in it; and these informants asking the said Margaret what it was that dropped from her, she bids them coop it up and catch it if they could. And this informant Henry Cornwall saith, that the said Margaret did confesse to him that she had twelve impes, and called them by their names; of which he remembers onely these following: Jesus, Jockey, Sandy, Mrit. Elizabeth, and Collyn.

The Information of Will. Dammon, Hen. Cornwall, Bevis Vincent, and Tho. Burles, taken upon oath before the said Justices, April 29, 1645.

These informants say, that upon the 21. day of April last past, they heard Margaret Moone confesse, that she was a witch, and that she had twelve impes, that she had killed a cow of Stephen Cookers, and had two cowes more of the said Stephen in handling; that she had killed a cow and a sow of Henry Robertsons. That she was partner with the aforesaid Eliz. Clark of Mannintree, in killing of a child of one Mr. Edwards of Mannintree aforesaid, and spoiling of 3 brewings of beere of the said Mr. Edwards. That she the said Margaret Moon spoiled a batch of bread of one Philip Berrimans; that she was the cause that one Philip Daniels horse broke his neck going down an hill in his wagon. And the said informant saith, that the said M. Moone did freely and voluntarily confesse unto him, without any question being asked, that she was the cause of the death of Johan Cornwall this informants daughter. And this informant saith, that the said Margaret Moone before his child fell sick, sent for this informant to do some work for her, and then she desired to buy an booke which he carried with him in his hand; and they agreed she should have the said booke for half a peck of apples: and as this informant went home he did eat one of the said apples, and was presently taken sick with an extreme shaking and pain in all parts of his body; and his informants wife knowing the said Margaret Moone to be a woman of a very bad fame and suspected for a witch, and had formerly been questioned at an Assize for the same, she flung away the apples. And this informant saith, that he continued in great extremity for the space of twelve weeks, and most part of that time deprived of his senses. And at the same time his wife was taken in the same manner, and is not yet perfectly recovered. And lastly this informant saith, that the next day after he had been at the said Margarets house as aforesaid, that his child (which the said Margaret confessed she was the death of) was taken sick with strange fits, and shriekings out, and so continued languishing for a moneth, and died.

The Information of Richard Caley of Thorpe, taken upon oath before the said Justices, April 29, 1645.

This informant saith, that being called into the house where Bevis Vincent, and Henry Cornwall were appointed by the neighbours of Thorpe aforesaid to watch Margaret Moone, the said Margaret did confesse before this informant, that she had by witchcraft killed a cow and a sow of one Henry Robertsons. And that one Henry Dorr being then called to write what she should confesse, the said Margaret refused to make any further discovery, before this informant; but fell upon other discourse, saying, that she had been told fourty times, that this informant thought in his conscience she was no witch: and that this informant knew that one William Caley his brother let the said Margaret an house about twenty yeers since, and afterwards warned her out of the said house; and that then she went into an house that was built for her by one Thomas Turner, and being also turned out of Turners house, that one Rawbood and his wife gave ten shillings more for the said house, then the said Margaret, and came and dwelt in the said house: But the said Margaret said, they (meaning the said Rawbood and his wife) had as good they had not medled with the house, for they did never thrive after. And this informant saith, that after the said Rawbood had taken the said house, he and his wife were alwayes lame or sick untill they died: and that the wife of the said Rawbood being a very tydy and cleanly woman, sitting upon a block after dinner with another neighbour, a little before it was time to go to church (and as he remembers) upon an Easter day, the said Rawboods wife was on the sudden so filled with lice, that they might have been swept off her cloaths with a stick; and this informant saith he did see them, and that they were long, and lean, and not like other lice. And this informant being asked, whether the said

Margaret were at this time sensible, he saith that she spake very plainly and very intelligently, discoursing of some things done long before, her memory serving her very exactly.

The Information of Francis Milles, taken upon oath before the said Justices, April 29, 1645.

This informant saith, that being imployed by the neighbours of Thorpe aforesaid, to search Margaret Moone who was suspected for a witch, she found three long teats or bigges in her secret parts, which seemed to have been lately sucked; and that they were not like pyles, for this informant knows well what they are, having been troubled with them herself. And this informant saith, that she asking the said Margaret for her impes, which sucked those teats: she said, if she might have some bread and beere, she would call her said impes; which being given unto her, she put the bread into the beere, and set it against an hole in the wall, and made a circle round about the pot, and then cried, Come Christ, come Christ, come Mounsier, come Mounsier: And no impe appearing, she cried out and said, she had devilish daughters which had carried her impes away in a white bagge, and wished they might be searched, for they were naught: And upon the searching of her daughters, this informant found that two of them had biggs in their privy parts as the said Margaret their mother had.

The Information of Mary Philips, Elizabeth Harris widow, Susan Burles and Philip Tumnor, taken upon oath before the said Justices, April 29, 1645.

These informants do all and every of them concur with Frances Milles in her said information, in that particular concerning the teats of the said Margaret Moone, and her two daughters; and the said Mary Philips doth also confirm and concur with that part of the information of the said Frances Milles, touching the pot, the circle, and the calling of the impes by the said Margaret Moone.

And this informant Mary Philips doth also say, that being sent for to search the said Margaret Moone, as she was coming towards Thorp aforesaid, and going over a broad foot bridge, this informant sensibly felt a great blow on her head, which strook her into a ditch up to the neck. And this informant and the said Francis Milles doe both of them say, That as soon as they came into the room where the said Margaret Moone was, she called these two informants, Mannintree rogues (they both dwelling at a town so called), and said, Who a devill sent for you? But I hope I have met with some of you.

The Examination of Margaret Moone, taken before the said Justices, the 29th day of May, 1645.

This examinant being examined to all the particulars charged upon her, in all the aforesaid severall informations, denies every particular.

The Examination of Judith Moone, daughter of the said Margaret Moone, taken before the said Justices, the 29th day of Aprill, 1645.

This examinant (being a single woman, and having such marks of a witch as aforesaid) saith, that about a fortnight before her mother was apprehended for a witch, the said Margaret bid this examinant goe and fetch a bundle of wood, and this examinant told her mother shee would not fetch any wood: Whereupon the said Margaret threatened this examinant, and told her shee had as good have gone for some wood; and that the next night as this examinant lay in her bed, she felt something come into the bed, about her legges, being at that time broad awake, and that shee searched to see what it should be, but could not finde anything.

The Information of Bridget Reynolds, the wife of Edward Reynolds of Ramsey in the said county of Essex, taken upon oath before the said Justices, the 3rd of May, 1645.

This informant saith, That she with some other women, were required to search Sarah Hating the wife of William Hating, Elizabeth Harvy widow, and Marian Hocket widow, who are all suspected for Witchcraft, and upon her said search (being a midwife) found such marks or bigges in their privy parts, that she never saw in other women: for Sarah Hating had foure teats of bigges in those parts, almost an inch long, and as bigge as this informant's little finger: That the said Elizabeth Harvy had three such biggs, and about the said scantling: And that the said Marian Hocket had no such bigges; but was found in the same parts not like other honest women. And this informant further saith, That the said Elizabeth Harvy said (since she was found with the said suspitious marks) unto this informant, That if she were a witch, she was so made by the said Marian Hocket; for that the said Marian brought unto her the said Elizabeth Harvy, three things about the bignesse of mouses, and willed the said Elizabeth to make much of them, for they were pretty things; which the said Elizabeth received: And the said Elizabeth told this informant, that ever since she received those three things which the said Marian delivered unto her, she hath been much torn and troubled in her privy parts, where the said bigges were found. And that the said three things were delivered to her the said Elizabeth about six or seven years since.

The Information of Elizabeth Durden, the wife of Edward Durden, and Mary Philips, taken upon oath before the said Justices, the 3rd day of May, 1645.

These informants do concurre in every particular with the said Bridget Reynolds, in her information touching the search of the said Sarah Hating, Elizabeth Harvie, and Marian Hocket: And this informant Elizabeth Durden further saith, that the said Elizabeth Harvie told her, that if shee were a witch, shee was so made by the said Marian Hocket.

The Information of Francis Stock and John Batilly, taken upon oath before the said Justices, May 3rd, 1645.

These informants say, that the said Elizabeth Harvie confessed to them with many teares, that shee had three marks, two before and one behinde (as is already informed by Bridget Reynolds and others), and that the said Marian Hocket made her have the said marks or bigs, by bringing of three things to her the said Elizabeth, and telling her, if shee would receive them, shee should never want so long as she lived; which three things have since made the said marks in her privie parts, and the said Elizabeth told these informants, that the said three things were of a reddish colour, and that since, the said Marian and the said Elizabeth falling out, she the said Elizabeth would have put away and sent home the three things which the said Marian brought to her, and that ever since the said things have tormented her in her bed, in the places aforesaid, as if they had pulled her in pieces.

The second Information of Francis Stock, taken before the said Justices upon oath, May 3d, 1645.

This informant saith, that about five yeers since, being one of the constables of Ramsey aforesaid, hee impressed William Hating, husband to the aforesaid Sarah Hating for a souldier, whereupon the said William threatened this informant very much, and not long after, this informant's wife told him, shee espied a snake lying upon a shelf in this informant's house, about three yards high from the ground, which falling down into the house, shee endeavoured to kill with a spade; and striking at it, the snake suddenly vanished away, and could no where be found: And this informant saith, that presently after his said wife was taken sick with extraordinary fits, pains and burnings all over her body, and within one week dyed: And further this informant saith, that within two or three dayes, after the death of his said wife, hee had a daughter taken sick after a very strange manner, who in all the time of her sicknesse, cryed out much on the said Sarah, the wife of the said William Hating, saying, that the said Sarah was the cause of her death, and dyed presently after; and that within two or three dayes after the death of his said childe, this informant had another childe taken sick in the same manner, and within a few dayes dyed also: And lastly, this informant saith, that about three quarters of a year after, he had a man-servant, that for some ill language given to him by John Hating, one of the sons of the said William and Sarah Hating, his said servant did beat the said John, and the very next day hee was taken sick, and so continued in a pining and languishing condition, crying out often of the said Sarah, that she had bewitched him, and was the cause of his death, which soon after ensued.

The Information of Francis Stock, and John Felgate, taken upon oath before the said Justices, May 3, 1645.

This informant John Felgate saith, that speaking with one Sarah Barton, the sister of the said Marian Hocket (which said Sarah is now imprisoned in the gaole at Harwich upon suspition of Witchcraft), who told this informant, that the said Marian had cut off her bigs, whereby she might have been the more suspected to have been a witch, and laid plaisters to those places: And the said Francis and John say, that the said Sarah Barton, told them, that the said Marian had given and delivered unto her the said Sarah three imps, and that the said Marian called them by the names of Littleman, Pretty-man, and Dainty.

The Examination of Marian Hocket, Sarah Hating, and Elizabeth Harvie of Ramsey within the County aforesaid, taken before the said Justices, May 3, 1645.

This examinant, Marian Hocket saith, that shee is not guilty of any of the particulars charged upon her, touching witchcraft, notwithstanding the severall accusations against her.

This examinant, Sarah Hating saith, that shee is not guilty of any particular wherewith shee stands charged in the information of Francis Stock and others.

This examinant, Elizabeth Harvie saith, that about halfe a yeer since, the said Marian Hocket brought three things to her house, two of them being smaller then mouses, and the other somewhat bigger and longer; and that the said Marian told this examinant they were pretty things, and would do her and this examinant good, if shee this examinant would keep them; and that afterwards shee was very much pained in those parts of her body where the said teats or bigs were discovered by the said searchers, as aforesaid.

The information of Robert Turner of St. Osyth Carpenter, taken upon oath before the said Justices, May 6, 1645.

This informant saith, that about eight dayes since, his servant was taken sick, shaking and shrieking, and crying out of Rose Hallybread, that shee had bewitched him: And this informant saith that sometimes his said servant, since hee was taken sick, as aforesaid, hath crowed perfectly as a cock; sometimes barked like a dog; sometimes violently groaned beyond the ordinary course of nature; and struggling with such strength (being but a youth), that four or five strong men were not able to hold him down in his bed; and sometimes sung divers and sundry perfect tunes: And that this informant could not perceive his mouth to open, or so much as his lips to stir all the time of his singing.

The Examination of Rose Hallybread, taken before the said Justices, the 6th of May, 1645.

This examinant saith, that about fifteen or sixteen yeers since, there was an imp brought to her house by one Goodwife Hagtree, which imp this examinant entertained, fed it with oatmeale, and suckled it on her body, for the space of a yeer and a halfe, or thereabouts, and then lost it: And this examinant further saith, that about half a yeer since, one Joyce Boanes (who is now also accused for Witchcraft), brought to this examinants house another imp, in the likenesse of a small gray bird, which this examinant received, and carryed it to the house of one Thomas Toakley of St. Osyth, and put the said imp into a cranny of the doore of the said Toakley's house, after which time the son of the said Thomas languished, and dyed, crying out of this examinant, that shee was his death: And this examinant further saith, that about eight dayes since, Susan Cock, Margaret Landish, and Joyce Boanes, (all which stand now suspected for Witchcraft) brought to this examinants house each of them an imp, (in all three) to which this examinant added one of her own imps; and then he said Joyce Boanes carryed the said four imps to the house of one Robert Turner, to torment his servant, because he had refused to give unto her this examinant, the said Susan Cocks, Margaret Landish and Joyce Boanes a few chips: And this examinant further saith, that the said Robert Turners servant forthwith fell sick, and oftentimes barked like a dog: And this examinant saith, that she believeth that the said four imps were the cause of his barking and sicknesse.

The Examination of Joyce the wife of William Boanes, taken before the said justices, May 6, 1645.

This examinant saith, that about thirteen yeers since, shee had two imps which came into the bed to her in the likenesse of mouses, and that they sucked on this examinants body; and that afterwards this examinant employed and sent the said imps to a farm house in St. Osyth, called Cocket-wick, where one Richard Welch then lived, where the said imps killed ten or twelve lambs of the said Richards: And this examinant saith further, that a little while after, shee sent her said two imps to the house of one Thomas Clynch, where they killed a calf, a sheep and a lamb: And this examinant also saith, that shee carried one of her said imps, called Rug, to the house of the said Rose Hallybread; and that her said imp Rug, with three imps of the said Rose Hallybread, Susan Cock, and Margaret Lindish, each of them sending one, were carried by this examinant from the house of the said Rose Hallybread, to the house of the said Robert Turner to kill the servant of the said Robert; whereupon his said servant hath oftentimes crowed like a cock, barked like a dogge, sung tunes, and groaned: And this examinant saith, that her said imp made the said servant to barke like a dog; the imp of the said Rose Hallybread inforced him to sing sundry tunes in his great extremity of paines; the imp of the said Susan Cock, compelled him to crow like a cock; and the imp of Margaret Landish made him groan in such an extraordinary manner.

The Examination of Susan Cock, taken before the said Justices the 6th day of May 1645.

This examinate saith, that about three or four yeeres since, one Margery Stoakes, this examinants mother, lying upon her death-bed, and this examinant comming to visit her, shee the said Margery desired this examinant privately to give entertainment to two of her imps, and withall told this examinant, they would do this examinant good; And this examinant saith, that the same night her said mother dyed, the said two imps came to her accordingly, and sucked on her body; And this examinant saith, that one of the said imps was like a mouse, and the name of that was Susan: that the other was of a yellow colour, about the bigness of a cat; and that the name of that imp was Besse: And this examinant saith, that she employed her said imp called Besse, together with the imps of the said Rose Hallybread, Joyce Boanes, and Margaret Landish, each of them one, to the house of one where the said impes killed ten or twelve sheep of the said farmer John Spalls; and that the cause of this examinants malice was, because she being with childe desired to have some curds of the said Spalls wife, which she refused, either to give or sell to this examinant: And further, this examinant saith that about a week since, she, together with Joyce Boanes, Rose Hallybread, and Margaret Landish sent four imps to the house of one Robert Turner, by the said Joyce Boanes to torment his servant, for that the said servant of the said Robert Turner refused to give this examinant a sack full of chips: And this examinant further saith, that she, together with the said Margaret Landish, sent her impe to the house of one Thomas Mannock in St. Osyth aforesaid, where their said impes killed six or seven shoots or hogges of the said Mr. Mannock; and that the occasion of offence was, because the wife of the said Mr. Mannock refused to give to this examinant such relief as she desired, telling this examinant, that shee was a young woman, and able to worke for her living.

The Examination of Margaret Landishe, taken before the said Justices the 6th day of May, 1645.

This examinant saith, that about eight or nine weeks since lying sicke by the fire side in her owne house, something came up to her body, and sucked on her privie parts, and much pained and tormented her: And this examinant saith, that if it were an impe that came and sucked her as aforesaid, that the said Susan Cock sent it to her: And this examinant denieth, that ever shee joyned with the said Joyce Boanes, Rose Hallybread, and Susan Cock, in the tormenting of the servant of the said Robert Turner, and doth utterly deny the sending of any impe to destroy or kill the hogges of the said Mr. Mannock, as the said Susan Cock hath charged her withall in the examination of the said Susan.

The Examination of Rebecca Jones of St. Osyth, taken before the said Justices the 9th of May, 1645.

This examinant saith, that about 24 or 25 yeares since, dwelling with one John Bishop, of Much-Clacton in the county of Essex as his servant, there came one morning one to the doore of the said John Bishop and knocked, and that this examinant going to the dore, shee saw there a very handsome young man, as shee then thought but now shee thinkes it was the devill; who asked this examinant how shee did, and desired to see her left wrist, which shee shewed unto him: and that he then tooke a pin from this examinants owne sleeve, and pricked her wrist twice, and there came out a drop of blood, which he took off with the top of his finger, and so departed. And this examinant saith that about a quarter of a yeare after, as shee was going to St. Osyth, (where this examinant doth now dwell) to sell her said masters butter, a man met with her, being in a ragged sute, and having such great eyes, that this examinant was much afraid of him; who came to this examinant and gave her three things like to moules, having foure feet a piece, but without tayles, and of a black colour, and bid this examinant nurse the said three things, untill he did desire them againe; And this examinant asked the said man, what she should give them to eate, and he told this examinant milke, and that they would not hurt her, and wished her not to be afraid of them: And the said man told this examinant, that those three things which he gave her, would avenge her on her enemies, and bid her murther some, but not too many, and he would forgive her; and then went away from this examinant: And this examinant saith, that the first time she imployed any of the said things, shee sent one of them to kill a sowe of one Benjamin Howes of Little-Clacton in the county aforesaid; and the said sowe was killed by the said impe accordingly: And this examinant saith, that the names of her three imps were Margaret, Amie, and Susan: And that a while after, this examinant and one Joyce Boanes, now in prison, did send each of them an impe to kill one Thomas Bumstead of St. Osyth aforesaid, who died about three weeks after. And this examinant saith, that shee beleeveth that the said two impes did kill the said Thomas Bumstead; and the impes name which this examinant sent to destroy the said Bumstead was Margaret: And that the impe which the said Joyce Boanes sent was a dun one like unto a mouse. And this examinant saith, that she did send another of her impes called Amie, to the said Bumsteads house, which did kill the wife of the said Bumstead within a short time after: And this examinant confesseth, that the cause of offence shee tooke so to destroy and kill the said Bumstead and his wife, was because the said Thomas Bumstead did beate the sonne of this examinant for eating up of some honey which he found about the house of the said Thomas Bumstead. And this examinant further confesseth, that shee did send her other third impe called Susan, to afflict the childe of one Mistriss Darcy of St. Osyth aforesaid: But did withall bid the said impe it should not hurt the said child too much, and come away againe: And this examinant saith, that the said imp is come again from the said Mistriss Darcies childe.

The Examination of Johan Cooper, widow, taken before the said Justices, May 9, 1645.

This examinant saith, That she hath been a witch about twenty yeers, and hath three familiars, two like mouses, and the third like a frog; the names of the two like mouses are Jack, and the other Prickeare, and the name of the third, like a frog, is Frog. And this examinant saith, that she sent one of her said impes to kill a child of one Thomas Woodward, which her said impe did kill a fortnight after. And this examinant saith, that shee did send her said impe called Frog, to kill two of John Cartwright's children, of Much-Holland in the county of Essex aforesaid, which said imp did kill the said two children within a fortnight or three weeks after. And this examinant saith further, that at another time shee sent her said imp Frog, to destroy the wife of one George Parby, of Much-Holland aforesaid, which did kill her within three dayes after.

The Examination of Anne Cate, alias Maidenhead, of Much-Holland, in the county aforesaid, taken before the said Justices, the 9th of May, 1645.

This examinant saith, That she hath four familiars, which shee had from her mother, about two and twenty yeeres since, and that the names of the said imps are James, Prickeare, Robyn, and Sparrow: and that three of these imps are like mouses, and the fourth like a sparrow, which she called Sparrow. And this examinant saith, that to whomsoever shee sent the said imp called Sparrow, it killed them presently; and that, first of all, shee sent one of her three imps like mouses, to nip the knee of one Robert Freeman, of Little Clacton in the county of Essex aforesaid, whom the said imp did so lame, that the said Robert dyed on that lamenesse within a half a yeere after. And this examinant saith, that she sent her said imp Prickeare to kill the daughter of John Rawlins, of Much-Holland aforesaid, which died accordingly within a short time after; and that shee sent her said imp Prickeare to the house of one John Tillet, which did suddenly kill the said Tillet. And this examinant saith, that shee sent her said imp Sparrow, to kill the childe of one George Parby, of Much-Holland aforesaid, which child the said imp did presently kill; and that the offence this examinant took against the said George Parby, to kill his said childe, was, because the wife of the said Parby denyed to give this examinant a pint of milke. And this examinant further saith, that she sent her said imp Sparrow to the house of Samuel Ray, which in a very short time did kill the wife of the said Samuel; and that the cause of this examinant's malice against the said woman was, because shee refused to pay to this examinant two pence, which she challenged to be due to her; and that afterwards her said imp Sparrow killed the said child of the said Samuel Ray. And this examinant confesseth, that as soon as shee had received the said four imps from her said mother, the said imps spake to this examinant, and told her, shee must deny God and Christ, which this examinant did then assent unto.

The Testimony of Sir Thomas Bowes, knight, which he spake upon the Bench, concerning the aforesaid Anne West, shee being then at the Barre upon her Tryall.

That a very honest man of Mannintree, whom he knew would not speake an untruth, affirmed unto him, that very early one morning, as he passed by the said Anne Weste's dore, about foure a clock, it being a moonlight night, and perceiving her dore to be open so early in the morning, looked into the house, and presently there came three or four little things, in the shape of black rabbits, leaping and skipping about him, who, having a good stick in his hand, struck at them, thinking to kill them, but could not; but at last caught one of them in his hand, and holding it by the body of it, he beat the head of it against his stick, intending to beat out the braines of it; but when he could not kill it that way, he tooke the body of it in one hand, and the head of it in another, and endeavoured to wring off the head: and as he wrung and stretched the neck of it, it came out between his hands like a lock of wooll; yet he would not give over his intended purpose, but knowing of a spring not farre off, he went to drowne it: but still as he went he fell downe, and could not goe, but downe he fell againe, so that he at last crept upon his hands and knees till he came at the water, and holding it fast in his hand, he put his hand downe into the water up to his elbow, and held it under water a good space, till he conceived it was drowned, and then letting goe his hand, it sprung out of the water up into the aire, and so vanished away: and then comming backe to the said Anne West's dore, he saw her standing there in her smock, and asked her, why shee did set her impes to molest and trouble him? to whom she made answer, that they were not sent to trouble him, but were sent out as scouts upon another designe.

Essex Elizabethan inn of the kind mentioned in the story of the Witch of Royston

Typical *torture room* with some of the implements used by Matthew Hopkins and his assistants

Matthew Hopkins interrogating two witches who appear to be readily confessing their guilt, without any form of inducement!

A *Cunning Man* being consulted by a client with a leg ailment. These *witch doctors* were found all over Essex and continued practicing until as recently as the beginning of this century.

A woodcut depicting a lady being visited by the Devil. See the story, *A Magical Vision*.

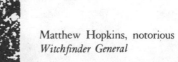

Matthew Hopkins, notorious *Witchfinder General*

Fanciful seventeenth century engraving of noblemen and women holding a Black Magic ritual

A glade in Epping Forest believed to have been used by *devil worshipers* in the seventeenth century

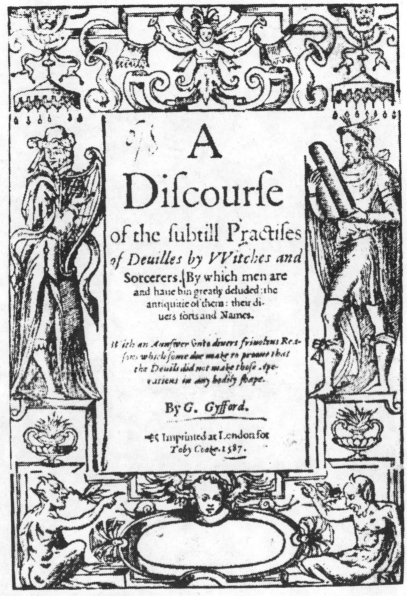

A Discourse

of the subtill Practises

of *Deuilles by Witches and*

Sorcerers. By which men are

and haue bin greatly deluded : the

antiquitie of them : their di-

uers forts and Names.

With an Aunswer vnto diuers friuolous Rea-

fons which fome doe make to proue that

the Deuils did not make thofe ope-

rations in any bodily fhape.

By G. *Gyfford.*

Imprinted at London for

Toby Cooke. 1587.

Discourse by George Gifford, preacher at Maldon, 1587
Almost as important as book by Reginald Scot

King James I of England who
instigated the harshest of all
Witchcraft Statutes in 1604. He
became skeptical about the whole
matter by the end of his reign.

Contemporary engraving of King James personally interrogating suspected witches

The *Witch Prickers*, with retractable blades, used by Hopkins so that the accused felt no pain and could thereby be said to be in league with the Devil

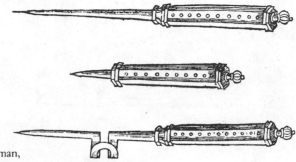

The *swimming* of Widow Coman, Coggeshall, 1699

A fanciful but widely held view of witchcraft in Elizabethan times

Essex witchcraft 400 years apart

Modern practitioners of *Wicca* conducting one of their age old rituals

the discovery of witches

by Matthew Hopkins

Although Matthew Hopkins's bloody and terrible activities are well known and documented, of the man himself we know surprisingly little except what has emerged from his persecutions and his writing. He was apparently the son of the minister of Wenham in Suffolk, but what his education, occupation, or pursuit were before 1644, when he was known to be living in Manningtree, Essex, it has been extremely difficult to ascertain. However, he can hardly have been unaware of the witchcraft tradition in the town in which he lived ("Manningtree was said to be one of the famous English sites of the Witches' Sabbats"—G. L. Kittredge), and according to his own words he decided to hunt down and prosecute these people after, as he puts it, he became aware that a group of local witches were meeting "close by his house" every six weeks and offering "their several solemn sacrifices . . . to the devil."

This story is doubtless just one more glib tale from this most untrustworthy of men—like his other story that these same witches, realizing that he was aware of their activities, attempted to kill him in his garden by letting loose a bear! There seems no doubt, however, that he nursed a particular fear of the devil (whom he believed in literally), and this, coupled with his fanatical Puritanism, gave him the impetus to begin his single-minded mission to wipe out witchcraft.

The several prints of Hopkins that still exist give us a fair idea of what he looked like, and it has been suggested that because of the manner in which he presented his findings, he may well have had some basic training as a lawyer. His qualifications as a witch hunter, however, were the scantiest—he had read King James's *Demonology*, which he accepted without question, and he knew of Bernard's *Guide to Grand-Jurymen*, which he used as it suited him.

His employment of torture and the "swimming" of suspects probably came from latent sadistic tendencies and also from a sense of frustration at what must have been a most undistinguished life until this time. Hopkins was, of course, paid a fee for his work (never less than five pounds and often much more), and no doubt his zeal was further enhanced by the thought of still larger commissions. Sometimes he was requested to attend to a village or town where witchcraft was suspected; more often than not he wrote to the magistrates of the towns where he thought there might be "work" for him, inviting himself in the most insinuating tones. Hopkins wrote this letter to the magistrate of a town in northeast Essex in 1645:

My service to your worship presented, I have this day received a letter to come to a town to search for evil disposed persons, called Witches (though I hear your Minister is farre against us through ignorance). I intend to come (God willing) the sooner to heare his singular judgement on the behalf of such parties; I have known a minister in Suffolk preach as much against their Discovery in a pulpit, and forced to recant it, (by the Committee) in the same place. I much marvelled such evil members should have any (much more any of the clergy) who should daily preach terror to convince such offenders, stand up to take their parts, against such as are complainants for the King, and sufferers themselves, with their families and estates. I intend to give your town a visit suddenly. I am come to Kimbolton this week, and it shall be ten to one, but I will come to your town first, but I would certainly know before whether your town affords many sticklers for such cattell, or willing to give and afford us good welcome and entertainment, as otherwise I have been, else I shall wave your Shire (not as yet beginning in any part of it myself) and betake me to such places where I do, and may persist without control, but with thanks and recompense. So I humbly take my leave, and rest

Your servent to be commanded,
Matthew Hopkins.

Hopkins certainly had his greatest "successes" in Essex but did not confine his activities to this county. In the year and a half when he was "hunting," he also visited Norfolk, Suffolk, Cambridge, Northampton, Huntingdon, and Bedford, and whenever the pressure of work called him on to other places he appointed assistants to carry on the examinations in his place. (One of these was a woman, Mary Phillips!)

In all, he committed several hundred people to trial, and of these nearly half were executed. Once the civil war had broken out in earnest, of course, his task was made easier still as the regular assizes were suspended and "justice" was dispensed by special commissioners. But unconfined and unqualified prosecution such as Hopkins was instigating could not fail to lead him eventually into disrepute. This came, mercifully, in 1646, when first a parliamentary news magazine, *The Modern Intelligencer*, and then several clergymen began to question his methods and the very noticeable loopholes being found in his depositions against suspected witches.

A Huntingdonshire clergyman, the Reverend John Gaule, who bitterly resented Hopkins's activities in his own county, also denounced him in a pamphlet, *Select Cases of Conscience*. Public support for Hopkins then began to pall, and his services were actively discouraged. Judges began to question him about his use of torture, and there were several heated wrangles about his integrity and the size of his fees.

In the autumn of 1646 Hopkins took himself back to Manningtree and into retirement. Within a year he was dead of tuberculosis. A rumor arose that he had in fact died as a result of being "swum" for suspicion of practicing witchcraft, but this has long since been proved to have little basis in fact.

Shortly before his death, Hopkins had attempted to answer his critics in a pamphlet, *The Discovery of Witches* (1647), which presented an insight into his reasoning and a justification for the harshness of his methods. This work, published "for the benefit of the whole Kingdom." is reprinted here to represent the Witch Finder General or the Hangman of Manningtree, as he was variously known. There is probably no more fascinating or bizarre essay in the entire history of witchcraft persecution.

Certaine Queries Answered, which have been and are Likely to be Objected Against Matthew Hopkins, in His Way of Finding out Witches

Querie 1. That he must needs be the greatest Witch, Sorcerer, and Wizzard himselfe, else hee could not doe it.

Answer. If Satan's kingdome be divided against itselfe, how shall it stand?

Querie 2. If he never went so farre as is before mentioned, yet for certaine he met with the Devill, and cheated him of his Booke, wherein were written all the Witches' names in *England*, and if he looks on any Witch, he can tell by her countenance what she is; so by this, his helpe is from the Devill.

Answer. If he had been too hard for the devill and got his book, it had been to his great commendation, and no disgrace at all: and for judgement in *Phisiognomie* he hath no more than any man else whatsoever.

Querie 3. From whence then proceeded this his skill? Was it from his profound learning, or from much reading of learned Authors concerning that subject?

Answer. From neither of both, but from experience, which though it be meanly esteemed of, yet the surest and safest way to judge by.

Querie 4. I pray where was this experience gained? And why gained by him and not by others?

Answer. The Discoverer never travelled far for it, but in *March*, 1644, he had some seven or eight of that horrible sect of Witches living in the Towne where he lived, a Towne in *Essex*, called *Maningtree*, with divers other adjacent Witches of other towns, who every six weeks in the night (being always on the Friday night) had their meeting close by his house, and had their severall solemne sacrifices there offered to the Devill, one of which this discoverer heard speaking to her *Imps* one night, and bid them goe to another Witch, who was thereupon apprehended, and searched by women who had for many yeares knowne the Devill's marks, and found to have three teats about her, which honest women have not: so upon command from the *Justice* they were to keep her from sleep two or three nights, expecting in that time to see her *familiars*, which the fourth night she called in by their severall names, and told them what shapes, a quarter of an houre before they came in, there being ten of us in the roome; the first she called was,

1. *Holt*, who came in like a white kitling.

2. *Jarmara*, who came in like a fat Spaniel without any legs at all, she said she kept him fat, for she clapt her hand on her belly, and said he suckt good blood from her body.

3. *Vinegar Tom*, who was like a long-legg'd Greyhound, with an head like an Oxe, with a long taile and broad eyes, who when this discoverer spoke to, and bade him goe to the place provided for him and his Angels, immediately transformed himselfe into the shape of a child of foure yeeres old without a head, and gave halfe a dozen turnes about the house, and vanished at the doore.

4. *Sack and Sugar*, like a black Rabbet.

5. *Newes*, like a Polcat. All these vanished away in a little time. Immediately after this Witch confessed severall other Witches, from whom she had her *Imps*, and named to divers women where their marks were, the number of their *Marks*, and *Imps*, and *Imps* names, as *Elemanzer, Pyewacket, Peckin the Crown, Grizzel, Greedigut &c.* which no mortall could invent; and upon their searches the same Markes were found, the same number, and in the same place, and the like confessions from them of the same Imps, (though they knew not that we were told before) and so peached one another thereabouts that joyned together in the like damnable practise, that in our Hundred in *Essex*, 29 were condemned at once, 4 brought 25 miles to be hanged, where this Discoverer lives, for sending the Devill like a Beare to kill him in his garden, so by seeing diverse of the mens Papps, and trying wayes with hundreds of them, he gained this experience, and for ought he knowes any man else may find them as well as he and his company, if they had the same skill and experience.

Querie 5. Many poore people are condemned for having a Pap, or Teat about them, whereas many People (especially ancient People) are, and have been a long time, troubled with naturall wretts on severall parts of their bodies, and other naturall excressencies as Hemerodes, Piles, Childbearing, &c. And these shall be judged only by one man alone, and a woman, and so accused or acquitted.

Answer. The parties so judging can justifie their skill to any, and shew good reasons why such markes are not meerly naturall, neither that they can happen by any such naturall cause as is before expressed, and for further answer for their private judgements alone, it is most false and untrue, for never was any man tryed by search of his body, but commonly a dozen of the ablest men in the parish or else where, were present, and most commonly as many ancient skilfull matrons and midwives present when the women are tryed, which marks not only he and his company attest to be very suspitious, but all beholders, the skilfulest of them, doe not approve of them, but likewise assent that such tokens cannot in their judgements proceed from any the above mentioned Causes.

Querie 6. It is a thing impossible for any man or woman to judge rightly on such marks, they are so neare to naturall excressencies, and they that finde them, durst not presently give Oath they were drawne by evill spirits, till they have used unlawfull courses of torture to make them say any thing for ease and quiet, as who would not do? but I would know the reasons he speakes of, how, and whereby to discover the one from the other, and so be satisfied in that.

Answer. The reasons in breefe are three, which for the present he judgeth to differ from naturall marks; which are:

1. He judgeth by the unusualnes of the place where he findeth the teats in or on their bodies, being farre distant from any usuall place, from whence such naturall markes proceed, as if a witch plead the markes found are Emerods, if I finde them on the bottome of the back-bone, shall I assent with him, knowing they are not neere that veine, and so others by child-bearing, when it may be they are in the contrary part?

2. They are most commonly insensible, and feele neither pin, needle, aule, &c., thrust through them.

3. The often variations and mutations of these marks into severall formes, confirmes the matter, as if a Witch hear a month or two before that the *Witch-finder* (as they call him) is comming, they will, and have put out their Imps to others to suckle them, even to their owne young and tender children; these upon search are found to have dry skinnes and filmes only, and be close to the flesh, keepe her 24 houres with a diligent eye, that none of her spirits come in any visible shape to suck her; the women have seen the next day after her Teats extended out to their former filling length, full of corruption ready to burst, and leaving her alone then one quarter of an houre, and let the women go up againe, and shee will have them drawn by her Imps close again: *Probatum est.* Now for answer to their tortures in its due place.

Querie 7. How can it possibly be that the Devill being a spirit, and wants no nutriment or sustentation, should desire to suck any blood? and indeed as he is a spirit he cannot draw any such excressences, having neither flesh nor bone, nor can be felt, &c.

Answer. He seekes not their bloud, as if he could not subsist without that nourishment, but he often repairs to them, and gets it, the more to aggravate the Witches damnation, and to put her in mind of her *Covenant*: and as he is a

Spirit and Prince of the ayre, he appears to them in any shape whatsoever, which shape is occasioned by him through joyning of condensed thickned aire together, and many times doth assume shapes of many creatures; but to create any thing he cannot do it, it is only proper to God: But in this case of drawing out of these Teats, he doth really enter into the body, reall, corporeall, substantiall creature, and forceth that Creature (he working in it) to his desired ends, and useth the organs of that body to speake withall to make his compact up with the Witches, be the creature Cat, Rat, Mouse, &c.

Querie 8. When these Paps are fully discovered, yet that will not serve sufficiently to convict them, but they must be tortured and kept from sleep two or three nights, to distract them, and make them say any thing; which is a way to tame a wilde Colt, or Hawke, &c.

Answer. In the infancy of this discovery it was not only thought fitting, but enjoyned in *Essex*, and *Suffolke* by the Magistrates, with this intention only, because they being kept awake would be more the active to cal their Imps in open view the sooner to their helpe, which oftentimes have so happened; and never or seldome did any Witch ever complaine in the time of their keeping for want of rest, but after they had beat their heads together in the Goale; and after this use was not allowed of by the Judges and other Magistrates, it was never since used, which is a yeare and a halfe since, neither were any kept from sleep by any order or direction since; but peradventure their own stubborne wills did not let them sleep, though tendered and offered to them.

Querie 9. Beside that unreasonable watching, they were extraordinarily walked, till their feet were blistered, and so forced through that cruelty to confesse, &c.

Answer. It was in the same beginning of this discovery, and the meaning of walking of them at the highest extent of cruelty, was only they to walke about themselves the night they were watched, only to keepe them waking: and the reason was this, when they did lie or sit in a chaire, if they did offer to couch downe, then the watchers were only to desire them to sit up and walke about, for indeed when they be suffered so to couch, immediately comes their Familiars into the room and scareth the watchers, and heartneth on the Witch, though contrary to the true meaning of the same instructions, diverse have been by rusticall people, (they hearing them confess to be Witches) mis-used, spoiled, and abused, diverse whereof have suffered for the same, but could never be proved against this Discoverer to have a hand in it, or consent to it; and hath likewise been un-used by him and others, ever since the time they were kept from sleep.

Querie 10. But there hath been an abominable, inhumane, and unmerciful tryall of these poore creatures, by tying them, and heaving them into the water; a tryall not allowable by Law or conscience, and I would faine know the reasons for that.

Answer. It is not denyed but many were so served as had Papps, and floated, others that had none were tryed with them and sunk, but marke the reasons.

For first the Divels policie is great, in perswading many to come of their owne accord to be tryed, perswading them their marks are so close they shall not be found out, so as diverse have come 10 or 12 Miles to be searched of their own accord, and hanged for their labour, (as one *Meggs*, a Baker did, who lived within 7 miles of *Norwich* and was hanged at Norwich Assizes for witchcraft), then when they find that the Devil tells them false they reflect on him, and he, (as 40 have confessed) adviseth them to be swum, and tels them they shall sinke and be cleared that way, then when they be tryed that way and floate, they see the Devill deceives them again, and have so laid open his treacheries.

2. It was never brought in against any of them at their tryals as any evidence.

3. King *James* in his *Demonology* saith, it is a certaine rule, for (saith he) Witches deny their baptisme when they Covenant with the Devill, water being the sole element thereof, and therefore saith he, when they be heaved into the water, the water refuseth to receive them into her bosom, (they being such Miscreants to deny their baptisme) and suffers them to float, as the Froath on the Sea, which the water will not receive, but casts it up and downe, till it comes to the earthy element the shore, and there leaves it to consume.

4. Observe these generation of Witches, if they be at any time abused by being called Whore, Theefe, &c., by any where they live, they are the readiest to cry and wring their hands, and shed tears in abundance and run with full and right sorrowfull acclamations to some Justice of the Peace, and with many teares make their complaints: but now behold their stupidity; nature or the elements reflection from them, when they are accused for this horrible and damnable sin of Witchcraft, they never alter or change their countenances, nor let one Teare fall. This by the way swimming (by able Divines whom I reverence) is condemned for no way, and therefore of late hath, and for ever shall be left.

Querie 11. Oh! but if this torturing Witch-catcher can by all or any of these meanes, wring out a word or two of confession from any of these stupified, ignorant, unintelligible, poore silly creatures, (though none heare it but himselfe) he will adde and put her in feare to confesse, telling her else she shall be hanged; but if she doe, he will set her at liberty, and so put a word into her mouth, and make such a silly creature confesse she knowes not what.

Answer. He is of a better conscience, and for your better understanding of him, he doth thus uncase himselfe to all, and declares what confessions (though made by a Witch against her selfe) he allows not of, and doth altogether account of no validity, or worthy of credence to be given to it, and ever did so account it, and ever likewise shall.

1. He utterly denyes that confession of a Witch to be of any validity, when it is drawn from her by any torture or violence whatsoever; although after watching, walking or swimming, diverse have suffered, yet peradventure Magistrates with much care and diligence did solely and fully examine them after sleepe, and consideration sufficient.

2. He utterly denyes that confession of a Witch, which is drawn from her by flattery, viz. *if you will confesse you shall go home, you shall not go to the Goale, nor be hanged, &c.*

3. He utterly denyes that confession of a Witch, when she confesseth any improbability, impossibility, as *flying in the ayre, riding on a broom, &c.*

4. He utterly denyes a confession of a Witch, when it is interrogated to her, and words put into her mouth, to be of any force or effect: as to say to a silly (yet Witch wicked enough) *You have foure Imps have you not?* She answers affirmatively, Yes: *Did they not suck you?* Yes, saith she: *Are not their names so, and so?* Yes, saith shee: *Did not you send such an Impe to kill my child?* Yes, saith she, this being all her confession, after this manner, it is by him accompted nothing, and he earnestly doth desire that all Magistrates and Jurors would a little more than ever they did, examine witnesses, about the interrogated confessions.

Querie 12. If all these confessions be denyed, I wonder what he will make a confession, for sure it is, all these wayes have been used and took for good confessions, and many have suffered for them, and I know not what, he will then make a confession.

Answer. Yes, in brief he will declare what confession of a Witch is of validity and force in his judgement, to hang a Witch: when a Witch is first found with teats, then sequested from her house, which is onely to keep her old associates from her, and so by good counsell brought into a sad condition, by understanding of the horribleness of her sin, and the judgements threatened against her; and knowing the Devill's malice and subtile circum-ventions, is brought to remorse and sorrow for complying with Satan so long, and disobeying God's sacred Commands, doth then desire to unfold her mind with much bitterness, and then without any of the before-mentioned hard usages or questions put to her, doth of her owne accord declare what was the occasion of the Devils appearing to her, whether ignorance, pride, anger, malice, &c., was predominant over her, she doth then declare what speech they had, what likeness he was in, what voice he had, what familiars he sent her, what number of spirits, what names they had, what shape they were in, what employment she set them about to severall persons in severall places; (unknowne to the hearers), all which mischiefs being proved to be done, at the same time she confessed to the same parties for the same cause, and all effected, is testimony enough against her for all her denyall.

Querie 13. How can any possibly believe that the Devill and the Witch joyning together, should have such power, as the Witches confesse, to kill such and such a man, child, horse, cow, or the like; if we beleeve they can doe what they will, then we derogate from God's power, who for certaine limits the Devill and the Witch; and I cannot beleeve they have any power at all.

Answer. God suffers the Devill many times to doe much hurt, and the devill doth play many times the deluder and impostor with these Witches, in perswading them that they are the cause of such and such a murder wrought by him with their consents, when and indeed neither he nor they had any hand in it, as thus: We must needs argue, he is of a long standing, above 6000 yeers, then he must needs be the best Scholar in all knowledges of arts and tongues, and so have the best skill in *Physicke*, judgment in *Physiognomie*, and knowledge of what disease is reigning or predominant in this or that man's body, (and so for cattell too) by reason of his long experience. This subtile tempter knowing such a man lyable to some sudden disease, (as by experience I have found) as *Plurisie, Imposthume*, &c., he resorts to divers Witches; if they know the man, and seek to make a difference between the Witches and the party, it may be by telling them he hath threatned to have them very shortly searched, and so hanged for Witches, then they all consult with *Satan* to save themselves, and *Satan* stands ready prepared, with a *What will you have me doe for you, my deare and nearest children, covenanted and compacted with me in my hellish league, and sealed with your blood, my delicate firebrand-darlings.*[1] Oh thou (say they) that at the first didst promise to save us thy servants from any of our deadly enemies discovery, and didst promise to avenge and slay all those, we pleased, that did offend us; Murther that wretch suddenly who threatens the down-fall of your loyall subjects. He then promiseth to effect it. Next newes is heard the partie is dead, he comes to the witch, and gets a world

1. The Divelles Speech to the Witches.

of reverence, credence and respect for his power and activeness, when and indeed the disease kills the party, not the Witch, nor the Devill, (onely the Devill knew that such a disease was predominant) and the witch aggravates her damnation by her familiarity and consent to the Devill, and so comes likewise in compass of the Lawes. This is Satan's usuall impostring and deluding, but not his constant course of proceeding, for he and the witch doe mischiefe too much. But I would that Magistrates and Jurats would a little examine witnesses when they heare witches confess such and such a murder, whether the party had not long time before, or at the time when the witch grew suspected, some disease or other predominant, which might cause that issue or effect of death.

Querie 14. All that the witch-finder doth, is to fleece the country of their money, and therefore rides and goes to townes to have imployment, and promiseth them faire promises, and it may be doth nothing for it and possesseth many men that they have so many wizzards and so many witches in their towne, and so hartens them on to entertaine him.

Answer. You doe him a great deale of wrong in every of these particulars. For, first,

1. He never went to any towne or place, but they rode, writ, or sent often for him, and were (for ought he knew) glad of him.

2. He is a man that doth disclaime that ever he detected a witch, or said, Thou art a witch; only after her tryall by search, and their owne confessions, he as others may judge.

3. Lastly, judge how he fleeceth the Country, and inriches himselfe, by considering the vast summe he takes of every towne, he demands but 20.s. a town, and doth sometimes ride 20. miles for that, & hath no more for all his charges thither and back again (& it may be stayes a weeke there) and finde there 3. or 4. witches, or if it be but one, cheap enough, and this is the great summe he takes to maintaine his Companie with 3. horses.

Judicet ullus

an experiment in necromancy

by the Reverend Ralph Josselin

The activities of Matthew Hopkins, although they created the greatest outburst of fanaticism against witchcraft that England had ever seen, also proved the turning point of witch persecution. Once the executions were over and the hysteria had subsided, the shamefaced local people and the law authorities realized how their own unconscious fears had been manipulated and their common sense abused. They vowed that what had happened should never be repeated.

The civil war was, of course, now over, and Oliver Cromwell was hard at work building his "better England," though not without problems. Before he could establish the commonwealth of which he dreamed, he had to invade and suppress the peoples of Ireland and Scotland. Subsequent attempts to create a parliament capable of running the nation proved unsuccessful, and in 1653 he decided to create a protectorate, with himself as lord protector.

A new Britain was in the making, and one of the many positive results was the rapid decline in the actual belief in witches and devils, though other superstitions were to remain, as they still do, very much a part of human existence.

Not surprisingly, with the decline of witchcraft persecution, records dealing with it in any form become fewer and farther between. At the birth of the protectorate, though, we find an Essex clergyman (and how often have we found men of the church as the most consistent chroniclers of witchcraft, if not the most unbiased?) recording in his diary a strange occult incident in the town of Colchester.

This man was the Reverend Ralph Josselin, a gentle and archetypal seventeenth-century vicar who ministered to the small parish of Earls Colne, not far from Colchester. If the Reverend Josselin had not kept a detailed diary of day-to-day life in his parish—with some asides on the national situation—that has survived to this day, he would certainly be completely forgotten. Though the diary is far from exceptional, the clergyman was alert to the changes of his period. He was much concerned with praising God even in the secret pages of his book, but he did record all manner of interesting tidbits.

Born in 1616 in the parish of Roxwell, near Chelmsford, Josselin was educated at Cambridge and appears to have entered the church thereafter, being appointed to the living at Earls Colne in 1640. His life was one of gentlemanly pursuits outside of his ministry, and his income seems to have come mainly from local property, inherited from his father, which he rented out to suitable tenants.

As far as we can tell, Josselin first began to keep a diary in 1644 and made a weekly entry thereafter until virtually the time of his death, in July 1683. After his death, the book passed into the hands of his son-in-law and was then completely lost to view until it emerged in the last century among the papers of the Victorian novelist Mrs. Oliphant. Today the work is interesting for the picture it paints of rural life and for its record of events too minor to have been noticed by the important chroniclers of the day. It shows us Josselin as a supporter of Cromwell, but he evidently believed that a king would eventually return and indeed lived to see Charles II reinstated in 1660. In the diary he makes only two specific references to witchcraft, but he gives somewhat more detail about a strange attempt by two Colchester men to find some lost property using necromancy. This entry, with an additional deposition to fill out the details, follows.

January 3, 1653.

This year has brought forth notable resolutions at home, in the dissolving of Parliament and the declaring of Oliver Cromwell as Protector, who is to rule by a council.

It is said that after many bloody fights we have made peace with the Dutch. The French have had a good year of it as have the Spanish. German diet still continues, they have crowned Ferdinand the 4th King of Romans. The Cossacks and Polish are in armies, and the Turks are against the Venetian. Things are somewhat calmer than formerly and discourses are of a general peace.

Sensible this was a new year to me, and a year of strange transactions at home and preparations for the like abroad, I pray the Lord keep me in soul and body without spot and without blemish.

Heard two strange passages of witchcraft about this area and I especially desired of God to protect us. On going to Colchester I did hear more of one story.

Of late one John Lock, a weaver, of that town did use witchcraft to declare and make known to one William Fayrcloth, a weaver also, the place where he should find certain yarn which had been stolen from him. He, Lock, did confess this sin in Court and was sent to gaol and was also to be placed in the pillory once in each quarter upon a market day for all to see and profit by.

The Reverend Josselin gives no further details of the trial in his diary, but a copy of the evidence of one of the witnesses, Elizabeth Fayrcloth, the wife of the man who had lost the cloth, still exists and is reproduced here.

Elizabeth Fayrcloth disposeth that on the night of November 8 she did see her husband and John Lock go into a room at the back of their house in Colchester and there prepare certain papers and say certain words by the light of candle only.

She said that Lock spoke in words which she did not understand and did raise his arms to the ceiling.

She was much afraid, but remained still in her place of hiding in case in moving she should be detected by her husband and John Lock. She saw a piece of paper pass between the men with symbols on it and drew a likeness of it for the court.

She said that when the men had finished their work, they carefully removed their traces as John Lock said it was Witchcraft and if anyone should find out they would be punished.

She had only spoken out because she was afraid that her husband might be carried off by the Devil instead of having his cloth returned.

an essex cunning man exposed

by Thomas Ady

As we have seen, the end of Hopkins's reign of terror put a stop to much of the witch persecution; however, the interest in the subject, particularly among writers, continued unabated. At least half a dozen major studies were to appear in the following ten years, of which Thomas Ady's *A Candle in the Dark* (1656) was perhaps the most important. Ady considered himself a disciple of Reginald Scot and set out in his work to answer the charges of all those who opposed his mentor, including King James (whom he did not believe was the actual author of *Demonology*), Thomas Cooper ("the bloody persecutor"), and William Perkins, the "arch enemy."

He was full of praise for George Gifford and showed himself a model of common sense and objectivity. "The grand error of these later ages," he wrote, "is ascribing power to witches, and by fooling imagination of men's brains without grounds in the scriptures, wrongfully killing of the innocent under the name of witches." Ady had obviously made a detailed study of the hysteria for his work and, having lived in Essex for some years, was well versed in the county's lore. In the course of the book he refers to a female diviner in Braintree who "gained money from deceiving beholders, until the reports thereof grew stale and fools had done wondering." Then he pours scorn on the value of any words obtained from "a poor wenche executed at the

Chelmsford Assizes who was compelled by the Inquisitor (by keeping her from sleep and with promises and threatenings) to confess that she was married to the Devil and that he lay with her many times in a man's body."

Ady's work reveals that he was particularly interested in the stories of "cunning men," or "witch doctors," who were supposed to be particularly prevalent in Essex. These male witches were credited with having similar powers to those of the female witches but were said to use them in a quite different manner. As we have seen, witches were almost invariably women (often old or widowed), but the cunning folk were mostly men, although they, too, were usually old and solitary beings.

The dividing line between the two must have been narrow, but it was undoubtedly the fact that the cunning man professed himself an opponent of witches and claimed to be able to counteract their work that earned him immunity, if isolation, from society.

Study of the sixteenth and seventeenth centuries shows that there must have been several hundred cunning men in Essex during this time, but as "men uphold them, and say, why should any man be questioned for doing good?" to quote John Stearne's *A Confirmation and Discovery of Witchcraft* (1648), there are no court records to study. However, in his recent study *Witchcraft in Tudor and Stuart England* (1970), Professor Alan Macfarlane has noted that "nowhere in Essex was there a village more than ten miles from a known Cunning Man. The county was simply covered by a network of magical practitioners, sometimes several in a town."

The main function of these men, it seems, was restoring health, finding lost property, and countering the spells of witchcraft. The very title under which these men practiced, "cunning," is an indication of the real nature of their skill; all were clever and ingenious souls who knew the rudiments of medicine and could diagnose simple affliction. They were also dedicated listeners to local gossip and knew who was reputed to be a witch, absorbing all the other tittle-tattle of rural life which they could then bring to bear when being consulted by a credulous laborer or his wife. They were always careful to avoid being

221

too specific, however, so that they could not later be charged with fraud if their magic failed, and they were more subtle in their manipulation of the supernatural than were the alleged witches.

It is interesting to note that long after the last witch trial had been held in England, the cunning men were still practicing their art. The last of these men, George Pickingale, was still being consulted in the early years of the twentieth century.

But now Thomas Ady returns us to the second half of the seventeenth century and records a case in which a somewhat dubious Essex cunning man is revealed as a fraud by his astute client. The story presents us with yet another dimension to the history of witchcraft.

A Butcher in Essex, having lost some cattle, resolved he would go to a Cunning Man to find out what had become of his animals. So he went to a notable, cousening knave that was (as common people say) skilful in the Black Art.

This deceiving witch, seeing his opportunity of gaining a fee for the purpose in hand, used his Conjurations in a room contrived for his usual impostures. Presently, a confederate came in where the two men were, covered over with a bull's hide and a pair of horns on his head.

The poor Butcher, now sitting and looking in a glass made for that purpose, beheld in it the terrible object. It was made less clear to his eye than if he had looked right upon the sight, but he was charged by the Conjuror not to look behind him, for if he did the Devil would be outraged.

Now this confederate, or counterfeit Devil, after the Conjuror's many exorcising Charms, or Conjurations, willed the Butcher to look East and West, North and South to find his cattle.

Thereafter, the Butcher sought much to find his cattle according to the Devil's counsel. But after much seeking and not finding, he perceived that it was a mere piece of knavery and returned to the Conjuror again and desired him to call up the Devil once more.

This the Conjuror did as formerly, but the Butcher had appointed his boy to stand near at hand outside the house with a mastiff dog. At the Butcher's whistle, the boy, as he was appointed, let go the dog, which came in presently to his Master and seized upon the knave in the bull's hide.

Then the Conjuror, and likewise the Devil, cry out, "For the love of God, take off your dog."

"Nay," said the Butcher, "Fight, dog—fight the Devil! If you will venture your Devil, I will venture my dog!"

After much entreaty he did call off his dog, and had thereby wittily discovered the cheating craft of Conjuring. He that acts the part as this Conjuror did, with the same intent to deceive, and to make silly people believe and repose confidence in his words (that is, in Charms and Conjurations to command the Devil, and to keep him in awe) is a seducing witch, as he was. But he that acts the same part, and causes people to wonder at him, and to think that he has really conjured the Devil, to this intent only to show to the world in a sporting way, how easily people are and have been deceived, is no Witch, but may be an instructor and enlightener of silly people.

And truly (if people were not so much naturally given to vain credulity, or believing of lies) those sort of Conjurors (so commonly prated of by silly people) would not have been heard of in the world, had not these deluders learned their cousening craft from the Popish rout, whereby they delude silly people, making them believe they do things really by virtue of words, as by the naming of the Trinity, and the several name of God, and of Christ, and by naming of Angels, Arch-Angels and the Apostles (just the same with Popish conjurations). Whereas their doings, as likewise the Popes, are all but cheating impostures, for if Conjuring Charms could keep the Devil in awe, why did he not submit to the Conjurors?

a magical vision

by "A Holy Sister"

Not until 1660, with the return to the throne of Charles II, did England again have a king. Charles was a dashing, amoral, fun-loving monarch who brought gaiety back into a land still lying dully under the severity of Cromwell's Puritan dictates. His influence was to generate the Restoration period, which, with its learning and brilliance, drove light into dark corners, not the least of these being the worst remnants of the fear of witchcraft.

The final actual trial for witchcraft in Essex was held in 1675 at the Essex Lent sessions. (The last such event in England, however, was not to occur until 1701, when the chief witness against the suspect, a London housewife accused of bewitching, was proved to have made up the whole story and summarily bound over to be "of good behaviour.") The Essex case concerned Elizabeth Gynn, of Great Dunmow, who was accused of bewitching to death a nine-year-old boy. From the records that still exist, the case seems to bear uncanny similarity to that of the very first Essex witch suspect, Elizabeth Lewys, back in 1563. Mrs. Gynn was accused of the boy's death by his father, and other neighbors presented testimony that she was widely believed to be a witch and had killed animals and inflicted pain on all those who had crossed her path. Unlike her predecessor, Mrs. Gynn was not able to plead pregnancy to avoid punishment; but she had no need to, for justice no longer accepted hearsay evidence, and the case was thrown out.

However, it would be wrong to imagine that witchcraft was now being dismissed or treated merely as a joke. (Suspicion concerning it has, indeed, survived to the present day, even with the clarification that the real witchcraft, an ancient religion called Wicca, devoted to the goddess of fertility, has little danger for anyone.) But at the time in question, witchcraft was being used in satire and black comedy.

Typical of the more lightweight treatments of the subject was the next item, a pamphlet published in 1673 entitled *A Magic Vision: or, A Perfect Discovery of the Fallacies of Witchcraft.* This fanciful little document, with its tale of an encounter with a wizard, satirizes the old witchcraft fears and is said to be the work of a "Holy Sweet Sister" which was "lately represented to her in a pleasant sweet dream."

There has been much debate about the author—it was for a time actually believed to have been written by a nun living in cloisters—but it now seems more than likely it was the work of a printer, Thomas Palmer, who had a press in Westminster and lived in Woodford on the boundary between Essex and London. Whatever the case, it makes for a contrasting study after all the seriousness and debate of previous contributions.

That there are Witches (in the common signification of the word) has been confidently asserted, and as briskly opposed by the ingenious pens of several modern Authors. Henceforwards none need doubt of it, that have but Faith enough to credit our relation of the following adventure; whereby we seek not to commit a Rape on any man's belief; but if any will persist in a state of infidelity, we leave them to be converted from their Errors by the horrors of some such like ghastly Apparition.

'Tis something above a month ago, that having trifled away the best part of a Morning, in amusing myself with Doctor Dee's 'Legend of Spirits', I resolved on a walk to dissipate those vain ridiculous imaginations, which had thence invaded my Brain. To this purpose I carelessly steered my course to a small Grove, whose stately trees view their Branches in the Christal streams of a Neighbouring Brook.

In which pleasing solitude I had not wandered half an hour but a sudden drowsiness seized my Spirits, and I perceived an intruding Boomstaffe that violently thrust itself between my legs, making me (spight of my Teeth) bestride it. Mounted (like a delinquent Soldier) on the wooden Pegasus, I presently felt myself fly swifter than a Parthian Arrow through the yielding Air, and without remembering the place where I was taken up, was set down again on my feet in the midst of a vast desert; where I could find no path. Seeing there no footsteps of humanity.

I presently fancied it to be some new World, and like an adventurous Columbus would needs discover further, but all my struggling endeavours only satisfied me in the impossibility of getting forwards, and to add to my astonishment, in a moment (as if I had journeyed to the Antipodes) Noon was turned to Midnight. I saw the Stars shine in the Firmament, with a faint blueish Fire like wasted Candles sunk into their Sockets; the Moon was in her full, but paler much than ordinary, she was thrice Ecclipsed, and thrice sunk down below her Circle.

The murmuring fountains were now grown mute, and the Birds had forgot their Chattering; not a Cock dared crow, and yet the Lions throughout the Wood trembled like the leaves of Asps, neither the Serpent's dreadfull hisses, not the howlings of Ravenous Wolves, nor the screechings of *Male ominous Ravens* could be heard, all Creatures had no more motion than was necessary to express their fear by, and the horror of an astonishing Silence that governed in every place, made it appear Nature was in suspense of some terrible accident.

My fear began to grow as great as that, which the face of the Horizon seemed troubled withall, when by the glimmering Moon-Light I saw ascending out of a vast Grotto or Cave situated at the foot of a Craggy Roc, over spread with Ivy and Bushes, a tall, venerable old man cloathed in a partly-coloured Vest of White and Green, with an austered countenance and swarthy Face, his Eyebrows thick as a Copse and long as a Horses main, were curiously turned back; and wound up about his Ears, a wall and frightful Eye he had, sunk above two inches into his Head, his Beard carelessly thrown over his left Shoulder, and his Temples anointed with Oyl of Night-shade. On his Head he had a large Hood of Vervain, and about him a Girdle of May-Fearn Artificially wooven in Tresses; upon his Gown, near his Heart was fastened a Bat and a Toad both half dead, and about his Neck he wore a Collar, set with seven several precious stones, each of which wore the Character of that Planet that governed it.

Thus mystically dressed, and carrying in his left hand a Triangular Vial full of May-Dew, with his right a Sappy Elder Rod, one end of which was well tipt with a mixture of all Metals, and the other served as a handle to a little Brazen Censer filled with the choicest fumigations, he kissed thrice the floor of his Grotto with a kind of superstitious Reverence, and having pulled off his right foot shoe, and flung it over his left Shoulder, and grumbling brought out certain words from the bottom of his Stomach; he went backwards Nine paces, till he came under the Boughs of an old Oak over-run with Missletoe. Four foot from this he drew three Circles one within the other, and the Earth obedient to his Necromantick charms, which ready trembling, put herself into those figures which he designed to have made in her. In these Circles he wrote with his Middle Finger, the names of his intelligences, as well of the age and Country as of the Year, Season, Month, Week, Day, Hour and Minute, each in its different Character and proper place, every one under its constellation, and with their respective due Ceremonies.

This tedious operation being dispatched, he put his Glass in the middle of the Circles, and opening it made a report louder than that of Cannon or Thunder, the small sharp end of his Rod, he plac'd between his fore-teeth, lay down with his face towards the East, and betook himself to his Repose. I (who you may think at that time had little mind to sleep) watch'd him very narrowly, admiring what might be the upshot of so many strange formalities. About the midst of his Nap (which exceeded not half an hour), I saw Seven Fearn seeds drop into the Vial, which when he waked he took out and put two in each ear, another into his Mouth, the Sixth again into the Glass, and the last he threw out of the Circles; but no sooner was it out of his hand, but I saw it encompassed by more than a Million (if my Arithmetic fail me not) of Mal-ominous Creatures, as well insects as others. He touched with his inchanting Caduceus, an Owl, A Fox and a Mole, which making a frightful Noise, instantly flung themselves into the Innermost Circle; And he with no less speed began to rip open their bodies with a brass Knife, and taking out their Hearts, he wrapt them up in three Bay leaves, and a little Moss, and swallowed them, he took away their livers, which he squeezed over an Hexagonal Vessel, and then reiterating the fumigations, mixt the Dew and the Blood together in a Basin, dipt in it a Glove of Virgin Parchment, which he put on his right hand, and after Four or Five horrible howlings, closed his Eyes, and thus began his invocations:

"*Onjura and confirmo vos Schamaim Athaliel Chiliarchus raquiem, Alchocodonean, Tapthathara, Tossossacan, Hamaguliel, Zonthonphandia, Heydonia,*" with a many more cracking, thumping blustring Terms which had not my fears frighted the Art of memory out of my Head, and the place been inconvenient for Writing Shorthand, I could have registered for supplying the courteous

Reader with terrible words, to still his bawling Children with. During all this Devilish Prayer, he was raised from the Ground above a hands breadth, and ever now and then would fix his Eye on the Nail of his left forefinger; his face was inflamed, and he foamed at the Mouth, like an over-ridden Horse.

But after this exercise concluded and many groanings and ghastly contortions, he fell prostrate on his face, and I heard in his Throat a humming as of many Voices together, from whence arising he became more strong than man, inso much that without stirring, he stood the monstrous shock of a horrible wind, able to blow a Mountain up by the Roots, he caught a falling Thunderbolt in his Hand, and put out a Cloudfull of Lightning; all of which dreadful Artillery (I perceive) was discharged to force the old Gentleman to abandon his Circle. But he with an undaunted resolution maintaining his ground, the Circles themselves began with an incredible swiftness to whisk about under him. This was followed by a storm of Hail redder than Blood, which gave place to a much more terrible torrent of Bituminous Fire, that roar'd like Mount Gibella when it burst, and seem'd to rend the Air with dreadful claps of Thunder.

This served as an Epilogue to all this tragedy of Horror for immediately a fair Light dissipated these sad meteors, and a brisk young man in a Flame coloured Mantle appear'd. He came riding post through the Air mounted with his right Leg on an Eagle, and the other on a Lynx, and in as Gentile and respective a manner, as if he had been one of Beelzebub's Pages of honour, presented the *Magus* with three small Vials full of Nobody knows what Liquor. The wizard in requital made him a present of three hairs; one pluck'd off from his Forehead, the other two from his Temples, whereupon he was gently struck over the Shoulders and between the Eyes with a small wand that his Spirit held, and then everything vanished, and methoughts it appear'd about that time, when Stars grown pale at the arrival of their illustrious Monarch the Sun, joined colour with the Heavens. I emboldened by this approach of day was just going to seek my way home.

But the old Magician it seems was unwilling we should part so, and therefore once more presented himself. He did not walk but glide along, and got home before I saw him stir, his Hand was so cold, that mine whereon he laid it, was benumb'd for a fortnight after. He neither opened his Eyes nor his Mouth, but in deep silence conducted me out of the wood, and over some Fields to the dreadful ruins of a long since dismantled Castle, where the ages for this 100 years have been labouring to carry the Chambers into the Cellars, under which in a deep Vault was his constant Residence.

As soon as we entered this enchanted Mansion, "Boast thyself young man" (said he turning towards me) "to have seen face to face the famous Agrippa, whose Soul by *Metempsichosis* heretofore was incorporated in the renowned Doctor *Faustus*, and long since inspired the Learned *Zoroaster* King of the *Bactrians*: Since (almost two ages) that I have disappeared to men, I have preserved myself with *aurum potabile* in such a vigorous state of Health, that no disease dared ever invade me. Every twenty years I swallow a quantity of the Universal Medicine, which renews my youth, and restores to my Body its decayed forces.

"Didst thou" (continued he) "consider the three Vials presented to me by the Prince of the Fiery Daemons: the first of them was full of this Elixir, the second of powder of projection, and the third of Oil of Bones. Nor art thou a little obliged to me since I have made choice of thee amongst all mortal Race, to be present at these mysteries, which I celebrate but once in four Lustres; and that thou mayst not be ignorant who it is has done thee this honour; let me tell thee. 'Tis (by my charms) in my power at my pleasure to render a Country fruitful or barren, I stir up Warts by breeding dissention amongst those Genii that goven Kings; I teach the Wolves *Pater Noster*, and the wizards how to manage the Sheers and turn the Seive; I send Jacks with Lanterns, and Wills with Wisps to Marshes and Fens, to allure benighted Travellers out of their way, over Hedges, and drown them in Ditches; I send out the Fairies and Elves to Dance and Revel together by Moonlight, and encourage the Gamesters to look under the Gallows for the Four of Clubs; I raise at Midnight the silent Ghosts from their Dormities, wrapt in a sheet to plague their negligent Heirs, for not performing those Vows they made to them at their Deaths; I command Spirits to haunt old Monasteries, and uninhabited Castles, and to strangle all that come to Lodge there, till some resolute fellows compell them to discover the treasure they so long have brooded over.

"I make those whom I would enrich find hidden wealth, and teach Thieves to burn Candles of Deadmen's Grease to lay Folks asleep whilst they Rob their Houses; I give the flying money that return again to the Pocket after 'tis spent, and cheat covetous Misers with a bagfull of dry Oak Leaves instead of Guineas and Charleses; I make those Amulets that render the wearers Musquet proof, and Philters to ingratiate Lovers with their Mistresses. 'Tis I clatter the doors when they are fast bolted, and invisibly humble the Dishes and Glasses without breaking them; I learn Mountebanks to drive away an Ague by writing *Abacadabra* on Virgin Parchment, and old Women to cure a Feaver by another charm equally Nonsensical and blasphemous; I awaken the Country Fellow on Midsummer Eve to gather his Herb fasting and in silence, and young Wenches to watch on *St. Agnes Night*.

"I teach Witches to assume the shape of Wolves and eat Children, to turn themselves into Hares, and be hunted all Day, and at night make their escape from the Hounds in at a Window, and when any happen to cut off one of the Legs (which tomorrow proves such an old woman's Arm) I forsake them; when they are tried I keep them above Water like bladders, that they cannot sink, and leave them in the power of Justice, yet at the Gallows allow nothing to Tuck them up but a rope; I send to the discontented and envious, the tall man in black with the Cloven Foot who makes them promises of great riches and other felicities. If they'll but make him a Fee of their Souls, and then blind them that take bargains of him; for when they agree for a term of Life of thirty years, I make them see the (3) before the (0) which I have placed after it; 'tis I that strangle those that raise me out of a wanton curiosity, and give me neither employment nor reward, but very civilly take leave of those, that when they have called me up, give me a hair, an old Shoe, or a straw; I take away from dedicated Churches the stones that are not paid for, and often demolish in the Night what was built in the Day.

"I make a *Conventicle* of Witches seem to those that are invited to Sabat, nothing but a troop of Cats, of which Marton is Prince; I send all the confederates to the offering, and give them the Goats Tail (seated on a Joynt stool) to kiss; I treat them splendidly, but allow them no salt to their meat, and if any stranger ignorant of their laudable customs offer to say Grace, I cause all forthwith to Vanish and leave him Five Hundred miles from his own home in a desert of Nettles and Bramble-bushes. I sometimes play the Pimp by sending plump Succubas to old Leachers' beds, and furnish with Incubusses those wanton Widdows that will not go to the charge of Dil——.

"I am the Sire of the Oak and the first that contriv'd the *Legerdemain* of the Changling; I convey Hobgoblins in the shape of a long piece of Marble, to lye by those that go to bed without making the Sign of the Cross; I teach *Necromancers* to destroy their Enemies by making a little image in Wax, which they throwing into the Fire or pricking, the original is sensible of those Torments they expose the Figure to; I make Witches insensible in those parts where the Ram hath set his Seal, and give a secret virtue to *Nolite Fieri*, when said backwards that it hinders the Goodwives Butter from coming, whom yet I teach to be even with the Hagg, by stabbling the Cream with a red hot Spit.

"I intrusted Bia—— to dispossess persons Bedivel'd, and white Witches to marvel the inchantements of Black ones; I taught plow Jobbers to lay under the ground of that Sheepfold they have a mind to destroy, a Lock of hair or a Toad with three curses that kills all the Sheep that pass over it, as also to stick a broken Needle in the threshold of the Bridal Chamber, or tie such a knot at the moment that the Ring is first put on, as shall make an eager lusty young Bridgroom impotent; I let loose the Hobgoblins against the Christmas Holy days and order him to roll a barrel, draw a Chain, or hurry a Coach along streets in the Night, that he might have the happy opportunity of wringing off their Necks that look out at Windows.

"I teach Crundal the composure of Charms, Lamens, Sigils, Talisman, spells, Christals, Pentacles, Magick Looking-glasses, and Geomantick Figures, how to find the Missletoe of the New Year, the wandering Herbs, the Gamahely, the Weapon Salve, and Magnetique Plaister; I send the Goblins, the Shodmule, the Nightmare, the Sprites, the Hobgoblins, the Hags, the Night bats, the Break-necks, the black Men and green Women, the Familiars, the Pugs, the Ghosts, and the Shadow. In fine I am the Prince of the Airs *Vice-Roy*, Deputy Lieutenant to the degraded Seraphin, the Fairy Protector, the Jew-Errant, the High Priest of the Holy Cross, the Genius of *Notredamus*, the Demon of Mascoon, and the Drummer of Tedworth. I am. . . ."

So would he have proceeded with a tedious Harangue of his power and Titles, had not a small spiritual officer in the shape of a Flitter-mouse interrupted him by a whisper in the Ear, which obliged the Magician to tell me, he must omit the rest he intended to have said, till another opportunity, for at present he was summoned for by a gang of Lap-Land Witches that came to treat with him about a new Bargain of Bottled wines, whereby they proposed to themselves to make very considerable advantages during these Wars, and saying thus, he mounts a flying Dragon that presented itself ready Bridled and Sadled, and in the twinkling of an Eye disappear'd.

When thinking to Ruminate a while on the strange Novelties of this uncoucht Adventure: I found myself in the before mentioned Grove, under the shade of a spreading Sycamore, carelessly laid along, on a rising Bank that was covered with a fresh green Mantle Embroidered with Cowslips and Violets, and have ever since strongly suspected not only this formidable apparition, but most other stories of that Nature to be nothing but Dreams.

the swimming of a witch

by the Reverend James Boys

Because of the barbarity of its trials and the harshness with which those
suspected of witchcraft were treated, Essex, more than any other area
of England, certainly deserved the enduring epithet of "The Witch
County." No other area could equal the persecutions and prosecutions
its people suffered during the years when the hysteria was at its height.
Indeed, it would be hard to find a similar area anywhere else in the
world (and that includes the terrible events at Salem, Massachusetts)
where the old, the crazed, the deformed, and those who merely upset
their neighbors ran such a risk of trial and execution on the flimsiest
and most circumstantial evidence.

Not surprisingly the county has never been able to live down this
dreadful era, and many towns and villages still bear the scars in the
form of old gibbet stones and memorials and in the constantly retold
witch stories. Nor would it be correct to say that the fear of witchcraft
completely died out after this time, for there were accusations made
against people until just before the Second World War. The last actual
witch hunt, however, took place just before the end of the seventeenth
century and resulted in the "swimming" of an old woman in the
manner so beloved by Matthew Hopkins.

This event occurred in June 1699 at Coggeshall, a small village not far from Colchester, and the unfortunate victim was a Widow Coman, who had apparently not long before lost her husband by drowning. She was subjected to be "swum" not once, but three times, and in the prescribed manner: she was stripped naked and bound with her right thumb to her left toe and her left thumb to her right toe and then cast into the village pond. If she swam, she could be declared guilty without any further evidence (obviously the devil had supported her in the water); if she drowned, her innocence was proved!

Although "swimmings" were fairly common in Essex, we have few descriptions of them and only one account of an entire sequence of events that culminated in this action—that of the Widow Coman. The story was recorded by the rector of Coggeshall, the Reverend James Boys, who served in the parish from 1679 to 1725 and appears to have still been a literal believer in witchcraft. He recorded the event on twenty-two pages of note paper that have amazingly survived the passing of time and are now in the possession of the Essex Archaeological Society. As stated at the beginning, witchcraft has continued as a tradition in the county to the present time, but here, as a fitting conclusion to our study, is an account of the very last time it took an innocent life.

A
BRIEF ACCOUNT
of the indisposition of the Widow
Coman of Coggeshall magna (in
the County of Essex) who was generally supposed to be a Witch.

Containing an exact relation of wt.
passed (in several visitations) between
her and the Reverend Mr. J. Boys
Minister of the parish: and some other
remarks which seem plainly to prove
the accusations of the Vulgar.

Penned down by the aforesaid divine
at the time of his performing those

visitations and afterwards transcribed
by the same person from loose papers.

June 4th, 1699, being Sunday I was requested about eight in the morning to visit the Widow Coman, at that time very uneasy and melancholy (as since suggested) upon the account of her Husband lately drowned in her well. When I came to her I found her under a very great disorder of mind (her pulse beating as true as my own or any other then present and in perfect health) and her eyes stared with a certain feirceness.

After some consideration I asked her whether she believed in God (the common report representing her as a witch). She replyed yes in God Almighty maker of heaven & Earth. I desired her to believe in Jesus the Son of the Living God. She answered she did not know him. I told her it was strange that such an ancient woman as she was did not know her Saviour, and that I was sorry she was so very ignorant. Whereupon I requested her to tell me (if she knew not Jesus) whether she knew the devil. She immediately replyed (without any hesitation) yes. I asked her whether she had seen him at any time? she answered yes, that he had broad goggle eyes and very rough hands. I desired her to let me see him (if she could help me to a sight of him) she said they were all gone out, for they told her they could not stay because they understood that I was to come. I enquired whither they were gone (humouring her discourse), she replyed towards Colchester, and that they would not come back till I was gone (whereupon I informed the standers by that it was worth their observation that if this woman spake advisedly, the Devil was forced to shun the presence of a servant of Jesus upon his own confession) but my business calling me that morning to go to Little Tey (which lyes a little out of Colchester road) I was entreated by some of the neighbours that heard her tell me thus not to go lest some mischief should befal me: but I went (as it was my duty) and found nothing amiss in going or returning.

After this she began to talk (as I thought) idely about a Kettle her relation had taken away from her and how she thought when it was carried out of the house, that the house had fallen upon her head. She talked also of sheets and Pillow-beers, insomuch that I thought that she was little less than crazy or mad, but enquiring amongst the standers by what the meaning of all these wild complaints should be, they informed me that her brother in law T. Everit had carried the Kettle away, and that Pudny her relation had the sheets. Whereupon I went to both and (finding it true) obliged them to bring her goods back thinking that being a widow and desolate she might fret too much and hurt herselfe for want of them.

Soon after (after some other discourse with her) I asked her whether she was baptized. She said yes and mentioned her Christian name. I requested her to tell me whether she knew what Baptism was (and immediately added) that there was a Covenant made then betwixt God and her Soul by which God obliged himself to pardon her sins and to save her by the blood of Jesus, and that she was bound thereby to repent amend and live up to the Gospel: and then enquired whether she had made any other Covenant with the Devil. She was so loth to speak to this point that I was forced to repeat the question very often unto her before I could get a fair answer, for she put me off abruptly saying that butter is eight pence a pound and Cheese a groat a pound, and would not seem to mind my question. But resolving with myself to have a pertinent answer, I urged her so long to tell me whether she had made a Covenant with the Devil that at last she did acknowledge that she had made an agreement with him and that he was her Master and sat at the right hand of God and upon my replying that if she was so engaged to him she must expect to perish with him, Yes said she, with very little concern upon her spirits, I must go directly to Hell down to Hell there is no help for it. I very mildly told her that God had created her and preserved her (she interupting me said Ay above sixty years) and offered his Son to be her Saviour, but what has this new master done for you? There is Mr. Cox, said she, who married Mr. Sparhawk's Daughter, I struck him on the Knee and made him lame. I made a hen in wax and hid it in Bundock's croft hedge. What did you do to this hen (I replied) did you stick pins into it? She answered yes. Now Mr. Cox being taken lame much about that time and complaining of a pain in his knee I began to think that there might be something true in the report that she was a witch, and importuned her to show me this hen, but she answered suddenly as before butter is eight pence a pound & cheese a groat a pound and changing her fancies thus almost every minute I gave very little heed to what she said in this rambling manner but being pressed very much by me to answer pertinently to my questions she was as one dumb for a while.

I then told her that I had read of a Devil that was dumb and that our Saviour cast him out and that (I made no doubt but) she might speak to me, whereupon she began to talk freely to me and did so for some time. Amongst other questions I desired her to pray and she repeated the Lord's prayer after me pretty well til I came to that part of the petition, As we forgive them that tresspass against us (which she then omitted and omitted ever after when requested to repeat that prayer after me) I told her I would go to prayer with her for I hoped that if she confessed her sin (tho it was very great) and would forsake it for the sake of Jesus God might pardon it. She answered I might if I would but, beginning to pray with the company, she broke suddenly out into a great laughter and talked with herself of pretty women, nor would forbear to make a noise till I had concluded & during the time of prayer had almost dressed herselfe with the assistance of another woman tho before she was (as was pretended at least) unable to rise.

Upon this I left her and after Afternoon Sermon I went to her again but found her eye very sharp & glaring and her pulse somewhat uneven & did then think she might have a fever in her brain and might stand in need of Physick, she talked sensibly to me in one moment and in another denyed what she said so that I gave little heed to her words imputing what she said relating to her being a witch to a distraction in her head, delusion of fancy or to the effect of some distemper coming or then upon her. Whereupon I prayed with her and recommending her to God's mercy departed desiring two or three of her relations to give her a Clyster and somewhat to cause sleep and sent them to Mr. White's (an Apothecary) for the ingredients of the one and Laudanam for the other. They applied the first but it did not stay long enough, the other caused some rest so that the next day (being Monday) she was in a good temper (as appeared by her eye and pulse) and discoursed as sensibly as any other but denying what she said before (complaining that alass she was light headed and said abundance of things which were not true).

Mr. Cox being then present I repeated to her what she had said of him; she persisted in the denial of it and would not confess that there was any hen or anything like it hid up in the place before mentioned, but owned that her husband (some years before) had killed a hen of her neighbour Pembertons and that it was likely that she might mean that. But when I told her that she mentioned this as an instance of what her master the Devil had done for her, she yeilded att last that theere might be such a hen but, it being late and she in bed, she desired to be excused from discovering where it was that night but that on the morrow she might go into the yard with the help of one of the women and then find it and send it to me. The occasion of Mr. Cox's being then present was not only her confession to me concerning what she had done unto him, but an account of what some of the women had brought unto him how that she had (of her own accord) enquired how he did, whether his lameness continued and said that she was against his removal to Stanham Street and that he should be lame and dye. The truth of this he was willing to enquire into (considering that his lameness came upon him as a Sciatica much about at the time he had in a passion said she should not come and live by him) and it was a satisfaction to him that he heard her confession attested to her face and that she had made a small acknowledgement that it might be true. Before I went from her I desired her to pray to God and she repeated after me the Lord's prayer, but mistook again at the same petition but (to the admiration of all there present) she uttered of her own accord this prayer which follows:—O Lord God Almighty have mercy upon my soul, create in me a clean heart and renew a right spirit that I may speak no evil and do no evil actions but may live in thy fear and keep thy commandments all my life in Jesus Christ. This was very surprizing to all the Company (especially to Mr. Parsons who came with an expectation of seeing a Witch). I did thereupon declare that one would almost think that something dictated the words unto her (she not being able to pray in the least the day before nor to repeat the Lord's prayer perfectly after another) and did hope that if she could pray so well she might by degrees be brought to confession and amendment, but instead of a confession she began to talk Philosophycally of three earths and worlds as if she had a perfect knowledge of them and being importuned (after all her ramble) to relieve Mr. Cox she replyed that God would not let her (an answer very inconsistent with her prayer). Having gained a sort of a promise from her that she would discover where the hen lay next morning and send it to me I left her.

The next day I had occasion to go to Colchester betimes and heard nothing from her til I came home and then Mr. Cox came to me and asked me what was done. I told him I was just come home and had received no messuage from her but that if he would stay til Wednesday nine a clock I would go with him. In the evening Mary Cox and Martha Appleton came to me and informed me that they with Susan Smith being with her in the night and observing how she nesled in the bed and grew very hot and uneasy desired her to tell them whether she had any Imps? And whether at that time she was not suckling of them? And that after many words and much persuasion she did acknowledge that she had and was at that time suckling of them. They requested her to inform them where or at what part she suckled them and she told them at her fundament. Susan Smith asked her whether she did not give them bread. She answered no, but added that Priscilla Deadman indeed fed hers with bread, but that she suckled hers with her own blood. They intreated her to acquaint them why she was so uneasy at that time, she answered that the bed was too hot for them (her imps) and it was that which made her uneasy; after some other discourse of that nature (she being in a good temper and as sensible as any of them) she confessed that she had taken a Lease not to go to Church for five years and that the time was out next Sunday and that then she would go to Church. I desired them to return to her and to keep a watchful eye upon her (because she had earnestly desired them to get her some pins) and to say nothing of what they had said to me but to dispose her if they could to declare the same to me and the company I should bring with me next day and to prevail with her to discover and send me the hen.

The next morning (wch. was Wednesday) at nine Mr. Cox and his Uncle Bufton came to me and (having by prayer recommended ourselves to God's protection and grace) we went to her. In the way Mr. Goldsmith and Mr. Grimes offered to go with us. I was the more inclined to accept of their company that the Sparks of the age might entertain more easily a belief that there may be that which we call Witchcraft. When I came into the room and began to mention our former discourse she denied all that she had said, and mentioning what the women had informed me and they attesting the same to be true to her head, she persisted in her denial with the greatest confidence imaginable. I found her pulse good her eye composed and understood by the women her nurses that her body was in a good condition, and then I appealed to Mr. Goldsmith and the rest of the company whether that they thought she was frantick or mad. He and the rest unanimously owned that she seemed to be very well in her health and as sensible and composed as any there present. I urged her therefore again to confess, but she denied all for some time, at last she gave some hopes of a confession but upon my declaring that I would burn the Imps if she would put them into my hands she became silent and would say no more. However I importuned her to confess and particularly insisted upon having the hen, she denying any such thing. On the sudden said she would go into the yard and shew it me and immediately went out through a crowd of people (there being a multitude in and about the house) and came to a woodstack, talking over the old story concerning the hen which her husband had killed. I searched (by her direction) an old payr of breeches and an old hose and other places but could find nothing.

She was for returning in, but Mr. Cox forced her to stay a while longer, she shreiked piteously upon it but would own nothing, but got in with little or no help tho she could not come forth without assistance on each side. When she was within I persuaded the women to take her into her bedroom and search her which they did but found no discovery of that nature, her flesh being strangely red and discoloured (beyond any that Mrs. Parsons had seen). I went into the room after the search was over and requested her once more to confess or to say in the name of God I renounce the Devil his Imps or Agents, I detest and abhor them and pray that all that have received hurt by me may be made well. But she refused to repeat any part of it, but said I might as well enable a Baby (with a beetle) to rive logs as her to say those words; that if I would give her my hat full of mony she could not do it; that life was sweet but that she could not say those words to save her life. Then Mr. Cox pulled out a paper with some words written in it and bade her say those words after him but she obstinately held her tongue and would not speak one word. Upon her refusal I stept to her again, called Mr. Cox, and forced her hand upon his lame thigh and then desired her to say after me these words:—I pray God that Mr. Cox's thigh may be well, but she continued for a while sullen and obstinately silent but at the last (after much importunity) she told me she could not. She then complained that her silver bodkin at Pudneys was not brought home (worth half a crown) and desired to have it. I promised her that it should be brought to her provided she would relieve Mr. Cox. She said that she could not; I replyed that it was right she should be just to Mr. Cox as that Pudney should be just to her and so I withdrew. Mr. Cox followed me out and advised with me what to do, whether he might force some blood from her. I told him I must leave that at present, that if he thought that her blood by the help of nature might give him relief (as in sympathy is done) he might do his pleasure but if an invisible agent was to assist & one Devil was to cure what another had hurt I would by no means consent to fetch blood for it was not lawful to go to the Devil for help or releife. However, I understood from Mr. Cox that after I was gone home he went into her room and urged her to say the same words, but she refusing to that degree that the whole company cryed out against her and said it was a shame she would not do so small a thing for him. He thought fit (by the persuasion of those present) to fetch blood of her, which he did by holding her hand and scratching her arm with his nails & then dipped his Handkerchief in the blood and carried it to his Father's house and there burnt it; but he told me it had not the usual smell of burnt linnen.

Soon after she was very impatient and desired to see me and said that she would give me one of her imps to burn, but in a little time she changed her mind and said it was too late. At the same time she was very desirous to see Mr. Cox but said she should not meet with so good fortune (neither he nor I going to her at that time when she was so earnest to have us come) she soon changed her tale and said that (as it happened) Mr. Cox could receive no benefit by her blood and never requested to see him any more. In this interval Mrs. Parsons desired her to say the creed, but when she was to say I believe in Jesus Christ, she said pish and would not say it but proceeded to say Pontius Pilate & being requested to repeat after her I believe in Jesus Christ she pished again and told her you do just as the boyes do, but she was often repeating tho he has had my blood he will not be much the better for it.

I went to her again and (as usual) requested her to repeat the Lord's prayer but she could not say As we forgive them that trespass against us, and told me though she was to be ganged she could not do it. Setting for some time by the bedside I observed that she looked very red, was in a great sweat and very uneasy. I asked her whether she was then suckling her imps. She told me yes she was. I desired to see them, she bid me look to my own family & not prevailing with her to make any confession I left her and visited her no more. But the mob (being headed by James Haines and some others) would swim her which they did several times and she always swam like a cork (as hundreds can testefie on oath)—and because the mob was so troublesome to her she said (when she was swimming) Yee see what I am, what need you swim me any more? Soon after, whether by the cold she got in the water or by some other means, she fell very ill and dyed.

Upon her death I requested Becke the midwife to search her body in the presence of some sober women which she did and assured me that she never saw the like in her life. That her fundament was open like a mouse hole and that in it were two long bigges out of which being pressed issued blood that they were neither piles nor emrods, for she knew both, but excrescencies like to biggs with nipples which seemd as if they had been frequently sucked. The women that laid her forth were desired to keep constantly by the corpse, but (after they had laid it on a clean sheet and covered it) they grew weary about midnight and must needs go to the fire-room and refresh themselves. They were gone about an hour and when they returned they lookt upon the corps and found the sheet under her all trampled and stained with blood as if some things like mice had been running to and fro upon it. This they all agreed in and (had there been an occasion) were ready to justifie it upon oath. She was carried to the grave in an ignominious manner and buried upon the North side of the churchyard upon the 27th. of December 1699. Her next relation S. Wharton's wife was under a terrible fear lest the imps should be sent to her and came to me for my advice. I told her that as she was a Christian she need not torment herself about them for they could not be entertained without her consent nor hurt her without God's permission; that if she was true to the Covenant of Baptism God would secure her; that if they offered their service she should let me know of it and I would do my best to fortifie her against them. This her uneasiness lasted for a little while and working off she came very well composed and (as I believe) never received any messages from them. The woman is now alive and can speak for herselfe.

Essex County was the center of the terrible witchcraft hysteria that blighted the English countryside from the mid-1560's to the close of the seventeenth century. This earned Essex, for all time, the epithet of "The Witch County."

Essex was rural, full of superstitious backwaters, strongly ruled by church and state, and the belief in witchcraft was more pronounced than in any other rural area. Wherever one turned, men, women, and children were put to death or imprisoned for the slightest hint of witchcraft. What passed for justice fell on the accused with barbaric savagery.

How did those who were present at the time view the events? What did they see, hear, and feel? How were their views shaped amid the hysteria? Did common sense and rationality prevail at all? Did anyone give a damn for justice and the basic human rights of man? These are the questions *The Witchcraft Papers* sets out to answer. Peter Haining has assembled some of the most important documents, trial reports, essays,